Language
Stories
&
Literacy
Lessons

Language Stories & Literacy Lessons

JEROME C. HARSTE
VIRGINIA A. WOODWARD
CAROLYN L. BURKE

Heinemann Educational Books

Portsmouth, N.H.

HEINEMANN EDUCATIONAL BOOKS INC.
70 Court Street, Portsmouth, New Hampshire 03801
Offices and agents throughout the world

10   9   8   7   6   5   4   3

LIBRARY OF CONGRESS CATALOGING IN PUBLICATION DATA

Harste, Jerome C. (Jerome Charles)
  Language stories and literacy lessons.

  Bibliography: p.
  1. Language and languages—Study and teaching.
2. Language arts. 3. Reading. 4. Children—
Language. I. Woodward, Virginia A. (Virginia Alice)
II. Burke, Carolyn L. III. Title.
P51.H34   1984   372.6   84-14256
ISBN 0-435-08211-6

Printed in the United States of America

Design by Wladislaw Finne

To literacy learning

Contents

Preface   ix

Introduction   xv

SECTION 1/LANGUAGE STORIES
1. Examining Instructional Assumptions   3
2. Rethinking Development   15
3. Lessons from Latrice   31
4. Race, Sex, Socioeconomic Status & Language   41
5. Examining Literacy Assumptions   49

SECTION 2/LITERACY LESSONS
6. An Overview: Searching for Reoccurring Patterns in Literacy   73
7. Organization   82
8. Intentionality   108
9. Generativeness   118
10. Risk-Taking   130
11. Social Action   143
12. Context   151
13. Text   164
14. Demonstrations   180
15. A Summary: Synthesizing New Patterns in Literacy   190

SECTION 3/TAKING OWNERSHIP
16. Conceptual Implications   199
17. Methodological Implications   221

Conclusion   229

Appendix   233

Bibliography   242

Index   253

Preface

A child doesn't need to know any linguistics in order to use language to learn; but a teacher needs to know some linguistics if he wants to understand how the process takes place—or what is going wrong when it doesn't. (Halliday, 1980, p. 11)

Language teaching and language learning are rooted in belief. If these processes are to be supported, teachers must come to understand the relationship between belief and theory and belief and science.

Because all too often teachers see theory and science as something college professors do, but they apply, this book attempts to demyth both theory and science. Theory, we argue, is fundamentally a set of beliefs upon which you are willing to act. It need not be, and most often is not, conscious, explicit, or formal in a hypo-deductive sense. Science, fundamentally, is the attitude that "I can find out." It is rooted in belief and the distrust of belief. It proceeds when beliefs suspected to be faulty are put in a position of vulnerability.

Unexamined belief is thought at rest. When examined in the course of teaching, it is at the same time a stopping place and a new starting place for science.

Curricularly, *Language Stories & Literacy Lessons* is an attempt to get teacher-researchers to think through the implications of recent insights into literacy and literacy learning. We found ourselves thinking through these issues as a result of a program of research which had as its function the study of cognitive processes involved in learning to read and write among 3-, 4-, 5-, and 6-year-olds. We hope teacher-researchers find the mental trip as fascinating and rewarding as we have found it.

Language Stories & Literacy Lessons is not a how-to-do-it curricular cookbook; yet, we argue it is clearly a language arts methods book of importance far beyond early childhood education. What the book does is to attempt to have readers experience what literacy, literacy learning, and the teaching and researching of literacy are by critically involving them in these processes. If we have been successful, this book will do more than just build language information for the preservice and in-service teacher-researcher. It will allow them to experience curriculum from the child's perspective: as the mental trip taken by the language learner during a literacy event. *Language Stories & Literacy Lessons* was written to invite reaction, discussion and, in Louise Rosenblatt's terms (1978), "a lived-through experience."

In some ways *Language Stories & Literacy Lessons* reflects a compilation of the most popular reports of our program of research; in other ways— and for those who have followed our work over the years—this volume will document our continued involvement in what we have come to call "the authoring process" in literacy. Some of the materials in this volume have appeared in *Language Arts, Theory into Practice, Research in the Teaching of English*, and in our Final Reports, *Children, Their Language & World: Initial Encounters With Print* (1981), and *The Young Child as Writer-Reader & Informant* (1983). Those interested in an in-depth discussion of our findings and in the taxonomies we evolved as heuristic devices for the study of literacy will find these earlier documents invaluable.

In a very real sense, *Language Stories & Literacy Lessons* is our attempt to involve readers in this "authoring process" by encouraging them to make the study of literacy and literacy learning their own. We see it as a significant contribution to the literature. We do not, however, wish to present it as something it is not.

Clearly we did not "discover" scribbling. Many people have noted that children scribble. Many people have noted that, while child language is different from adult language, it is systematic and organized. Clearly we did not "discover" the rule-governed nature of children's speech or even "invented spelling." Many people, in fact, have already noted a lot of the things we note about written language and written language learning. We claim few discoveries.

You may, then, ask, "Why read this book?" "What does it contribute?" Although it is difficult to put oneself in historical perspective, we have decided, in thinking about how to answer this question, that what we do that hasn't been done before is to put these discoveries in a broad theoretical frame that's radically different from before. While we didn't "discover" scribbling, what we did discover is that the process of scribbling bears sociolinguistic and psycholinguistic similarity to the highly prized processes we call reading and writing. All of a sudden scribbling isn't just "cute"; we see it as an unfrozen form of the very process characterizing our involvement and growth in literacy. Children, we argue, attend to the cue complexes we attend to. They do not outgrow strategies. There are, in that sense, no developmental stages to literacy but rather, only experience, and with it fine-tuning and continued orchestration. While we didn't "discover" invented spelling, what we did discover is that the process which undergirds the generation of invented spellings is the very process which undergirds our own spelling efforts. Past research has suggested that "invented spelling" was a stage on the way to conventional spelling. We see it as a specific instance of a more generalized strategy, called "functional writing," which is rooted firmly in the psychological limits of human cognition and memory. "Functional spelling" isn't a characteristic of early literacy, but of literacy at every age.

The "authoring cycle" we introduce is characterized by a search for text in context, the negotiation of meaning—both between other language users in the literacy event, and within and across communication systems—the risk of taking one's current best shot, and the fine-tuning of text with text. The cognitive strategies we identify as constituting this "authoring cycle" allow language users to learn written language *in the process of using* written language. The multimodal nature of literacy allows language users to shift perspectives and to alter their sociological and psychological stances during the course of their involvement in the literacy event. By psychologically and sociologically shifting perspectives, language users can triangulate their knowing. In use then, language and language learning are not only continuous but have self-correcting devices built into them. This process, we argue, is the same for the 3-year-old as it is for the adult. It is why the process of language learning and language learners can be trusted; why teachers need only support, not intervene, in it.

Following Kuhn (1970) we call what we did an "invention" rather than a "discovery." Kuhn distinguishes between "discovery" and "invention" by saying that the former involves the identification of facts, and the latter the generation of paradigm wherein knowledge takes on heightened significance. Kuhn uses the example of oxygen. Several persons had already discovered oxygen, that is, identified its existence. But Lavoisier's theory of oxygen combustion replaced phlogiston theory and in so doing, not only demonstrated the significance of the discovery of oxygen, but also opened new vistas of understanding and exploration.

The theoretical perspective we build in this volume, somewhat like Lavoisier's theory of oxygen, allows us to see "scribbles" and "invented spellings" in a new light—a light which says that persons studying what preschool children know about reading and writing have a good deal more in common with cognitive psychologists studying the adult reading and writing process, literary critics studying reader response and interpretation, and semioticians studying all kinds of signs and how it is that sign functions are established, than we've ever been able to see before. This very light, then, allows us to see some past gaps as dysfunctional. All of a sudden we have new colleagues. What were once gaps between disciplines, between theory and practice, between researchers and teachers, were a function of our perspective, and not inherent in literacy and literacy learning itself.

Consequently, the theory we build permits us not only to ask new questions but to seek answers to them in new ways. Are we misguided in our current efforts to get written language learners to write like Palmer, spell like Horn, and use grammar like Warriner? We think so. We now see the goals of the language arts curriculum, at all levels, as exploration and expansion of communication potential. Conventional control may be an outcome, but it is not a criterion of entrance to or exit from the process. Language is one of several communication systems. Just as Copernicus helped us see that the earth was not the center of the universe, so our theory helps us see how verbocentric our approach to literacy has been. Our old perspective has limited our vision; with a new theoretical stance, new potentials for literacy, literacy learning, and literacy instruction exist. These, are of course, radical shifts. Importantly, discovering *what* past discoveries mean in a conceptual assimilative sense generates rethinking and redirection.

Equally fundamentally then, our theoretical perspective has led us to reexamine teaching: its relationship to learning, curriculum, and even its status and future. Lots of teaching models equate teaching and learning. We see this as problematic. There is much that the child has learned. But all that children know about language has not been taught. Curriculum is often thought of as a course of study—content to be taught, skills to be mastered. Such thinking about the language arts curriculum becomes curricular. Even when a process perspective has been taken, the question curriculum still tried to answer was what process to use to move children to convention.

When the goal of the language arts curriculum is seen as the exploration and expansion of human potential, not the control of convention, then growth can be seen as continuous, and the curriculum as the mental trip that the language user takes during a literacy event. From our perspective, what we ought to do, curricularly, is to establish an environment in which the child can *experience* and *come to value* the psycholinguistic and sociolinguistic activities we associate with successful written language use and learning. This does not mean that convention—correct spelling, correct grammar—is not important, but rather that it is a fringe benefit of socio-psycholinguistic involvement in the authoring process. Curriculum, in this view, can never be formulaic. If curriculum is what happens in the head of the language user, and is dependent on the transactions which occur in particular contexts of situation in light of the personal history of literacy which the language user brings to the situation, then teaching is theoretically based, a process of active decision-making, and theory and the use of the child-as-informant become self-correcting strategies. The development of "teacher-proof" materials is out of the question. While teachers must plan, their "paper" curricula must be written, metaphorically, in pencil.

The sociopolitical tenor of our times, which calls for "back to the basics" and uses the "content covered" as the criteria of good teaching, is out of synchronization with what we know about children, and what the teaching of literacy involves and ought to involve. Just as we would never think of going back to the basics in medicine (blood-letting), so we should never think of going back to the basics in the teaching of reading and writing.

We have learned much about literacy and literacy learning. Those who advocate going back to the basics in reading and writing ought to reflect on their own school experiences. How many stories do they remember writing? How many workbook exercises do they recall when they think back on their "great moments in reading" during their elementary school years? More pointedly, how many manuscripts of their own do they have in progress at this very moment? To glorify the English exercises which teachers paraded before us in the name of literacy is to romanticize a day and a curriculum that never were, as well as to run the risk of passing the dysfunctional strategies which we were taught on to our children. That is not to say that there is not still more to learn; nor is it to say that we have not been doing an increasingly better job of literacy instruction; but, it is to say that the literacy demands and potentials of our society have greatly increased, and to suggest that we could greatly improve the teaching of reading and writing by applying what we currently know.

This volume, then, has been written to and for our teacher and researcher colleagues in hopes of expanding their thinking and stimulating a collaborative pedagogy. Since we list only three authors, few will recognize the collaborative nature of the research program we report and the research agenda we set. Teachers from the United States, Canada, and Australia have freely shared their language stories and literacy lessons, and in so doing, have become informants in their own right. Doctoral students have pushed our thinking, and by using parallel constructs to study literacy with both less and more proficient language learners, they have greatly fine-tuned our understanding of the theoretical significance of what we, together, have found. Without the critical, but generative, insights of this thought collective (Fleck, 1979), we could not make the statements we do. We have tried to acknowledge these debts in the body of the volume. While there are many others whom we need to acknowledge, few are as important as the children who were our informants, the Proffitt Foundation, the National Council of Teachers of English, and the National Institute of Education, without whose support and cooperation this work would never have been possible. In closing we wish to express our thanks to the parents of our informants, the Monroe County School Corporation, the Indianapolis

Public Schools, the Early Childhood Learning Center, Little People's Prep, Indiana University, the administrators in these organizations, and the many others who in one way or another assisted us in this "authoring."

October 1983

Introduction

A LANGUAGE STORY

A theology student in preparation for the ministry traveled to neighboring congregations to work with local pastors. On one such trip he observed the pastor of the local congregation give a "Children's Sermon" as part of the regular worship service.

All of the children were called to the front of the church and the pastor began his sermon:

Children, I'm thinking of something that is about five or six inches high; that scampers across the ground; that can climb trees; that lives in either a nest in the tree or makes its home in a hollowed-out portion of a tree's trunk. The thing I'm thinking about gathers nuts and stores them in winter; it is sometimes brown and sometimes gray; it has a big bushy tail. Who can tell me what I'm thinking of?

Knowing the proper church behavior, the children remained quiet and reserved. No one ventured an answer.

Finally, Robert, age 6, slowly and ever so tentatively raised his hand.

The pastor, desperate for a response so he could go on with the sermon, said with some relief, "Yes, Robert, what do you think it was?"

"Well," came the response, "ordinarily I'd think it was a squirrel, but I suppose you want me to say it was Jesus."

A LITERACY LESSON

We call such an experience a "language story." Its virtue as a life vignette is that it accents some important aspects of language and language learning, and therefore helps us understand how language works.

The story which the theology student shared is a particularly good language story because it helps us understand that the setting in which we find ourselves affects the kinds of responses we give.

Robert knows that the language we use depends on the context in which we find ourselves. When we are in church we do not expect to talk about squirrels, we expect to talk about Jesus. Robert knew that the thing which his pastor was describing was a squirrel. Yet, given the fact that he was in church and listening to a sermon, the response "Jesus" seemed more predictable than did the response "squirrel."

Robert's response shows us what a sensitive language user he is. In order to come to his decision, Robert used not only all that he knew about squirrels, but also all that he knew about churches and pastors.

Not only does Robert know what topics are appropriate and inappropriate in church, but the style of his language reflects the setting in which he finds himself. Think of how masterfully Robert has phrased his answer under these awkward circumstances. Here he is in church, a place where he is supposed to behave. He is talking with a pastor, a person who is the leader of his church. In this difficult situation, Robert had better phrase his response politely, and our young diplomat does: "Well, ordinarily I'd think it was squirrel, but I suppose you want me to say it was Jesus." Robert acknowledges the fact that his pastor is the leader of his congregation by implying that if the pastor were to insist, he would set aside his "ordinary thinking."

Under a different set of circumstances we would expect Robert to respond differently. If he were at home, and if one of his friends were doing the questioning, the possibility that Jesus was the desired response would never have occurred to him. And not only would the content of his response be different, but his phrasing would be different.

Language varies according to the topic, the persons involved, and whether it is written or spoken. The language used in church is different from the language used when talking with one's playmates; the language we find in books is different from the language we find on street signs. Language which sounds right at home may sound funny in church. Children learn naturally to make adjustments in their language by having many opportunities to be present in different kinds of settings where language is being used. Successful language users adjust their language to meet the demands of the setting in which they find themselves.

Robert's response is more than just amusing or cute. It tells us that he is a growing, sensitive, and effective language user who has had lots of opportunities to compare, contrast, and use language in a wide variety of settings.

Instructionally, if the language and the language strategies we use vary according to the context of situation, then curricula should reflect this principle, as well as provide multiple and varied opportunities to explore how language users adapt reading, writing, and thinking processes to the circumstances of language use.

ABOUT THIS VOLUME

Language Stories & Literacy Lessons reports what we make of the language stories we collected from young children over the course of a program of research studying literacy before schooling. As a result of this work we are convinced that there is still much to learn about literacy as a learning process throughout life. Further, we are convinced that standard research procedures and experiments only obscure the real characteristics of this process.

What educators need to know, we think, is how written language users come to experience and value the strategies involved in successful written language use and learning and how such knowledge can lead to further exploration and expansion of the human potential. This statement suggests that young children are written language users and learners prior to coming to school. Further, it raises the possibility that children have much to teach us about successful written language use and learning. By comparing, contrasting, and evaluating the strategies involved in children's literacy learning prior to their going to school, we can evaluate the adequacy of current instruction procedures, as well as adduce directions for the future. Before we abandon the natural learning process, we had better understand it. Learning, Frank Smith (1983) tells us, is not an occasional thing. Clearly, we cannot assume that written language learning is a school-related phenomenon, which, if properly "motivated," begins when the child walks through the school's doors.

The title, *Language Stories & Literacy Lessons*, is meant to suggest that we have much to learn by using the child as our theoretical and curricular informant. "The Child as Informant" is our call to the profession to go beyond kid watching to the active examination of current assumptions about language learning and instruction.

Section One, "Language Stories," represents our attempt to make theoretical and curricular sense of the stories we collected. They are the basis from which we will proceed theoretically and curricularly until we encounter informants whose behaviors defy the explanation given in these attempts at theoretical sense-making.

Many may find our conclusions disturbing in light of what it is they think children know about reading and writing prior to coming to school. Others, who already think children know a good deal about reading and writing prior to coming to school, will find us supportive, but challenging. One reviewer of our research report wrote:

This is some of the most important and exciting educational research I know. Its challenges to traditional assumptions about research, learning and teaching are relentless, even shattering. These challenges do not spring from carping negativism but from a positive appreciation of the powers of children as learners. This research is at once highly philosophical and enormously respectful of the concrete: observations of individual children, writings, drawings, conversations. It deserves the widest possible audience.

We have purposely tried to extend the thinking of even our friends—true kid watchers. To enjoy "the language story" but not to search actively for "the literacy lesson" is to reduce children to "cute," curriculum to "that which keeps children happy," and naturalistic research to "soft." Some "whole language teachers" think making something "fun" justifies the activity. Others collect data and assume the data speak for themselves. All too often these friends—well-meaning and humanistic educators—end up not being as critically supportive of either themselves or of us as they might be.

We wish to help such educators get their theoretical act together; to move beyond cute, fun, and soft, to "sound." Any in our profession who fail to search for the literacy lesson in the language story need help in understanding what a vulnerable position they put themselves, the children they teach, and their profession in.

We would be charlatans, however, if we propose what we conclude as "truth," and ask educators simply to replace their old set of beliefs with our new set. This would do little more than condone past servitude, and serve only to freeze the profession at a 1984 level of Big Brotherhood. Most assuredly there is more to learn. The introduction we used in a report to the federal government on our findings still holds:

We began our study of what 3, 4, 5, and 6-year old children know about written language with a good deal of optimism, assured that they know much more about print than what teachers and beginning reading and writing programs assume. In part this optimism was founded in a body of research which preceded our current work. . . . In part it was founded on our own work . . . and the work of doctoral students with whom we have had the good fortune to work. . . . What the results of our effort have taught us is that we began not being optimistic enough; that children know much more than we or past researchers have ever dared to assume, and that many of the premises and assumptions with which we began must give way to more generous perspective if research and understanding are to proceed. (Harste, Burke, Woodward, 1981, p. 2)

Teachers are often surprised to find, after becoming familiar with our current position, that as preschool and elementary teachers we engaged in some of the practices we no longer condone. Our only justification is that, given what we knew at that time, such activities made sense. We now know more . . . and knowing more, we no longer engage children in such activities.

Outgrowing one's current self is not easy. It was not easy for us; it will not be easy for other educators. We were able to do so by reflecting what we believed through the theoretical prism we made of what young children were doing. This, then, is why we believe that one of our major findings, that the child can act as an informant, can become a professional self-correcting strategy of major and long-term import.

This volume does not propose a new method of teaching reading and writing to young children unless building from what the child already knows is a "new method." Even at that, we recommend no single set of experiences, nor any single classroom organization. What we attempt to do is to identify and explicate language and language learning principles that undergird theoretically based reading and writing instruction.

Good theory and good teachers interact, making better instruction and better teachers. Ten years from now we would be pleased to hear that teachers, using the child as their informant, had unearthed all of the conceptual flaws in our thinking. Even as of this moment we are pursuing new child-as-informant studies in hopes of identifying such flaws; readers would be foolish indeed if they did not do the same.

Section Two, "Literacy Lessons," introduces more formally our program of research. In this section we attempt to illustrate the key patterns in language and language learning which we see in the language stories we collected. These patterns do not speak for themselves, but in transaction with us and with the history of literacy which we bring to the setting, do convey a powerful message. It is these patterns which have caused us to rethink literacy as we respectfully, but critically, stand on the shoulders of those who have preceded us. Some readers may prefer to start their reading of this volume here, where we provide an overview of our program of research.

Some think the value of our work is that it provides a theoretical rationale for justifying what insightful teachers and researchers have been doing and saying all along. Recent experience would suggest, however, that without theoretical support, accumulated linguistic truths may be ignored and dropped from the curriculum. Complex processes like literacy and literacy learning can be explained simply, but to do so does not reduce the complexity of the original process. Simple theories have led to simple-minded instruction. The result is a profession and a nation at risk; restrictively labeled children, educators, and education.

Productive theories of literacy attempt to capture key transactions involved in the process, thus pointing out what is and what is not worthy of attention. Past models of literacy and literacy learning did a good job of explaining literacy under laboratory conditions. Unfortunately, few persons except psychologists spend much time in the laboratory. When these theories were applied to classrooms they explained so little of what went on that gaps between theory and practice often occurred. We call for a closing of such gaps by arguing that in the end, they fail to serve our profession.

These theories receive a fundamental blow when reading and writing are observed under natural conditions. "Natural conditions" does not mean in the "wild," unless that is where our informants happen to live, but rather in homes, on the job, or wherever else people are using literacy to get on with the business of living. New explanations of literacy and of literacy learning evolving from such observations constitute practical theory. We encourage teachers to follow our example and call for a collaborative pedagogy.

Children who grow up in a literate society make good informants. If the lessons these children teach us are heeded, classrooms can become natural language learning environments and teachers can become theoretical informants. Theory, too, is a self-correcting strategy. Since both our children and our profession are at stake, the study of literacy and literacy learning is much too important to be left in the hands of persons who rarely come in contact with children. These are the themes of Section Three, "Taking Ownership."

We would like to think that *Language Stories & Literacy Lessons* is the blueprint for a quiet revolution. Through it we attempt to restore professionalism to teachers and to teaching. We will try to convince readers of this volume that not to make a decision is to make one through default, that research is not simply the business of testing hypotheses, but rather the business of getting hypotheses to work in exploring and expanding the nature of literacy, literacy learning, and literacy instruction. These we see as the real and potential lessons of studying young children.

Section One
Language Stories

Chapter 1

Examining Instructional Assumptions

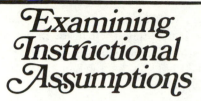

Both teachers and learners operate on the basis of language assumptions. Teachers are asked, before seeing the sty in their students' eyes, to first know themselves.

Alison, age 6, could hardly wait for first grade to start. Her mother explained her anxious anticipation tongue-in-cheek, saying, "She's caught it from me! She's no more enthusiastic than *I* am that school is going to start!"

A letter from her new teacher welcoming her to her new classroom made her impatience even more obvious.

Finally the day came when Alison and her mother could privately go to find her room, meet the teacher, and explore the school. Alison was in ecstasy! She got to register her name and birthdate on the class birthday cake, explore the reading center, tell about her summer, find out what supplies to buy, and clarify both for herself and her teacher what bus she would be riding. Alison was now more than ready.

So was her mother. This teacher was a marvel! She obviously loved children and was insuring that they would have a good year. Alison had already made her mark on "her new classroom."

That was some time ago. School is now in full swing. Alison is still enthusiastic. She loves school—the books, the teacher—and willingly shares her observations and experiences:

"Recess is *'the pits'!*"

"The boys chased me today and I fell. Do you know my friend was being so *'unconcentrative'* that she didn't even come to help?"

She also brings home her reading and writing worksheets, her art work, and other items produced or completed each day in school.

We would like to share these with you as we think that they are typical of many of the language activities found in first grades. They may even be better activities than those found in many classrooms, though we wish to argue that they are not good enough; that they reflect unfounded assumptions about written language growth and development, and that they debilitate rather than facilitate the process of language literacy.

3

Figure 1.1. Underwriting
(Alison, Age 6.4).

IDENTIFYING THE TEACHER'S ASSUMPTIONS

One of the first activities which Alison completed is that shown in Figure 1.1.

When questioned at home about why she had elected to draw the bottom half of her body, Alison responded, "It's okay, teacher said so. Someone asked and teacher said we didn't have to draw our 'whole self' if we didn't want to."

The teacher, in all likelihood, responded in this manner assuming some children wanted to draw their heads rather than their complete figure. It is interesting to note that Alison, given the option, elected to draw her bottom half and leave her top half unrepresented, extending, as it were, off the page.

At first, we might think, "A creative response to a good instructional activity." But is it? After all, this was an activity designed to help children learn to control the reading/writing process. Did it do for language what it did for art? In order to answer this question it becomes necessary to examine the activity more closely. We need to identify what teacher-held assumptions underlay the creation and selection of this activity.

This is readily done by identifying the set of written language principles related to learning which undergird this activity as opposed to other activities which might have been selected. We can easily think of both more open and more closed activities which were available options to the teacher. For example, the teacher did not elect to give the children a sheet of paper, ask them to draw a picture of themselves and then write or pretend to write an autobiographical story to share (a more open activity), nor did the teacher focus the children's attention upon an isolated letter or letter-sound correspondence pattern (a more closed activity). An analysis, then, of this activity and of the teacher's responses to it, suggests the following assumptions about written language learning:

Assumption 1: One of the first tasks in learning to read and write is to be able to discriminate visually between the letters of the alphabet.

This is best taught by activities such as underwriting which force the child to attend to the distinctive features of each letter.

Assumption 2: Language activities designed for children should be manageable to insure completion and hence success.

One way to accomplish this is to use simple whole texts which contain a limited number of basic vocabulary items (Here I am. My name is . . .).

Assumption 3: Errors should be marked to give corrective feedback and to stop bad habits from forming (see the teacher's correction of *s* in Figure 1.1).

Assumption 4: Initial language activities should be personally meaningful to the child.

This is best done by focusing on topics of interest to the child (in this activity, the topic self).

Assumption 5: Children do not need as much support in art as they do in writing.

The incorporation of art allows for self-expression and creativity.

The question now becomes, "In order to make these assumptions, what does one have to believe?"

The more obvious belief underlying Assumption 1 is that children need to be able to note differences between the various letters of the alphabet in order to read and write. Less obvious perhaps is the implicit belief that first graders do not already possess this ability to discriminate between the letters of the alphabet, i.e., that visual discrimination of letters must be formally taught.

Each of these beliefs merits investigation. They may be as much folklore as developmental givens. The rampant popularity of a belief is never a criterion for acceptability, but rather for testing.

A rather extensive listing of further beliefs which we have identified as inherent in this single instructional activity is the following:

Access to the reading/writing process hinges on mastery of the distinctive features of print (see Assumption 1).

The word is the key unit in language (see Assumption 2).

Words selected for initial instruction must be chosen on the basis of frequency of usage (see Assumption 2).

Errors must be pointed out by a guiding adult since children do not have information which they can use for self-correction (see Assumption 3).

The goal of early language learning is an error-free performance on basics since without this children will never be able to access the process (see Assumption 3).

Activities which make personal sense support the child's access to basic literacy processes (see Assumption 4).

This means, insofar as language learning is concerned, that topics should be chosen carefully so that children

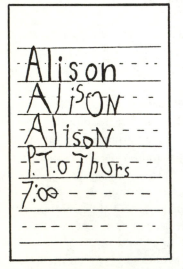

find them personally meaningful but that the actual language introduced must be carefully selected and controlled by the teacher (see Assumptions 2 and 4). Art is an easy activity for the child (natural); reading and writing are hard activities (unnatural) (see Assumption 5).

Art is learned; reading and writing must be taught (see Assumption 5).

Creativity must wait upon control. Because children have already learned the basic forms of art, i.e., they have control of the basic conventions, creativity can be expected. Once children control the conventions of written language, they can and will become creative written language users as well (see Assumption 5).

Some may argue that this kind of analysis is highly speculative, and infers much from a single instructional activity. With this we would have to agree. These same persons would feel more comfortable, as indeed we would, if the identified language learning principles reoccurred in subsequent activities. To show that this is indeed the case, three additional activities completed during the first week of school are illustrated.

The activity illustrated in Figure 1.2 is closely tied to that already discussed in Figure 1.1. In this instance, children were given ditto master copies of story parts, of which the page shown is one. The children were asked to arrange the pages in order, paste them to the blank pages of a stapled book, draw a picture to fit the text, and overwrite the script on each page. Though this assignment involves more procedures, what has been said about the beliefs inherent in the first activity holds for this activity too. The significant creative decisions about the written language—the writing of the story—have been made by the teacher. The student is left simply to recreate the decreed text order and to copy the print. Only the art is left open to the creative efforts of the student.

The activity which generated the product illustrated in Figure 1.3 initially appears somewhat different, but closer examination indicates that it too shares the beliefs reflected in the first two assignments. This assignment is a Parent-Teacher Notice which the children were asked to copy off the blackboard and take home as a reminder of an upcoming meeting. In this instance, the teacher gave the children a sheet of lined paper with their name on it. She asked the children to underwrite their name twice, and then to copy the message written on the blackboard.

An analysis of the beliefs which guided this activity suggests that all of the original beliefs still hold, and that a further clarification has been achieved. Presumably the teacher is concerned with how Alison spatially controls the writing of her name and feels that she needs to practice it. Often this concern for the child's inability to stay within the lines is predicated on the belief that handwriting signals muscle and eye coordination and that such coordination is prerequisite to learning to read and write.

Figure 1.4 illustrates this teacher's application of the language experience approach to teaching reading. Rather than transcribe what the children have actually said, Alison's teacher has transformed each new suggestion into a common pattern for the purpose of teaching the word *we* and controlling the complexity of the syntactic patterns used. After the teacher composed this text, she gave each child a ditto copy of the class-contributed "language experience story" and asked the class to circle the word *we* each time it appeared. Although the instructional activity has changed, the underlying assumptions governing the activity remain intact from the first three lessons.

An analysis such as we have been doing here is intended to indicate that what Alison's teacher believes about the reading and writing process strongly affects both her choice of instructional activities and her handling of such activities. Her behavior is orderly, consistent, and predictable. This is so in spite of the fact that she maintains that she is eclectic and applies "a variety of approaches to the teaching of reading." Despite the supposed surface structure variety in activities, her invariant assumptions continue to show.

From data such as these, we have come to believe that looking at teacher behavior in terms of beliefs held and assumptions made is more cogent and powerful than looking at behavior in terms of the supposed approach being used (Harste and Burke, 1977). This teacher presumably changes her approaches, but because she does not change her beliefs, her classroom practice is unaffected (as is, in all likelihood, the outcome of her instruction, but that's another equally important and complex issue which we will not develop here).

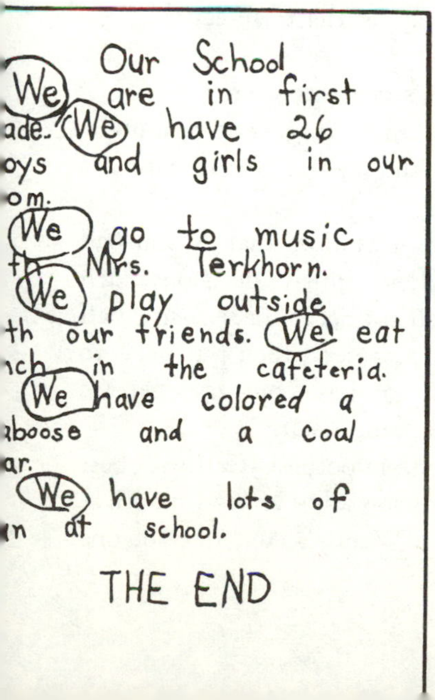

These data support the position that the teaching of reading and writing is theoretically based, that all of us as teachers have a theory of how to teach reading and writing in our heads which strongly affects our perception and behavior. We define theory simply as a set of interrelated beliefs and assumptions through which perception and behavior are organized. What this means practically is that in order to change behavior we must change beliefs. To that end we will now turn to an examination of the language encounters which Alison had prior to and outside of her school-related experiences.

IDENTIFYING THE LANGUAGE LEARNER'S ASSUMPTIONS

Reading. Alison, we wish to argue, has been a user of written language for a long time. One of the earliest instances of Alison's use of

Figure 1.4. Class-Contributed "Language Experience Story" (Alison, Age 6.2).

written language occurred when she was 3 years old. At the time, Alison and her family were on the way to the zoo. As they approached the beltway which would take them to the zoo, Alison's father, pointing to an overhead sign signaling "West 465," asked, "Alison, what do you think that says?"

Alison responded, "It says . . . uh . . . 'Daddy, turn right here to go to the zoo.'"

While some might argue that this isn't reading, we wish to disagree. Alison has made a decision which puts her in the semantic ball park. She assumes that the print *out there* relates to the activity in which she and her family are engaged. And she's right in all but the pickiest sense. Alison's response demonstrates her expectation that written language is meaningful. We do not know how or when children come to this important conclusion. All we know is that children as young as 3 have already made it, and that somehow readers who end up in remedial classes have lost it or lost faith in it.

We believe it is through the expectation that written language makes sense that control is gained. Once the sense-making intent of written language has been perceived, ideation and hypothecation become the process forces of control. To illustrate this point further, we can share another one of Alison's early encounters with print. This encounter occurred on a "dessert trip" to Baskin-Robbin's. She was 4 years old at the time.

After eating her ice cream cone, Alison looked around the room attempting to find a trash can where she could deposit her soiled napkin. After exploring logical locations, she found it, studied the wooden flap engraved with the word *PUSH*, performed the required action, and deposited her napkin.

Alison's mother, who had been observing her problem-solving behaviors now asked, "Alison, what does that say on the trash can?"

"Push," came the response.

"How do you know?" came her mother's next question.

To which Alison responded by taking her index finger and running it over the *P*, the *U*, the *S*, and the *H* in turn, and saying, "Because it's got all the right letters!"

It was from knowing what written language does that Alison had grown in her control of the form. From earlier cognitive decisions, such as that illustrated in the trip to the zoo which put her in the semantic ball park, she could and did test language hypotheses which put her—to carry the metaphor another step—not only on base, but gave her the metalinguistic control to speak about the game itself.

The importance of this process of ongoing hypothesis-testing is best illustrated by yet another language story. Alison was 4 years, 1 month at the time. In this instance she was shown a Wendy's cup, like the one

Figure 1.5. Wendy's Cup (Alison, Age 4.1).

illustrated in Figure 1.5, and asked, "What do you think this says?"

Alison ran her finger under the word *Wendy's*, and responded, "Wendy's," and under the word *Hamburgers*, and said, "Cup." Alison then paused a moment as if in reflection, and added, "That's a long word with a short sound!"

In this instance, the hypothesis which Alison has formulated about graphic-sound correspondence is an incorrect one. Yet her very mention of it signals us that she has also formulated the correct alternative and is attempting to orchestrate this decision with the sense-making intent she knows exists.

Need we help her? Not in a traditional corrective sense. All we need to ensure is that she has continuing encounters with the process, for each encounter will allow her to test out the validity of her current hypotheses and to reconstruct a new set at a level far above our assumptive imaginations.

Alison was reading before she went to first grade. Her first-grade teacher, through the use of standardized tests, has placed her at the preprimer level. At home she reads such texts as *It's the Easter Beagle, Charlie Brown* (Schulz, 1976)—she's not likely to encounter equivalent print settings in school until fourth grade.

Why the discrepancy? It's those assumptions again. The tests Alison has taken in school strip language of its context, forcing her to deal with letters and words not only outside of a supportive linguistic environment, but also outside of a supportive context of situation. Without the latter, Alison has neither a point of anticipation, nor a point of contextualization.

Written language learning is a social event of some complexity, and written language use reflects the orchestration of this complex social event. Both the complexity and the orchestration support the development of user control. Knowing that Alison is the reader she is would leave us puzzled at her production of backward *s*'s in writing (as illustrated in Figure 1.1) unless we give up the assumption that control of form is prerequisite to the language process. It is because Alison is, and has been, a reader and a writer that she has a growing control of its form, and not vice versa.

Writing.   Alison is, and has been, as impressive a writer as she is a reader. Her explorations of written language began long before what she produced became representational in any adult sense. What Alison reaffirmed in her movement into writing is that children must encounter the language process in its complexity in order to learn control. As with reading, it was Alison's early access to what written language does which allowed her that control.

One evening, at 4 years, 3 months, Alison encountered a wordless book and made up an appropriate story. The next evening, wanting to reread the book, she asked her mother, "What was that story I read last night?"

"Well, I'm sure I don't know. If you want to remember your stories, you need to write them down. Then you can reread them whenever you want to."

Alison's story about Daddy coming home and taking the family to McDonald's (in Figure 1.6) was placeheld by using the letters of the name simply reshuffled in order. For months, whenever she encountered this book, she would get her paper out and faithfully read this text, with minor variations:

*One day Daddy came home and
he said, "Hi Family, I'm home,"
and he's gonna take us to
McDonald's. I'm gonna have a
Fun Meal.*

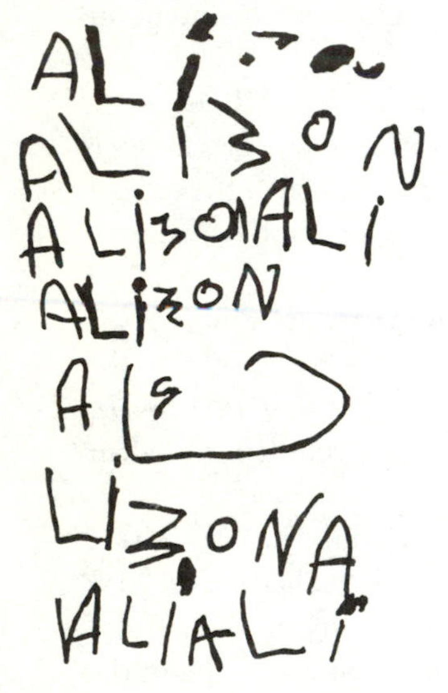

This sample illustrates Alison's public announcement of her discovery of the finite symbol system in written language; namely, that one continuously reorchestrates the same set of letters to produce an infinite set of words. Alison, as was always the case, demonstrated this growth using print of high personal worth—her name.

As with reading, adult recognition of the writing process often seems to hinge on how representational or conventional the product is. This is clearly unfortunate, for it leads to the dismissal of early writing efforts as unworthy of attention.

Alison is clearly a writer, orchestrating aspects of this particular social event much as any writer would. She has already grasped a lot: the meaning relationship between picture, text and her world; directionality (both top-down and left-to-right), the function of print in this setting; the organizational scaffolding of a story; the use of structure components to placehold meaning. Each of these insights is a signal of her developing written language literacy. The fact that her writing is not yet representational (the symbols she uses to placehold *McDonald's* or *Daddy* do not look identifiable as such to our literate eyes) is not nearly as significant as are these other factors.

Alison's orchestration of these multiple insights is clear evidence of

*Figure 1.6. Story to Wordless Book
(Alison, Age 4.3).*

her sophistication. In light of all that she has managed to do, why should the questions most frequently generated about her accomplishments be, "Did she spell correctly?" and "Did she make her letters right?"

At 4 years, 8 months, Alison placeheld all written messages using a cursive script such as that illustrated in Figure 1.7. While a first look at Alison's product might indicate that she knew little about writing, such a conclusion would turn out to be assumptive and false. What this product represents is simply Alison's testing of alternative available hypotheses. Although we cannot know specifically what she is testing, we can feel fairly comfortable in light of her earlier behavior in saying that she has tentatively set aside some of what she already knows (her knowledge of letterness and the finite symbol system of English) to test other aspects of the process. Alison has not had a setback. Current models would suggest that she evidences linear growth and is bringing more and more aspects under control in an incremental fashion. Data such as these clearly challenge extant notions of development.

If one views each instance of written language use as the orchestration of a complex social event, then what the initiate written language user is faced with is a problem of some magnitude. As the language user perceives various elements in this event, new hypotheses are generated and tested. These hypotheses are concerned with pragmatics (what the rules of language use are relative to a particular situational context), semantics (how I can say what I mean), syntax (how I get the flow of my message captured on paper), graphics (how I represent what I wish to say), and the orchestration of these systems (how I draw on all these systems simultaneously). Within each of these areas there is, of course, a range of hypotheses which need formulation and fit. Additional hypotheses arise as the user orchestrates more and more elements. What looks like regression, given the assumptions underlying one theory, signals growth from another theoretical perspective.

*Figure 1.7. Cursive Story Script
(Alison, Age 4.8).*

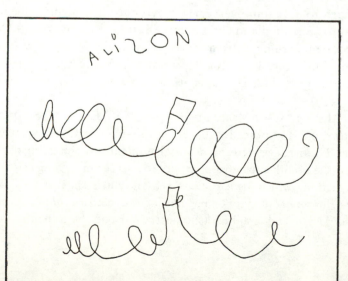

Figure 1.8. Signatures (Alison).

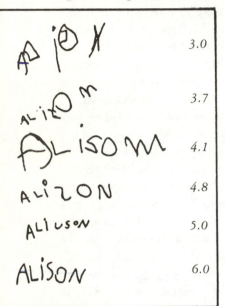

	3.0
	3.7
	4.1
	4.8
	5.0
	6.0

*Figure 1.9. Finger Puppet
(Alison, Age 5.6).*

Growth, while constant—and we believe this to be the mode for *all* of us as written language users—looks sporadic because of the postulates which undergird our assumptive yardsticks. Current yardsticks divert attention away from growth and toward "developmental stages," which attempt to calculate growth by marking surface level features of conventional form. Such a focus draws our attention away from the universals of written language literacy, which operate across language users at all ages and simply express themselves in a variety of alternative forms. It limits our thinking about literacy. Literacy becomes a step-by-step progression of control, not a vehicle for exploring and expanding our world.

As an example, let's take spelling, often measured as a simple yes-no decision. Alison has used the conventional spelling of her name since she was 3 years old, as is illustrated in Figure 1.8. Yet her most interesting signature is not her first or last, but the one she experimented with during a two-week period shortly after she turned 5. At this point, when Alison wrote her name, she added a *u* in the middle. When asked why she added the *u*, she replied, "Because I wanted to." After several weeks of experimenting with this signature, she abandoned it in favor of the spelling her parents had elected at her birth.

Isn't it fascinating? Everything Alison had discovered about print compelled her to say that there ought to be a *u* in her name. And there well could be. It was one of the options her parents could have taken when they selected the original spelling of her name.

Alison feels very comfortable with what she's discovered about how print operates. Like all of us, she's most satisfied and most interested in her latest discovery and tries it on for fit. Similar trends will be seen in the writing of all of us—a favorite word, a favorite syntactic pattern, a favorite organizational style. The issue is not so much what is being tested or how much conventional congruency is achieved, but that the universality of growth, and fit, and continued growth is expressed.

At 5 years, 6 months, Alison was asked to make a finger puppet out of paper, to add a smiling face, and to write about something that made her happy. She produced the product illustrated in Figure 1.9. Without apparent warning, Alison moved so naturally from the writing illustrated in Figure 1.7 to that represented in Figure 1.9 that her behavior quite surprised us. She has continued to write in this latter fashion ever since.

Alison's "What Makes Me Happy" (MN I C FLOMRS—When I see flowers) is an impressive display of rule-governed, orchestrated behavior. The message is the product of her integrated processing of pragmatics (she used language appropriate to this setting), semantics (she said something which made personal sense), syntax (she managed to capture the flow of her thought on paper using the standard conventional form of wordness), and graphics (she abstracted out the salient letter-sound

DRerbRe M I JoveoN Your PRessAlison

Figure 1.10. Letter to Grandmother (Alison, Age 6.0).

Text Translation: "Dear Grandma, I loved your present. Alison."

Figure 1.11. Underwriting (Alison, Age 6.4).

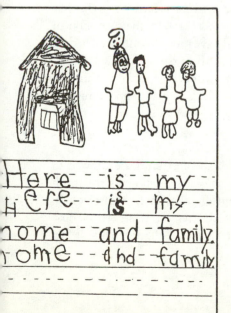

relationships which undergird written language and placeheld these relationships with letter forms). Given such a magnificent breakthrough, we find it quite frustrating that the only comment made by one professional, with whom we shared this piece, was that her "W's were upside down."

On her sixth birthday, Alison wrote her grandmother a letter thanking her for the present which she had sent. Once again Alison's knowledge of written language proves to be extensive, showing a complex mapping of letter-sound relationships, syntax, and meaning. When her writing here is compared to that done on the finger puppet, it becomes clear that Alison also has some awareness of the function of written language in alternative settings. That is, her letter sounds like a letter, while the message on her puppet was a response to the implied lead, "What makes me happy . . ." We might also note Alison's conventional spellings of *loved* and *your*, indicating that she is using not only a phonetic mapping in her spelling, but also a visual memory of what these words look like. Alison orchestrates these elements so smoothly that they go easily undetected as the magnificent achievements which they are. The fact that such phenomena are sorted out so readily by children at such an early age leads us and others to conclude that, "Writing is Natural" (K. Goodman and Y. Goodman, 1979).

Alison's behavior here is a vivid display of the interrelatedness of reading and writing. It is through having encountered the words *loved* and *your* in reading that Alison fine-tunes her writing strategies. Alison simultaneously orchestrated spelling by the way it sounds, by the way it looks, and by the way it means. All of the growth illustrated in the examples above occurred prior to Alison's entrance into first grade— growth which went untapped in the instructional activities which Alison's teacher provided for her.

When Alison returned home from school with the written product

HoRos Mi Hos ADND FoMLE

*Figure 1.12. Uninterrupted
Writing
(Alison, Age 6.4).*

shown in Figure 1.11 her father gave her a piece of paper and asked her to write, "Here is my house and family," the very script which she had underwritten on the school worksheet.

Alison, we lamentingly report, burst into tears and said, "I can't write."

After being comforted, she was told, "Sure you can, you've been writing a long time now."

"But I don't know how to spell and write good," came the still tearful reply.

"Oh, yes you do. You're only in first grade. If your writing looked like ours, there would be no reason for you to be there. You know we can read anything you write."

With this Alison produced the text illustrated in Figure 1.12.

We say, "How sad that Alison had to have this moment of doubt." Her assumptions did not match the instructional assumptions being addressed and hence she decided she was wrong. In this instance instruction was a debilitating rather than a facilitating experience.

CONCLUSION

Data collected from Alison and some sixty-seven other 3-, 4-, 5-, and 6-year-olds (Harste, Burke, Woodward, 1981, 1983) leads us to conclude that many of the instructional assumptions currently made by teachers are faulty at best and debilitating at worst. In no instance—and our data have been collected from boys and girls in high, middle, and low SES, black and white, small town and urban inner-city families—would the assumptions underlying Alison's instruction have been appropriate ones from which to operate instructionally.

The error in the instruction provided by Alison's teacher was that her instructional assumptions were never tested through the provision of open-entry student activities which could have provided alternative data and led her to challenge her own beliefs. All of the activities given to Alison by her teacher effectively forced Alison to operate within the teacher's assumptive bounds, never providing her the opportunity to demonstrate what decisions she, as a language user, was interested in and capable of making.

What we recommend instructionally for both teacher and pupil is such open-entry language activities in which constraints are allowed to evolve in a risk-free language environment, where each in a sense (both teacher and pupil) can become an assumption taller than themselves. In many ways, the real issue which this chapter addresses is: Whose written language assumptions should be tested—the teacher's or the language user's?

Chapter 2
Rethinking Development

Young children are written language users and learners long before their writing looks representational. A new set of criteria for understanding the evolution of literacy is proposed.

Researchers studying what young children know about print have found children in a state of "cognitive confusion." After many years of work in this area, however, we have yet to find a child who is "cognitively confused." In this chapter we discuss three perspectives which we believe to be imperative in shaping a new theory of literacy learning. These three perspectives are: confusing product with process, confusing growth with experience, and confusing convention with language.

ON CONFUSING PRODUCT WITH PROCESS

Figure 2.1. Uninterrupted Writing and Uninterrupted Drawing Samples (Marvin, Age 3).

Recently we asked a preschool teacher to have her 3-year-olds sign in each day to help her keep attendance and to help us trace written language growth and development. We made booklets for her so that the children could write their names on a clean page each day. When we offered her more booklets, she said, "This isn't working. The children aren't writing."

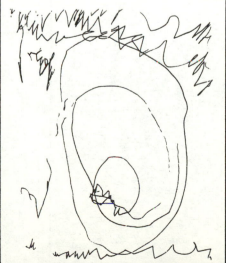

Figure 2.2. Uninterrupted Writing (Taisha, Age 4).

Figure 2.3. Uninterrupted Writing and Uninterrupted Drawing Samples (Terry, Age 3).

Figure 2.1 presents two typical products which this teacher was using in reaching her decision. In Uninterrupted Writing, Marvin was asked to write his name and anything else that he could write. In Uninterrupted Drawing, Marvin was asked to draw a picture of himself and to write his name. (Demographic information as well as a description of the tasks we used in this research study can be found in the Appendix to this volume; for more in-depth discussion, readers are referred to our original research reports.) Marvin's signature in Uninterrupted Writing closely resembles his signature at the bottom of Uninterrupted Drawing. When we contrast Marvin's writing with his art (top portion of Uninterrupted Drawing), we have to conclude, despite his teacher's evaluation, that not only is Marvin writing, but he has made important distinctions between art as a communication system and writing as a communication system.

Teachers and parents often view early drawing in much the same way that they view early writing, demeaning both by calling them "scribbles." When the product becomes representational or stereotypic, then, and only then, do they become excited. A typical example is Taisha (see Figure 2.2).

Since Taisha's representation of her name as well as her representation of *people*, *houses*, *snow*, and *rain* coincide with adult notions of how these ought to be represented, these forms become valued. For many adults, literacy means "to represent the world on their terms, with their templates."

A first argument we wish to make is that the young child is a written language user long before his writing looks representational. We will argue that the decisions which the young child makes are, both in form and in kind, like those which we make as literate adults. When we confuse product with process we fail to note the onset of literacy and, in so doing, also fail to appreciate the real literacy achievement made by 3-year-olds.

Uninterrupted Writing

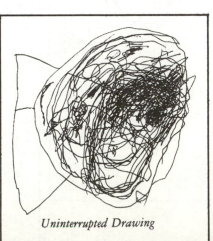

Uninterrupted Drawing

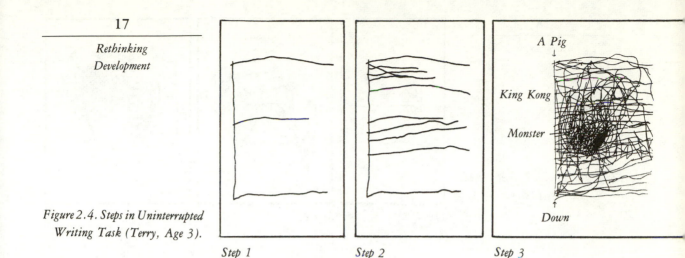

Step 1   *Step 2*   *Step 3*

*Figure 2.4. Steps in Uninterrupted
Writing Task (Terry, Age 3).*

To develop this point we will examine the products which Terry, another 3-year-old, produced in Uninterrupted Writing and Uninterrupted Drawing (see Figure 2.3).

When we share these products without identifying which one is drawing and which one is writing, adults often initially find it difficult to say which is which. If, however, we examine the processes involved in producing these products (see Figures 2.4 and 2.5), these confusions disappear.

The first four marks Terry made in Uninterrupted Writing form the letter *E*, which Terry says is his name. Note that at age 3, Terry has invented a mark which he takes to represent his name. Later, we will show that Terry consistently uses this mark to sign his name across written language encounters. Terry added a few more lines (Step 2). Significantly, these markings are linear, and, as is illustrated in Figure 2.5, quite different from the lines he added during Uninterrupted Drawing. Terry wrote for twenty-five minutes in producing the product in Figure 2.4. When asked to read what he had written (Step 3), Terry read, "A pig . . . King Kong . . . Monster . . . [and] Down," pointing to the places marked in Figure 2.4.

Terry's Uninterrupted Drawing contrasts sharply with his writing. Art for Terry is global and circular and as such, contrasts with the linearity of what writing is for him. Terry began his self-portrait with the letter *E* (Step 1). Interestingly, Terry's art, like his writing, also evolved from the letter *E*, his name. Terry's subsequent decisions here, however, are quite different from those he made during writing, as is illustrated in his emerging product (Step 2).

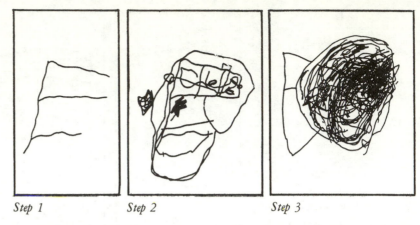

*Figure 2.5. Steps in Uninterrupted
Drawing (Terry, Age 3).*

| Step 1 | Step 2 | Step 3 |

*Figure 2.6. Name Writing Across
Tasks (3-Year-Olds).*

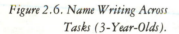

Uninterrupted Drawing		Uninterrupted Writing
H	Heather	H H
E	Terry	E
~~	Marvin	~~~
ooooooo	Shannon	ooooo
mmmm	D.J.	mmmm
4+9 T T	Towanna	T T T T T
10	Robert	o o
MMMM	Latrice	4
OOO	Jerry	OOO
MMMM	Tasha	MMMM

Art is often thought to develop ahead of writing, and many even argue that children learn letter forms from their work in art. Terry's writing challenges that view. The decisions which Terry has made about writing facilitate his growth and development in art, and vice versa. The relationship here is a reciprocal one which becomes mutually supportive to written language literacy in the broadest sense.

We have found that by the age of 3 all children in our study could, under certain conditions, distinguish art from writing. Their decisions in writing, as in art, are systematic and organized. We found further that all 3-year-olds had developed a marking which to them symbolized their name. This marking acted as any symbol acts, serving to place-hold meaning during writing, and to reconstruct that meaning during reading.

Figure 2.6 shows the consistency of the markings of our 3-year-olds in representing their names from one writing to another. And, lest we forget, these are the writings of lower- and middle-class black and white children, not of upper-class children who supposedly have some school literacy advantage. We believe it is also important that we recognize these writings for what they are. They are not pseudo, preliterate marks or acts, but, both in form and in process, the stuff of real literacy, being invented from the inside out.

A second argument we wish to make is that in order to judge the quality of a literacy experience one must judge the quality of the mental trip taken, not the arrival point per se. To illustrate this argument we will use some of the selected examples collected from a story writing setting we used in our research (see Figure 2.7). In this setting the child was given a paper and pen and told, "Today, you will write a story and I'll write a story. When we are done, we'll read our stories. You read your story to me and then I'll read my story to you."

In response to our request we received a variety of products. Jason drew a picture. Natasha also drew a picture, but not before she had written, "This is a puppy." Vincent wrote, "I like candy," using a rebuslike combination of writing and art.

If we, as adults, expect children to write when we ask them to write, then we would be more pleased with Natasha's and Vincent's work than with Jason's. What we wish to argue, however, is that to use such a criterion sells short both the child and the cognitive operations involved in real literacy.

Jason, when asked to read what he had written, read, "A ghost flying through the air. A dog barking. And when the ghost saw him, he came down and he bumped him on the nose!" In so doing, Jason demonstrates that he not only understands the rules governing what he is to do in this setting, but also the notion of storiness. What Jason has elected to do in this instance is simply to move to an alternate communication system to placehold his meaning. This option is one which we, as literate adults, can also make when writing.

Vincent, age 6, when asked to read what he had written, read the expected, "I like candy." Natasha, age 6, likewise read the expected, "This is a puppy." But it is important to understand that each child has communicated ideas in sentence form using graphics as symbols to placehold meaning. Vincent, like Jason, negotiated the contract on the floor from writing to drawing when he believed he could not spell candy. Importantly, neither Vincent's nor Natasha's products show knowledge of storiness, while Jason's product, despite its less conventional form, does. So from a process perspective, the products which we might initially favor do not appear to be as good.

Given this single instance, we cannot realistically say if Vincent or Natasha have a notion of storiness or not. All we do know is that in this situation, they decided to respond in a particular way which didn't obviously show it, and that their way of responding differed from at least one other child, namely, Jason.

Trying to get ideas down on paper can be a constraining factor, especially if schools demand correctness of form. Our hunch is that both Natasha and Vincent decided to play it safe, so the product does not express all that they know, but is rather a function of their decision-making given the constraints which they perceive to be operating in this particular context of situation.

A third argument we wish to make is that writing is not a monolithic skill. Language varies according to the circumstances of its use. Different settings mandate different products. Michelle at age 6, in what was our seventh session with her over the four-year period we studied her, was asked to write her name and anything else she could write. A transcript of her conversation with the researcher during the production of her product in Figure 2.8 illustrates the key cognitive operations

*Figure 2.7. Story Writing
(Composite).*

Jason, Age 5

Natasha, Age 6

Vincent, Age 6

*Figure 2.8. Uninterrupted
Writing (Michelle, Age 6).*

*Transcription (as read by child):
Michelle Morrison
Where is this (flower)? It is in the
(grass). Where is the (grass).
It is in here.*

involved in her written language use and learning.

After initially writing *Where*, Michelle asked: "Did I write *where?*"

The researcher responded: "Yes."

Michelle: "I forgot how to write *tiger.*"

Researcher: "You write whatever you can."

Michelle: "It begins with *T* . . . [writes *t*] . . . but, I want to know how."

Researcher: "You write whatever you want to write."

Michelle: "I don't know how. . . . Is an *h* after this [pointing to the *t*]?"

Michelle writes *is*, squeezing it in between the *e* in *where* and the *t* in *this*.

Realizing she has a word card with *tiger* written on it, Michelle starts to leave the table, saying, "I'll be right back."

The researcher stops her, saying: "You write it how you think it is."

"I wish you'd tell me some words. I can't remember *tiger.*"

"You do the best you can. You'll remember it's *tiger*," responds the researcher.

Michelle responds, "I don't know what to write. Can I write a picture? . . . Can I write a picture, if I don't know how to spell it?"

"You write whatever you like to write."

Michelle writes *This* and draws a flower. She then writes *It is in*. She reads to herself, "Where is this flower. It is in." She writes *the*, and draws some grass.

Again she reads the whole thing: "Where is this flower. It is in the grass." She writes her second *Where*, rereads all her writing, writes *is the*, and then draws another clump of grass. Without rereading she writes *It is*, saying the words to herself as she does so. After reading all she has written, Michelle writes *in herer*.

She then reads her completed text: "Where is this flower? It is in the grass. Where is the grass? It is in here."

Throughout this literacy event we can see Michelle clarifying for herself the expectations for her writing under these conditions. She wants approval to get her word card so she can spell correctly and, later, to draw instead of write. Once she has made her decision to draw the words she cannot spell, she moves freely between writing and art to placehold meaning. By listening to Michelle we get a good picture of what constraints she sees operating in this setting. It is important to understand that this significant literacy event would have been lost if we had examined only product and not process. By watching Michelle write this product, however, which in itself means little, we can uncover the orchestrated literacy decision-making event which undergirds it. Strategies and constraints which are frozen in adult writing once again become visible.

Figure 2.9. Letter Writing Composites (Michelle, Age 6).

Transcription (as read by child):

Dolly with her treasure chest. Come with cradle and stroller and doll rocker, sleeper outfit, baby seat, little love panties and powder set.

The next day Michelle was asked to write a letter. Before this research session began, Michelle had shown the researcher the Sears catalogue and the doll she wanted for Christmas. The researcher used Santa as the person to whom Michelle should write her letter (see Figure 2.9).

Michelle writes *DAE* and asks, "Does it spell *dolly?*"

The researcher responds, "You write it the best you can."

After writing *with*, Michelle reads, "Dolly with," and then writes *hr*. At this point she asks, "Does this spell *her?*"

The researcher responds, "You're doing nicely writing this letter." Michelle sounds out *tr* and *ch*. She writes *ch* and crosses it out, saying, "Oh, is that right for *treasure?*"

The researcher says, "If you make a mistake you can cross it out." Michelle writes *thr chchrt*, and decides to cross out the final *rt*, as she asks, "Does that say *Treasure Chest?*"

The researcher responds, "You're doing well. You keep writing your letter."

After rereading, Michelle says, "I know how to spell *come.*" Michelle reflects as much to herself as to the researcher, "You make funny *e*'s." As she makes another she says, "You make little circles and color it in," obviously loving not only the experience, but her new-found style.

Michelle writes *come with* and once more rereads her evolving text.

Michelle asks, "Does *cradle* start with *k* or *c?*" Michelle writes *KdL*, asking, "Does that say *cradle?*"

After writing *And*, Michelle once more rereads her text.

She writes *stLL* and asks, "Does that spell *stroller?*"

As she finished writing the letter, Michelle continued reading her text, making self-corrections and asking the researcher for reassurance that she was doing it right. When her message was complete, Michelle said that she was not going to use periods. She put her name at the top of the page, probably because of the first-grade practice of putting your name at the top of all papers (previously in the Letter-Writing task, Michelle had followed the convention of putting her name after the message). After finishing all her writing she was still not tired of the task, and she elected to draw a picture at the bottom of the letter.

In this letter-writing context as contrasted to the Uninterrupted Writing task, Michelle made several literacy decisions. From reading the catalogue she was aware that the doll and all the things it came with were formatted graphically in a specific way. In writing letters over time, Michelle always used the graphic form for signing her message and had never negotiated a move to pictures. As she wrote this letter she was testing out her ideas about following the catalogue's graphic format. This forced her to test her ways of spelling to include both spelling as it sounds and spelling as it looks.

These examples show us that Michelle demonstrates good graphophonemic knowledge. As a writer, she is also actively engaged in the reading process. As a writer, Michelle herself is her own first reader. Attention span is not an issue when personal involvement and choice are an integral part of the process.

After writing her letter, Michelle paused, as if reflecting. Dejectedly she said, "Don't send it to Santa. I know it's not correct." Using the product, not the process, as the standard by which she judges her success in literacy, Michelle has all too willingly adopted the adult expectation that the product is the important indicator of "what I know." The adult focus on product in the environment in which Michelle is growing up begins to confuse her about what writing is. This focus seems to convince Michelle to value form over function and to reorder her literacy learning priorities accordingly.

But more positively, Michelle seems aware of different writing demands in different writing settings. Through working with us over the course of our research, Michelle learned that when she wrote with us, as opposed to when she wrote with her parents or in school, she could set aside certain concerns. She learned that she was allowed to and expected to experiment, to take risks, and to actively use all she knew about language. Under these conditions, Michelle came to understand and discover what real literacy was all about as we did.

With a focus on product, we not only fail to see growth, but also to make and take the opportunities for literacy which abound around us. With a focus on product, we deny language users such as Michelle their most powerful language learning strategy: namely, active involvement— the kind of involvement which demands that they bring to bear all they currently know about language to test yet another new hypothesis. It is only when children are engaged in this way that both they and we can go about the business of understanding written language literacy. At bottom, written language literacy involves "the saga of learning how to mean" (Halliday, 1973) via markings which placehold and sign meaning. Understanding this process is as central to our growth as it is to that of the child's.

We began this section, "On Confusing Product With Process," with a language story telling about how a teacher, on the basis of surface feature form, rejected a sign-in activity as a valuable literacy learning experience. We close with the request: "Let them 'sign in,' please!"

ON CONFUSING GROWTH WITH EXPERIENCE

Most 5-year-olds can correctly identify the basic colors.
Most 6-year-olds can write their names.
Most 7-year-olds have a reading sight vocabulary of approximately 215 words.

Despite the fact that we seem to have no trouble responding to such statements, and despite the fact that such statements are capable of statistical verification (that is, we can test populations and come up with numerical counts and percentages), such statements, we would like to argue, are not useful predictors of accomplishment. The relationship which these statements feature, that between *age* and *accomplishment*, is based upon a loose correlation between *age* and *experience*.

The languaging of the children in our study demonstrates that experience is the operational factor in this pair. Experience makes the evolution of literacy predictable. This argument becomes clearer when we add a fourth statement:

Most adults can read.

While this statement is as verifiable as the first three, some of the pitfalls in its underlying reasoning are more easily visible. What does this "fact" lend to our assessment of any individual adult who does *not* demonstrate an ability to read? We cannot assume lack of age, but we should begin to ask questions about opportunities and experience.

Age pales into insignificance in the adult example. And it should also begin to pale when the language users we are interested in are children. Age has always been a convenience, an easier factor for language researchers and curriculum developers to manage than experience. But age is a dangerous criterion precisely because it does not consistently covary with the operational factor of experience.

Let us look at some responses which children gave when reading items common in their environment.

Reading responses have been ordered in Figure 2.10 in relation to their approach to the conventional response to the item. For Dynamints, the trend is from a *functional* response, through a *categorical* response, to a *specified* response. When we examine the ages of the children who made these responses, we can see no clear age trends.

We will pay particular attention to Tyler and Michelle, the two youngest readers, as we look at their Jello, Crest, and Wendy's environmental print readings. In the readings of Jello we again find responses which range from functional, through categorical, to specified, with a dispersal of ages. Just as she does with Dynamints, Michelle seems to have the experiential edge on Tyler. An examination of the functional responses to this print environment is supportive of our age thesis. Both "We eat food" and "It should be a telephone number" are descriptors of selected past encounters which these readers feel should be related to this encounter.

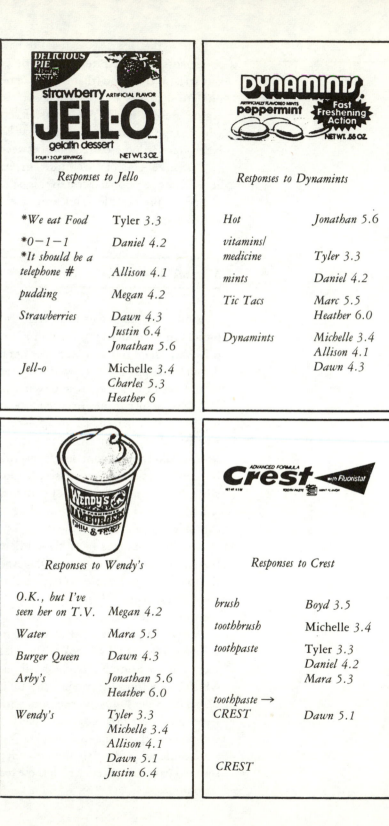

Responses to Jello

*We eat Food	Tyler 3.3
*0−1−1	Daniel 4.2
*It should be a telephone #	Allison 4.1
pudding	Megan 4.2
Strawberries	Dawn 4.3
	Justin 6.4
	Jonathan 5.6
Jell-o	Michelle 3.4
	Charles 5.3
	Heather 6

Responses to Dynamints

Hot	Jonathan 5.6
vitamins/ medicine	Tyler 3.3
mints	Daniel 4.2
Tic Tacs	Marc 5.5
	Heather 6.0
Dynamints	Michelle 3.4
	Allison 4.1
	Dawn 4.3

Responses to Wendy's

O.K., but I've seen her on T.V.	Megan 4.2
Water	Mara 5.5
Burger Queen	Dawn 4.3
Arby's	Jonathan 5.6
	Heather 6.0
Wendy's	Tyler 3.3
	Michelle 3.4
	Allison 4.1
	Dawn 5.1
	Justin 6.4

Responses to Crest

brush	Boyd 3.5
toothbrush	Michelle 3.4
toothpaste	Tyler 3.3
	Daniel 4.2
	Mara 5.3
toothpaste → CREST	Dawn 5.1
CREST	

Figure 2.10. Reading Environmental Print (Composite).

Figure 2.11. U.S. Mail Logo.

Figure 2.12. Gas Station Logos.

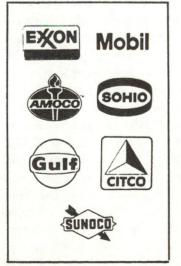

Tyler is saying, "Hey, you're supposed to eat this." Daniel and Alison are saying, "This is crazy, they made the name look like a phone number." All three of their readings are the direct outcome of their personal functional knowledge of the world.

The Crest example is an instance in which Tyler seems to have a slight experiential edge on Michelle—Michelle's response is functional, while Tyler's is categorical. In reading this product label he is not in danger of being considered immature (as do all those studies which say that boys developmentally lag behind girls), as he was with his readings of Dynamints and Jello.

Now let's see if we can even the odds even more, not only between Tyler and Michelle, but between them and some of their older research mates. What happens when the children are asked to read an item which is brand new, where the experiential opportunities are severely restricted for everyone?

Wendy's as an item had only been physically available in the environment for about a month and television ads about it had been available for about a week before the readings. Tyler and Michelle are both successful at competing under these circumstances, despite the dispersed age ranges in this situation.

Now before we acquiesce to the danger of concluding that there might be a simple and direct relationship between an increase in experience and the production of a specified conventional response, we need to consider the reading which several of our language users gave to the graphic U.S. Mail logo.

As a response to the U.S. Mail logo (see Figure 2.11) our informants read both *gas* and *gas station*. The fact that several of them concurred in their reading assured us that they shared a focus on a common experiential background which we (older and wiser, as all researchers are) were unable to spot. We were forced to go out and reexperience gas stations, to confront them actively as our subjects obviously were doing, instead of simply encountering them, in order to perceive the significance of their outline configuration, limited text, style of lettering, geometric logo designs, and predominance of red, white, and blue coloring (see Figure 2.12).

This experience was enough to make us think that we should be able to "fill up" at the post office. While the researchers' experience of both the U.S. Mail insignia and gas station logos was of longer duration than that of our informants, their present experiences were more acute. The currency, strength and commonality of their confrontations had led them to an agreed upon alternative response.

We encountered another mystery when our Bloomington and Indianapolis subjects were asked to read a highway sign displaying the name of their town (see Figure 2.13). Some children in both cities gave the

Bloomington   Indianapolis

Figure 2.13. City Marker Signs.

reading "book." While phonic analysis might seem to offer some explanation for the Bloomington sign, it loses all its promise in relation to the Indianapolis sign. In this instance, one of our informants filled in the experiential void of the researchers. By giving a reading of "Sesame Street" to the Indianapolis sign, this young person showed us that a number of our informants possessed experience which we simply lacked (see Figure 2.14). In this instance, the researchers' ages worked as a clear obstacle to their experience. Our informants tended to display a greater facility in producing conventional adult responses in their readings of environmental print than they did for either their own written stories or for a published picture storybook.

It is quite easy to draw the assumption from these data that these two continuous texts are more complex than the environmental text and are therefore simply more difficult to read, an assumption which does not, however, hold up so well under continued examination. As the U.S. Mail logo example has already indicated, even the most spartan of environmental print settings is replete with graphics from alternative communication and signaling systems: container shapes, logos, color relationships, pictures, and print. These present a complex communication processing environment. Cue complexes are selectively perceived as a function of their transaction with the reader's experiential knowledge. Even when, in our attempts to understand, we limit examination to the print environment alone, the linguistic complexities are greater, and the subjects' responses more varied, than common sense would predict. The U.S. Mail logo turned out to be the most lexically constrained text environment with which our readers were confronted, and even it was composed of something more extended than a single word. The other text environments were much more complex; they contained multiple syntactic and semantic units scattered over the item's surface. These text environments presented messages which included brand name, generic category, ingredients, amounts, and directions for use. All these mes-

Figure 2.14. Sesame Street Sign on
Book Cover.

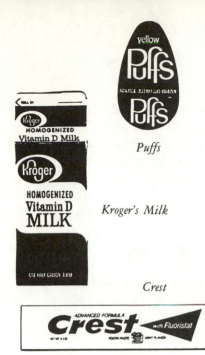

Puffs

Kroger's Milk

Crest

Figure 2.15. Examples of Complex
Text Environments.

Figure 2.16. Corrected Workbook
Page (Jason, Age 6).

sages were weighted for significance by their placement on the package, as well as by the size, shape and coloring of their letterings. Through this virtual forest of competing cues and messages (see Figure 2.15), our subjects moved with credible composure, familiarity, and with a display of individual interest.

These young language users displayed the flexibility and confidence necessary to make individual decisions which can only come with the accumulating effect of personally significant experimental confrontations with environmental print, confrontations which were initiated on the day their mothers pulled their first diaper out of the Pamper's box, and which continued through feedings from the well-marked jars of Gerber's Baby Food right up to their first historic encounters with the Golden Arches of McDonald's. So, if they read boxes more conventionally than they read books, it just might be that it is not because environmental print is less complex than continuous text but because it is more familiar.

Why can most 5-year-olds identify colors and most 6-year-olds write their names? Because they live in environments which provide many meaningful and pleasant encounters with such processes.

What is one of the most valuable gifts we can give language users? We can litter their environment with enticing language opportunities and guarantee them the freedom to experiment with them.

ON CONFUSING CONVENTION WITH LANGUAGE

In first grade, Jason's teacher corrected his spellings of *heel*, *glass*, *broom*, *toys*, *car*, and *mitt* (see Figure 2.16). She also corrected any faulty notions which Jason might have developed about the current practicality of authors who put together reading workbooks; we note particularly the teacher's correction of Jason's "cau" to "ox." In third grade, Jason's teacher corrected everything she knew how to correct, including his sentence structure and spelling (see Figure 2.17). Her spelling corrections appear on almost everything except *ogre*, a word which she obviously didn't know how to spell either.

From an instructional perspective, what all of Jason's experiences have in common is a concern for convention. This concern pervades written language instruction. It guides teachers in making decisions about "good handwriting," "correct spelling," "good grammar," and "well-formedness of stories."

Language conventions are defined as socially agreed upon rules of expression which have as their function the facilitation of communication. Notice that there is nothing in this definition which defines them as barriers to communication. We can communicate—and do so quite creatively—whether or not our speech or writing is conventional. Con-

Jason THE Oger Sept 21, 1979

Once upon a time an Oger went
to town and caught 6 boys for supper.
And he said they were good. He wet to
town and he got 6 more but they
got lost and got away when the oger son them
runing he got his 7 large boats and
chased them. The boys came to a room.
Luckily the king came bie and stoped
and cut Ogers had off tok the boys back
home and thay livd Happly ever after.
the end

— proofreading is just
as important
as writing.

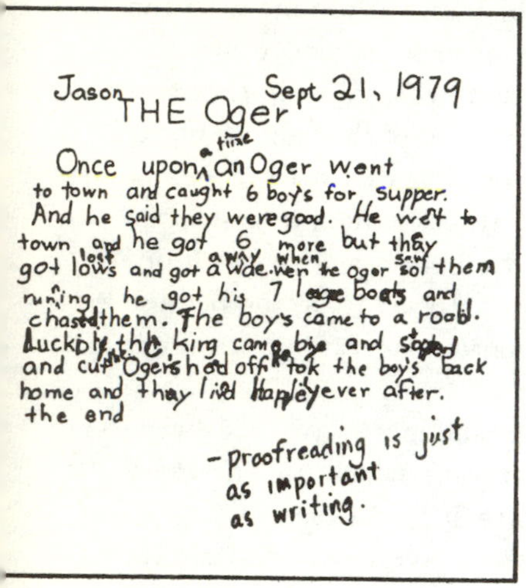

*Figure 2.17. The Oger (Jason,
Age 8).*

ventional control does not free creativity, and when overemphasized, it has quite the opposite effect. James Joyce broke the canons of convention with his stream of consciousness writing and in so doing, taught us a process by which to mean. So have Alison, Mike, and Charvin, all age 4.

Conventional control has been the bifocals through which we have viewed growth and development in language. This is more than just a poor prescription for eyeglasses; it also makes it appear as if growth to convention were the goal of the oral and written language curriculum. It causes us to see convention when we wish to see language, and in the process, to confuse not only ourselves but our students. When convention is the lens, we fail to see linguistic growth as continuous throughout the life of the language user and so, fail to appreciate linguistic achievement after convention has been reached.

A case in point is Alison's signature over a four-year period. Alison had written her name more or less conventionally since she was 3. Yet a far more interesting signature was the one she wrote at the age of 5 when she penned A-L-I-U-S-O-N. At 5, everything she knew about letter-sound correspondence compelled her to put a *u* in her name. She experimented with this form for a couple of weeks and then elected the optional spelling her parents had chosen.

At 7, however, she produced A-L-L-I-S-O-N as her signature. Since this signature was put on the flyleaf on a book being dedicated to the church library, Alison's mother was less than ecstatic with her decision to write her name with two l's. When she asked, in exasperation, "Alison! Why did you write two l's?" Alison replied, "You can, you know; some people write Alison that way."

Alison is an active language user; standard conventional form is for her one option among many. It is far more interesting to map the range of hypotheses which children like Alison test about language than it is to assume that convention is the sole option, and nonconvention either failure or carelessness. Convention and nonconvention are more a function of experience and perspective than of practice.

Probably no data better illustrate this point than do the cross-cultural data which we have collected. To observe that Alison does not control the conventions of her language is to focus on one act, but to miss the event.

Language, whether oral or written, is a social event of some complexity. Language did not develop because of the existence of one language user, but of two. If we are to understand language, we must see it as an orchestrated transaction between two language users which has as its intent to convey meaning in a given context of situation. Pragmatics is the system of language which joins language users, not only through convention but through negotiation and discretion. This perspective is as important for our understanding of reading as it is for our understanding of writing. We have purposely selected a reading example to illustrate this point since convention is as big an issue in reading as it is in writing.

When we examine the set of responses we received after showing children a carton of Kroger's milk (see Figure 2.18), we can readily agree that all the "milks" and "Krogers" are responses which answer the question we asked, namely, "What does that say?" while "Some milk goes in there," "A milk box," "Box that hold milk," and "A milk can," are better responses to questions such as, "What goes in there?" and "What is this?"

While clearly in these instances the children have not answered our question, what they have done is far more interesting. They have, like us on certain occasions, chosen to answer a question other than the one we posed. We do this all the time. In fact, it is a classic strategy used in passing doctoral qualifying examinations and essay tests more generally. The children here, like us, have exercised their options. That is, under certain conditions, they either negotiate or reinterpret the communication contract put before them. What at first then, may appear to be an unconventional response, from another perspective falls well within the range of conventional options, given the setting.

Convention has largely been viewed as relating to the graphophonemic and syntactic systems of language, but this is misguided. Oral and written language use involves the orchestration of not only graphophonemic and syntactic systems but of semantic and pragmatic systems. One cannot even begin to explore what hypotheses are being tested about convention at these levels until one understands the nature of the communication contract which has been agreed upon. Convention is a function of context and involvement in the language process.

Engaging in the languaging event, that is, deciding to use paper and pencil or whatever, leads not only to the development of convention, but to the realization that one can build upon those conventions that others have used which have addressed similar issues. The relationship is one between personal convention and social convention. A personal convention is a decision reached because of a need experienced while participating in a language event.

It is Charvin's decision to placehold separate concepts with blobs using space and distance (see Figure 2.19); this personal convention underpins his notion of wordiness and reflects his schematic readiness for understanding that concept as we know it.

It is Mike's decision to placehold meaning by using space, like Charvin, and by using a combination of letters and picturelike symbolic forms. This decision not only builds on Mike's knowledge of how to represent meaning through a series of pictures, but incorporates what he knows about both art and writing. It is these border scrimmages

PRINT SETTING:
KROGER MILK

*Some milk
    goes in there* (Nathan, Age 3)
Milk   (Tyler, Age 3)
Milk   (Michelle S., Age 3)
Milk   (Michelle M., Age 3)
Milk   (Boyd, Age 3)
Milk   (Daniel, Age 4)
Milk   (Dawn B., Age 4)
A Milk Box   (Jeremy, Age 4)
*Box that holds
    milk in it.* (Megan, Age 4)
Milk   (Alison, Age 4)
Milk   (Jonathan, Age 5)
Milk   (Charles, Age 5)
Kroger   (Teddy, Age 5)
Milk   (Mara, Age 5)
Milk   (Dawn, Age 5)
A Milk Can   (Heather, Age 6)
Milk   (Leslie, Age 6)
Milk   (Emily, Age 6)
Milk   (Justin, Age 6)
Kroger's   (Denver, Age 6)

*Figure 2.18. Reading Response to
Kroger's Milk.*

between systems (art and writing) which are often the most developmentally interesting. Mike's decisions, at 4 years of age, are a set of real writing decisions like those many of our ancestors came to make, which further reflect the literacy level they attained. Having come to his decision in a literate society, however, Mike is now ready to use the linguistic information which bombards him, not through wholesale adoption but rather, like us, through linguistic discretion.

It is important to understand in this regard that a very delicate balance exists in each of us between personal and social convention. Some of what is social convention will always elude us. We are always reminded of this fact whenever we send a final draft manuscript away to be published. We can never believe all the changes the publishers make—even with nonconvention aside! But it is personal convention which gives our language its style and makes it our own. Language convention, like language, is socially invented in a supportive environment which makes such discoveries available; it is not an heirloom like a grandfather's clock which is passed along from generation to generation, but rather, more like a civilization whose heritage is passed along by those immersed in it. And sometimes it is our personal convention, as in the case of James Joyce's stream of consciousness writing, which leads not only us, but others to new ways to mean.

Conventions are quite simply fringe benefits, artifacts of written language use in a community of written language users, not prerequisites to, nor criteria for, language use. If we can accept them for what they are, we will find that language conventions are interesting as fringe benefits of involvement in a literacy event.

CONCLUSION

In this chapter, we have suggested that the most prevalent view of language development can be represented by a formula which states that: AGE in relationship to CONVENTION indicates GROWTH.

In contrast to this view of development, we would suggest a new formula in which EXPERIENCE is seen as TRANSACTING with PRINT SETTINGS, the results of which lead to new levels of PSYCHOLINGUISTIC AND SOCIOLINGUISTIC ACTIVITY. Because this process is cyclic and ongoing throughout life, the nature of literacy itself is forever changing, creating new personal and societal potentials for all of us.

*Figure 2.19. Uninterrupted
Writing (Composite).*

Charvin, Age 4

Mike, Age 4

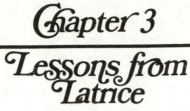

Chapter 3
Lessons from Latrice

A three-year-old demonstrates that language, for her, is a social event and that her literacy decisions are rooted in the same social foundation as ours. Latrice's experiences demonstrate that writing must be observed as a process and that, at best, the written product is but a dinosaur track.

Mary Hill (1980), a professor of reading and writing at Westminster College in Pennsylvania, asked teachers who were attending her graduate seminar to survey other teachers about the amount of reading and writing being done in their classrooms. The survey was designed specifically to explore the number of opportunities teachers provide children for uninterrupted reading and writing.

One of the teacher-researchers reported that:

The kindergarten teacher in her building said, "None," in response to a question about the amount of time which children were provided just to look through books and read, or pretend to read, them. Regarding time given children to interact with paper and pen on their own, the kindergarten teacher was again reported to have said, "None," but qualified her answer by saying, "but we do creative endings to stories orally."

In the first grade, the teacher reported not having time for uninterrupted reading now, but that during the second half of the year ten minutes per week would be provided. About uninterrupted time for writing, she also reported, "None now," but added, "We do get into this later in the year."

The second-grade teacher wanted clarification: "You mean time I read to the children, and they listen?"

The third-grade teacher reported, "None." She qualified her answer, however, by saying, "But I used to have it every day when I taught in the country and life was less complicated."

The school also had a remedial reading teacher. For fun, the graduate student asked the remedial reading teacher the same set of questions. Her answer: "I'm afraid these questions don't apply to our situation."

Although this is, of course, only a partial report of the data, we have reason to believe it is somewhat typical of what goes on in all too many schools and classrooms in this country (Graves, 1975; Applebee, 1981; Durkin, 1977; NAEP, 1980). Children are not given the time that they should be given to write or to interact with books.

In thinking through why this is so, we seem to find two principal reasons: One is the belief that such uninterrupted time is not useful. For many teachers, uninterrupted reading and writing time is wasted time, given what else might be done. The issue really is "time on task." But, unfortunately, the belief prevails that children learn very little from non-directed as opposed to directed activities. Their choice within the process and their ownership of the process are not seen as important.

One of our graduate students started setting aside uninterrupted reading and uninterrupted writing time in her preschool classroom. Initially, she met with a good deal of resistance to her idea from the other teachers with whom she works. After she initiated these programs, however, they became extremely popular not only with children, but also with parents. Currently, we're happy to report, other preschools in the area are following suit.

The second most prevalent reason why children are not given uninterrupted reading and writing time is that, while such time is perceived as useful, children are not perceived as ready for these activities; that before children are able to make the most of such experiences, something more "basic" has to be learned or already be in place. Often this means letter-sound knowledge. Sometimes it means oral language.

Because of our experience, we consider these positions and attitudes unfortunate. They do a disservice not only to children, but also to the evolution of literacy. Until the beliefs which underlie these notions are changed, beginning reading and writing programs do as much, if not more, to inhibit written language growth and development as they do to facilitate it. The issue centers on our understanding of the literacy process. To illustrate this point, we report data collected from a single language user. Our informant is Latrice, an inner-city black child who comes from a low socioeconomic area. Latrice has all of the characteristics of the children about whom one Chicago inner-city teacher, having listened to us extol what it is that young children can do, said, "Well, okay, that's fine, but what about the children I work with. . . . They don't have language."

We're really not sure what this teacher would have said about Latrice. Initially, even we found Latrice more difficult to understand than other children her age. Her products looked less clear to us; her development less conventional. Given the seventeen 3-year-olds we studied over the course of our program of research, Latrice was developmentally the least experienced written language user of her age whom we encountered.

Figure 3.1. Uninterrupted Writing, Drawing, and Name Samples (Latrice, Age 3).

Uninterrupted Writing

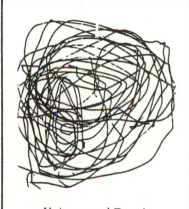

Uninterrupted Drawing

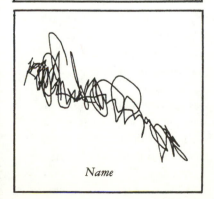

Name

We asked Latrice to write her name and anything else that she could write (see Uninterrupted *Writing* in Figure 3.1). We then asked Latrice to draw a picture of herself (see Uninterrupted *Drawing* in Figure 3.1). We asked Latrice to write her name on her picture. Latrice turned the paper over and wrote what she declared to be her name (see *Name* in Figure 3.1).

The first thing we notice in comparing the product of Latrice's Uninterrupted Drawing to that of her Name is that she has organized her art differently from her writing. Art for her involves a wide circular marking which is centralized and cohesive. Writing, on the other hand, is linear, involving an up-and-down stroke. We have found that all children, by the age of 3, differentiate between writing and drawing. Some children use circles for writing and a linear up and down stroke for art, but, more importantly, whichever marking form they select, the decision is consistent, systematic, and even rational.

Theoretically, what this means is that by age 3, children have made a conscientious decision, reflective of and appropriate to the context of situation in which they find themselves. Latrice is no exception. What look like scribbles are not scribbles at all but organized and systematic reflections of decisions which she has made about how the written language and artistic systems are organized.

This explains why the word *scribble* is inappropriate when it is associated with children's writings. *Scribble* suggests that the response is unorganized . . . unintentional . . . random. It is not. Nor is it, we will argue, "pseudo-writing," or "mock-writing," or "nonrepresentational" writing, or any of the other demeaning terms often tagged onto the written efforts of young children.

One of our graduate students was an art major before coming to do work with us, and she has said that she has no problem calling Latrice's first effort art. Nor do we have any problem calling Latrice's second effort writing. It is our hope that when children's writing is recognized for what it really is, we can go about the business of appreciating and valuing it.

Latrice and her age-mates made a clearer distinction between art and writing when we asked them to draw first and then write, than they did when we reversed the tasks. Because adults typically see the 3-year-old as able to draw but not necessarily able to write, they more typically ask children of this age to draw rather than to write. Pragmatically, drawing is the usual contract a 3-year-old comes to expect: Given a 3-year-old, an adult, a paper, a pen, and an oral request, the contractual expectation is one of DRAW. When we buy into the pragmatic expectation children bring to the setting by asking them—after they are engaged in fulfilling the expected contract—to write, the request itself semantically highlights what it is we want, and as a result we get more 3-year-olds to engage in the contract we desire.

If a 3-year-old is given a pen and asked to write without first engaging in drawing, about 25 percent of all 3-year-olds will draw rather than doing what is asked, which is to write. If the contract is clarified by asking what the 3-year-olds expects, almost all children will make the distinction wanted. We say "almost all" because Joan Chubb, a research assistant on our project, found that if a 3-year-old is given a pen, as opposed to a crayon, and asked to write, the confusion is reduced (see Harste, Burke, Woodward, 1981). Children at 3 know that usually pens are used for writing and crayons for drawing. In fact, when Joan asked one of her 3-year-olds to write with a crayon, her young sophisticate said, quite matter-of-factly, "No. I need a pen."

Here we see a dynamic transaction between context of situation, pragmatics, and cognitive processing. When all of these elements are allowed to transact as they normally do in natural language situations, the child reads these complex cue systems as signs and uses them to reach an orchestrated decision. When we compare Latrice's picture (Uninterrupted Drawing in Figure 3.1) with her efforts under the condition: "write anything you can write" (Uninterrupted Writing in Figure 3.1), it initially looks more confused. Most of this confusion, however, is a function of the fact that we are looking only at the product. When we look at the process there is no confusion.

We initially asked Latrice to write her name. Latrice began by meticulously making some downward and sideward strokes, seemingly attempting to make the letter *L* (see Step 1, Figure 3.2). The linearity of her markings, given what we already know, leads us to conclude that she is engaging in the contract we requested, namely, writing.

When pushed to write anything else she could write, Latrice picked up her pen and, using a free-flowing circular motion, all but obliterated this initial display of literacy (see Step 2 in Figure 3.2). Again, knowing what we already know, that Latrice organizes art differently from writing, we suspect she has negotiated the contract in this gesture by moving from writing to art.

Midway in this second effort, Latrice said, as much to herself as to the researchers, "Gonna write an *i*." Without seeking a clean spot on the paper, she produced a line with a dot attached to the top (see Step 3 in Figure 3.2). Latrice dotted the *i* with such savagery that, even later, when she had written still more, it is clearly visible.

At this point, Latrice announced she was "gonna make a dog." She then did so, using a movement we now recognize as art (see Step 4 in Figure 3.2). Latrice got very involved at this point and, at each progressive stage, her picture became increasingly tied and busy. The result is the final product we saw earlier, in Figure 3.1.

Let us now analyze this language event and identify what insights it provides into literacy and literacy learning. When we look at the process, we can trace Latrice's moves from writing to art to writing to art. At a minimum we know that Latrice already knows that art and writing are communication forms which can be produced with paper and pen. But she knows more than this, for she moves freely between them in an effort to mean. Importantly, moving back and forth between art and writing buys her time. She never has to stop the process. She is much better off than the child who has lost this freedom, who writes a word, stops, who cannot proceed, who is so concerned with editing that the process is paralyzed. No one, Atwell (1980) reminds us, can edit a text before producing one. To the extent that current school practices support this dysfunctional notion of composing in either reading or writing, it must be stopped.

It is important to understand that Latrice's decision to move between art and writing in order to mean is a process strategy used by many if not all good writers. It is a keep-going strategy. That is one of the reasons why we find charts and maps and diagrams and pictures in books and newspapers and other texts. Text production is not print production per se, but rather, an orchestrated set of multimodal cues carefully laid forth in an attempt to placehold and potentially sign one's meaning.

Latrice knows some things about writing right now which, if her experience in school is typical, she will "unlearn" and then have to "relearn" in order to become proficient later on. One wonders what would happen if the strategies taught in schools would allow children to

Figure 3.2. Steps Involved in Uninterrupted Writing (Latrice, Age 3).

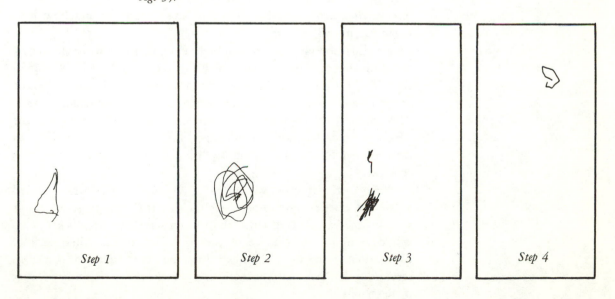

Step 1   Step 2   Step 3   Step 4

build on what they already know, rather than forcing them to refocus their attention. The paranoia we and our students have about print and correctness is a rather dysfunctional outcome of most current instruction.

But, back to Latrice. She demonstrated that she has a schema for writing which includes both writing and art. Equally important, but likely to be overlooked, is the fact that, given a paper and pen and a request to write, Latrice picks up the pen and makes a mark on the paper. She could attempt to eat it . . . she could stick it in her ear . . . she could get up and close the door. She doesn't, and neither do other children her age. They, like Latrice, write.

Latrice already understands that making marks on paper is a form of social action; that given a certain kind of language (namely, a request to write), one does so by responding physically, by making marks on paper. This is very important and complex learning.

If we ask ourselves, "How does she know this?" we will have to conclude that she already has a schema for writing. And if we push ourselves even further, we will have to conclude that the only way she could have gotten such a schema was by being or having been a writer—either vicariously or directly—at some point prior to the encounter in which we see her. Latrice, like us, has a history of literacy. There is no other way to explain her knowing what to do, given the task we gave her, and her performance.

At one level, then, Latrice's schema for writing includes a general readiness to make marks on paper given a particular kind of language request. But at a more specific level, Latrice already differentiates art from writing and is beginning to take note of its cultural form. Latrice is only 3, but from her involvement as a reader and writer she has discovered much about how written language works and how it is organized in this culture.

It is also important to note that each set of markings represents a new and different concept: her name, a dog, a picture of herself, her signature. In addition to all of the other things Latrice does, she also writes the way it means, using space and distance to placehold and separate ideas. This conceptual coordination of space seems an early precursor to the development of our notion of wordness and syntax. It also reflects an early notion of abstract thought: "I'll let this mark represent this thought."

When Latrice finished writing, she was asked to read what she had written. All her reading responses fell within the semantic set of things she said she was writing when she was engaged in that process. This would seem to be evidence of the fact that, despite their lack of conventional form, her markings are serving her much as our markings serve us in that they conserve memory and make the retrievability of that memory possible.

Nor is this all we can learn from Latrice. On another level, it is important to note the role which speech plays in this writing event. Latrice's initial written response to our request, "Write your name and anything else you can write," was linear marking on paper. She then moved to art. Before she once again engaged in writing she announced, "Gonna write an *i*."

One way to look at her oral language here is to note that it serves an organizational function which directs her writing. Once she completed the making of her *i*, our continued request, "Write anything you can write," again moved her to comment: "Gonna make a dog." Once again her speech shows evidence of a plan. Speech during writing, we have found, almost always reflects the presence of a plan, either being abandoned or in operation.

There has been a long, unfortunate history of separating reading from writing, speaking from writing, art from writing, and reading, writing, speaking, and listening from each other. One must, in light of our data, pause to ask, "Why?" Clearly the cause must be that, theoretically, researchers have seen these areas as distinct. Each has been assumed to have different origins, and their joint participation in language operations has been considered to be of no basic psychological import. Even when written language and speech are closely linked in one operation, as they are in reading and writing, they are reported as if one did not exist, or treated as if they are separable processes belonging to two completely different classes of phenomena. This is unfortunate, since language is a multimodal event. And so is language learning.

There is not a separate section of the brain that handles writing and another section that handles reading. If all one studied in writing was writing there would be no way to understand the process. Writers, Atwell found (1980), spend almost as much time reading during writing as writing. Language curricula, we believe, ought not violate what we currently know about language use and learning. To do so is a blatant form of anti-intellectualism.

Observations of children in the experimental situations which we set up show that children gesture, act out, draw, and speak during the fulfillment of a request to write. Speech and the use of alternative communication systems arise spontaneously and seem to assist the child in planning. These activities do not lie outside the writing process, but are an intimate and integral part of that process. To call them "intrusions" is to fail to understand theoretically the literacy process.

Nor is this the case only for young language users. Adults use speech the same way Latrice does when they write. Adults talk to themselves during writing . . . argue with themselves . . . and often give initial forms of paper in speech form. Writing occurs over time. Dialogue with colleagues prior to, during, and after making a mark on paper is also an important part of the process.

To study writing, as we have in the past, by looking at the markings left on paper is to study dinosaur tracts without the benefit of observing the beast or his habitat. While this is understandable given the nature of paleontology, it is inexcusable given the nature of written language literacy. What it leads to is the confusion of convention and literacy. A focus on process leads to the identification of the psychological and sociological strategies involved in successful written language use and learning. This is the basis of instruction, not convention.

Art is an integral component of writing. So are drama, reading, and speech. The lines we adults draw between the expressions of language and other systems of communication are arbitrary. No proficient teacher or learner can focus on these separate categories without destroying the event itself. Latrice knows this. Unfortunately, we need to "relearn" it as do, all too often, the students with whom we work, who have been systematically taught to abandon what they once knew. While we do not know everything about the literacy process, there is much that we can do today to theoretically update our language curricula.

Now, having taken some time to look at the written language process, let's summarize what we know about Latrice and her literacy learning:

1.   We know she knows that writing serves a pragmatic function, a doing, a social action of a particular sort.
2.   We know that she knows that one can placehold thoughts with marks on paper.
3.   We know that she knows that the formation and placement of those marks bear a relationship to intended meaning and conceptual reality.
4.   We know that she knows that, while both art and writing serve a semantic placeholding function, both are organized differently and both can be used for purposes of communication.
5.   We know that Latrice has been a reader and a writer prior to this particular encounter and that she has learned a good deal from these encounters.
6.   We know that Latrice, faced with print, makes a series of highly complex and orchestrated decisions. These decisions involve the use of pragmatics, context of situation, semantics, syntax, and symbols in a truly sign-semiotic sense.

It is important to note that Latrice has learned all these things prior to any formal instruction because she has had opportunities to engage in the process on her own. As Halliday has noted for oral language learning (1975), and as Latrice has so aptly demonstrated for written language learning, each of these encounters with written language has provided her with the opportunity to learn language (that is, how to get things done by making a variety of written responses to a variety of requests), to learn about language (note her growing control of language about language, particularly "make" and "write"), and to learn through language (ever exploring and expanding her world—which, by the way, is what real literacy is all about).

As adults we often view literacy through the bifocals of convention. For that reason it is important for us all to meet Latrice. She can help readers of this volume as she has helped us. Most continuums in language end with conventional control, whether the topic is literacy, spelling, grammar, or story form. This is unfortunate. Control of form cannot and should not be equated with either the onset or the attainment of literacy. If and when it is so equated, we do not have a growth and development continuum, just a magic trick—now you see it, now you don't. Control of form is a social event. It occurs late in the authoring cycle when we wish to "go public." That is when we all need editors.

Literacy must be said to be present when we have evidence that a decision has been made which would not have been made if written language were not present. The orchestration of a complex set of cues represents growth in literacy, not convention, correctness, nor even success. These are illusionary artifacts of experience and involvement in the process from someone else's perspective. Defining literacy from the informant's perspective is important for our understanding of functional literacy, and equally important for our continued understanding of literacy beyond convention. It is only when we take a definition of literacy such as this one seriously that we can recognize written language growth as continuous and universal for all of us. What marks the difference between Latrice and us is not the kind of decisions we make, but the quantity of information we have leaned to use and orchestrate as a sign potential. And it is important to see Latrice as fast gaining on us. Given a more experienced teacher, or a more experienced researcher, or a more experienced writer, or a more experienced reader, our efforts too could be and certainly would be dismissed as scribbles.

Latrice, given her performance, demonstrates a real access to literacy. It is a disservice both to Latrice and to our present understanding of literacy if her important literacy achievements are viewed as "precursory", "pseudo," or as some form of "emergent readiness." They are none of these. They are the process artifacts of real literacy and must be recognized as such. The best any of us can do is to take our current best shot. It is only by recognizing the importance of the written language hypotheses which Latrice is testing in relation to the orchestrated demands of literacy that we can come to a decision about what experiences we can provide her which will facilitate her continued exploration and growth.

Our task as reading and writing educators is not so much to direct her learning—for clearly Latrice demonstrates that she has a viable and important agenda of her own—but to facilitate her testing of those written language hypotheses which she demonstrates she is currently interested in solving. That is why uninterrupted reading and writing opportunities are so important.

Latrice is only 3 years old. But she is already a sophisticated written language decision maker. She has two years left before she enters kindergarten, two years left to explore written language on her own as a participant learner in a community of written language users, two years before she faces a teacher who will probably provide her no time for uninterrupted reading and writing because "she's not ready for such experiences."

Even more incredibly, she has five years left until third grade when, to paraphrase the teacher Mary Hill's teacher-researcher interviewed, "life in the city is so hectic that there is no time." And heaven help her if she ends up in some kind of remedial reading and writing class, because having opportunities to orchestrate for oneself the written language event somehow does not even apply to this situation.

Thank goodness she is coming into your classroom and that you understand.

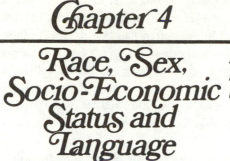

Chapter 4

Race, Sex, Socio-Economic Status and Language

A new perspective is suggested concerning the relationship between literacy and the circumstances of one's birth.

In designing our research we, like many other researchers, blocked on certain key variables. In a review of the literature, we saw factors such as sex (girls are better readers than boys), race (black children are more likely than whites to end up in need of remedial instruction), setting (inner-city children perform less well on national assessment tests than do children from suburban areas), and age (children are ready for formal reading instruction at the age of 6) as relevant.

But now, more than ever before, we question the importance of these variables. Given the characteristics of the responses to environmental print on which we coded—sex, race, and setting—they failed to distinguish between or among age groups. If girls are better readers than boys, this is not evident in the quality of their responses to print at the 3-year-old level, the 4-year-old level, the 5-year-old level, or the 6-year-old level. If blacks are more likely than whites to end up in remedial reading classes, this is not evident from the responses made by black and white children at particular age levels. If inner-city children have more difficulty than suburban children in learning to read and write, this, too, is not evident in the quality of the responses they make to environmental print.

Because we had recently completed research using the environmental print task with children coming from middle to high socioeconomic status families, we were able to compare the response characteristics of children in this sample to those in our earlier sample. Again, no significant differences were found. If parental socioeconomic status is a factor, this factor did not show up in response patterns at these particular age levels.

Nor did children coming from single-parent families seem to be at a disadvantage in relation to children coming from two-parent families.

Many lower SES children from single-parent families in which the parent was on welfare were seemingly as provided for, in terms of the quality of the written language encounters they were having, as were *some* high SES children coming from two-parent homes.

Some lower SES families took what money they had to buy books, go to the library, or even save to go to the ballet; others did little. Fortunately, the children often had better ideas of how to use reading and writing functionally than did their parents. One parent, for example, reported that he did "nothing" to help his child learn to read and write. Later in the interview he reported that his son "drove him nuts" by playing cop and writing out tickets when family members did anything wrong—like leaving dishes in the family room or coming late to supper.

Many middle- and upper-class homes, on the other hand, were far from ideal literacy learning environments. Because both parents worked, many children in these homes were left with baby-sitters or involved in preschool programs that had little or no interest in literacy. While the homes were supposedly better literacy environments, little of this benefit automatically shifted down to the children in any directly observable way. There did not, in this regard, seem to be big distinctions between lower-, middle-, and upper-class homes. Some homes, whether upper- or lower-class, were rather sterile literacy environments, while others were filled with ongoing written language events and were seemingly hard places in which to avoid print involvement.

Some lower-, middle-, and upper-class parents seemed bent on "teaching" their child to read and write, yet this factor did not seem to distinguish between children's performance on our tasks other than to make these children initially reluctant to demonstrate what they knew. The result of our experience leads us to conclude that lower and upper socioeconomic status, as it relates to literacy, is more a "mental attitude" than it is anything else. If the parent or parents perceive themselves to be middle class, despite their residence in a lower socioeconomic neighborhood, they tend to provide middle-class kinds of literacy-related experiences for their children—books, visits to the library, plays, etc.

Telephone interview data collected from the parents of children in our sample, although incomplete (32 parent interviews/48 children), does suggest that homes provide varying "cultures" for literacy and literacy learning. Several factors seem to be identifiable as distinguishing these alternative home literacy learning cultures.

The most salient home factor relating to literacy learning is one we have termed "availability and opportunity to engage in written language events." Homes where books were out and readily available, where paper, pens, pencils, crayons, magic markers, and other instruments were handy, where children seemed quite naturally to be included and involved, seemed to provide the key conditions for children to go exploring and for parents to involve themselves in using and encouraging reading and writing, whether they "technically" reported that they knew what they were doing or not. In fact, some of the worst disasters in terms of literacy development for both parents and children seemed to occur and revolve around those times when the parents set out to formally "teach letter names," "teach the alphabet," or engage in other schoollike reading and writing tasks. The quantity of literacy materials (number of books, for example) does not seem to be the key element but rather, that what materials there are, are highly accessible, so that both parents and children have to be more or less constantly tripping over them. When paper and books were in the way, children used them, often coming up with quite creative uses (writing out a menu for supper, writing traffic tickets, writing notes, posting signs on doors, labeling their toys during play). When there were books in the family room, children were read to, an activity which seemed to be equally initiated by both parents and children. If the books, pens, and paper were not in the way, literacy activities were much less frequent and only occurred on "high occasions" as one parent called them, meaning when new books arrived, when a trip to the library was made, or when the child was asked to contribute a picture or something to send along in a letter. Some homes stored quantities of little-used literacy materials. Others made creative and concentrated use of more minimal quantities of readily accessible materials.

Because we were working with 3-year-olds in a local preschool program one morning per week, we decided to follow up on this insight. Before we made any physical changes in the classroom we observed the space and attempted to map where children spent their time. Once we had this data we attempted to "litter the environment with print." We brought the book corner out to the center of the room, added a writing table with different kinds of paper, writing instruments, envelopes, and stamps, put a pad of notepaper for taking messages by the play telephone in the home area, initiated a "Sign-In" activity whereby children kept their own attendance, and in general tried to accent and highlight reading and writing activities.

Although this particular 3-year-old group met only once a week, and the study was not done very formally in that we increased the amount of literacy activities which previously had been available, the data we collected suggest that children spent from three to ten times the amount of time they had normally spent in direct reading and writing activities. This did not include any measure of the amount of time children were not directly involved, such as overhearing a message read to the teacher by some child who had taken it on the telephone.

If there is a second home factor which seems significantly related to some early literacy advantage, that factor has to be called "inclusion." Whether by design or default, children who were reported as always being "dragged around" on shopping trips, trips to the courthouse, trips to the doctor's office, trips anywhere, whether or not the trip matched the child's developmental interest or not, seemed to have an advantage. These same children who were reported as always "under foot," who naturally got included in cooking and setting the table, who were reported as writing out shopping lists and reading them during shopping, who were given paper and pen to write a letter to grandmother while a parent wrote letters or sent bills, who were given the occupant mail to open and read while the mother opened and read the rest of the mail, seemed to be at an advantage. Most of these activities had no great literacy teaching design behind them in the parent's eyes, but were done more by virtue of the fact that the child was about, and involvement seemed natural largely because it was the only logical way the parent had for going about the business of the day.

Interestingly, the other thing that strikes us while looking over this parent interview data is the fact that all children at this age seem to have an almost natural affinity for books and for paper and pencil activities if the environment makes these things available. This observation was further borne out during data collection. Despite the quality of our research tasks, which could hardly be considered exciting literacy events, children were eager to participate, did so quite freely, and were often sorely disappointed when the week of data collection was up. Because of the nature of these tasks, children could make of them what they wanted and obviously found the experience rewarding.

This does not mean, of course, that all children start at the same place at the time of formal language instruction. It does mean that knowing the child's sex, race, level of parental income, parental educational level, or where the child lives are poor predictors of what the child knows and can do in terms of literacy. Given our experience, we must conclude that one must approach all children as if they know quite a bit about reading and writing regardless of the circumstances of their birth. Working from that assumption, open-ended activities should be designed in order to allow children to demonstrate, use, and build upon the knowledge they have already acquired about literacy.

Children's response characteristics do seem to vary as a function of age, with older children making an increasing number of expected or conventional responses in both reading and writing. One is immediately struck by the seeming differences between 3-year-olds' responses as a group across tasks and those of 6-year-olds'. Figure 4.1 contrasts some of these differences. The reading responses of 3-year-olds look much less conventional than do the reading responses of 6-year-olds. The writing and drawing samples of 3-year-olds are much more difficult to understand than are the more conventionalized products of 6-year-olds. The story well-formedness of 6-year-olds over 3-year-olds is equally striking. There came a point during our research project when team members who volunteered to work with the 6-year-olds' data were considered to be taking the easy way out, avoiding a real challenge. In comparison to the 3-year-olds' samples, the 6-year-olds' data was, as one member of the research team observed, "duck soup." In retrospect, this attitude is interesting, especially in light of the fact that many of the children whom we came to perceive as "very sophisticated 6-year-olds" were likely to be in formal reading and writing programs at school which assumed they knew nothing about written language.

One important observation that can and must be made, given the sheer weight of this data, is that this is a period of phenomenal literacy growth for all children. To squander this period as many homes do is sad indeed and speaks directly to the need for parent literacy programs like the one which Mary Hill (1980), an early member of our research team, has developed and field-tested.

There is more to be said about age as it relates to literacy growth, however. In further analysis of the data, we have found that differences reside more frequently in the product of literacy than they do in the process of literacy.

Of particular interest in understanding why one might think of age as a noncorrelate of written language growth and development is the fact that when children have equal opportunity, the characteristics of the responses across age show no difference. Age, rather than being the main factor, seems to correlate with the number of, or opportunity for, language encounters. The real variable then may be encounters rather than age. Age typically falls out as a factor, not per se, but because it generally provides an index to the number of encounters possible. When the number of encounters possible is held constant, age fails to distinguish among or between response characteristics.

We do not wish to overemphasize the number of encounters and their relationship to literacy, however. Children obviously can learn a good deal from a single significant encounter. We found, for example, that once children had gone through our first condition on the environmental print task, almost all the responses they made in the second and third conditions fell within the set of responses they made in the first. Said another way: If you take all of the responses that children initially make to environmental print in the first condition and identify this as a semantic field, well over 97 percent of their responses to this print on subsequent days, even when presented in random order, fall within the set of choices they made on the first day. Obviously children are rapid learners. Once they have had an encounter, their subsequent encounters are governed at least in part by their understanding of what worked the last time. From a processing perspective the research setting itself acts as a sign which obviously allows them access to appropriate schema, including response strategies.

Given this phenomenon it may not be the encounter at all that is the key variable but rather the quality of the encounter. Language and language learning are social events. When the encounter which the child has permits feedback, then learning can take place. To illustrate, using a

Figure 4.1. Responses of 3- and 6-Year-Olds: A Product Comparison Across Tasks.

3-YEAR-OLDS

Task: *Environmental Print*

PRINT SETTING

-Brush Teeth
-Toothpaste
-Teeth
-Wash Your Teeth
-It's got a name on it.
-Toothpaste
-It's called Aim
-I don't know
-Crest
-Cavities
-Toothbrush
-Toothbrush

6-YEAR-OLDS

PRINT SETTING

-Crest
-Toothpaste
-Crest
-Crest
-Toothpaste
-Crest
-Crest
-Crest
-Crest
-Crest
-Crest
-Crest

3-YEAR-OLDS

Task: *Language Experience Story*

Heather (*as dictated by child*)
Trick or Treat. Candy Mints.
They goes driving. They
go hunting. They going to
drive down the spoon. I like
cottage cheese. Cottage cheese.
I like faces. I like everything.
My Daddy.

6-YEAR-OLDS

LaShell (*as dictated by child*)
One day it was three little
bears. They had pork chops.
Then they went to a park.
Then a little girl came to the
little house. She ate the father
pork chops. She said, "Oh, it
is too hot!" Then she ate the
mother pork chops. Then she
said, "It is too soft."

written language example: if the child sees a door marked "Janitor" and she enters thinking it is a girls' lavatory, no one needs to tell her she's made a mistake, and yet feedback is provided. Or if an adult says "No, that's not the lavatory," then she can reason and rethink and thus also get feedback. This same process of feedback also works each time the child makes a correct decision, that is, when she sees a sign which says "Girls" and enters, and indeed it is a girls' lavatory. In our research task, given

3-YEAR-OLDS

Task: Uninterrupted Writing

6-YEAR-OLDS

(DuJulian, Natasha)

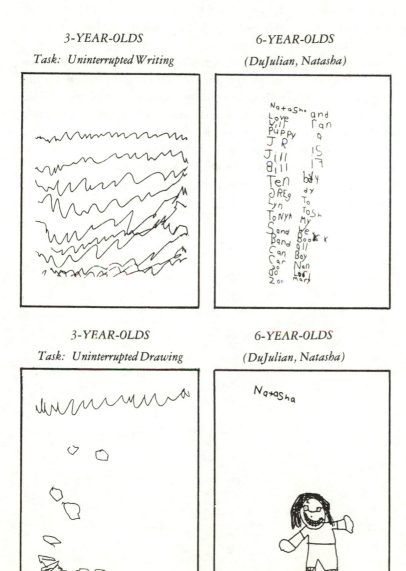

3-YEAR-OLDS

Task: Uninterrupted Drawing

6-YEAR-OLDS

(DuJulian, Natasha)

its format, not all naturally available feedback was provided, and hence qualitative improvement in responses across conditions was neither always possible nor observed. This does, however, raise the important issue of what responses to environmental print or other written language literacy events would look like under normal conditions where natural feedback was possible.

This issue is an important one to pursue since currently, there is much research in reading and writing which suggests that "time on task" is a key variable in literacy learning. Our experience would suggest that not all encounters are of equal worth, and that the quality of the encounter must be studied in conjunction with time on task if simplistic formulas are to be avoided.

Because of these findings and insights we need to challenge the view which holds that sex, race, setting, and socioeconomic status are significant correlates of literacy. They are not, nor should they be taken to be, causal factors. If they were, knowing these factors one could make near-perfect predictions. No such cause-effect relationships are evident in our data. Rules of thumb based on correlations must give way to theoretically based principles of language learning. We have begun, we believe, to identify some of these more promising principles.

Chapter 5
Examining Literacy Assumptions

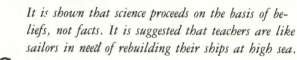

It is shown that science proceeds on the basis of beliefs, not facts. It is suggested that teachers are like sailors in need of rebuilding their ships at high sea.

INTRODUCTION

This chapter will address methodological and conceptual issues involved in researching and teaching literacy as a socio-psycholinguistic process. By process we mean the cognitive stances language users assume, and the strategies or cognitive activities language users engage in, during a literacy event. We label this process "socio-psycholinguistic" because we see language as sociologically rooted, and language learning as understandable only when viewed within its social context. Psycholinguistic processes have their genesis in the literacy demonstrations made available to language learners as they encounter members of their interpretive community engaged in the psychological and sociological actions associated with literacy.

Theory and methodology not only provide a structure for research and instruction, but are in themselves structuring. "Data" do not exist "out there" ready to be picked up, but constitute the results of a transaction which occurs when teacher or researcher meets child. What teachers and researchers believe about language and language learners constitutes a set of constraints as well as potentials for the study of literacy. Teachers and researchers must not only be cognizant of the structure-structuring relationships of their beliefs, but develop methodological stances where reflexivity and self-correction are possible.

What we wish to do in this chapter is to challenge existing assumptions about literacy and literacy learning in an effort to both demonstrate and explore the transactive potentials of theory and methodology in the study of literacy. We believe that researchers and teachers must proceed from theory, and further, that this theory must constantly be subject to reflection and change. In this chapter we elaborate our position that the observation of ourselves and of children in language situations can function as a self-correcting strategy in the pursuit of a practical theory of literacy and literacy learning.

EXAMINING METHODOLOGICAL ALTERNATIVES

KNOWLEDGE AS THEORY, NOT FACT

At an intuitive level the goal of science is to identify a set of basic immutable facts upon which a discipline's knowledge might be built. While this thinking seems reasonable, upon examination it proves untenable.

In a series of papers, Peirce (1931—1958) slowly convinced the scientific community that such a "fact-seeking agenda" was unworkable, since any "fact" contains countless assumptions which first have to be verified.

Peirce argues that science can only proceed on "belief," or a "network of belief," since there is no way to arrive at "fact." Kuhn (1970) labels such a network of beliefs "theoretical paradigms," and sees paradigm shifts as occurring once evidence is gathered that a belief is faulty, which then occasions a new statement of belief from which to proceed and a new theoretical stance.

A large number of thinkers in this century have formulated the problem of knowledge in similar terms. Especially striking is Otto van Neurath's famous simile:

Scientists are like sailors who have to rebuild their ships at high sea, without being able to seek port. Each plank in the hull may be jettisoned in the process, but it is not feasible to jettison all of the planks at the same time. (As quoted by Skagestad, 1981, p. 19)

Scientists or not, educators too must act; they cannot wait around until all the data are in. But just as they must act, they must also realize that what they are acting upon is "belief," not "truth" or "fact." While "sailing their ship at high sea," it behooves them to examine the beliefs out of which their ship is built.

As professionals we not only have the right, but also, we suppose, the responsibility to make assumptions. But—and one must hastily add the but—as professionals we have the responsibility constantly to put the assumptions underlying our beliefs to the test. Because beliefs affect our world view, the research stance we hold does make a difference.

TOWARD A COLLABORATIVE METHODOLOGY

Although we began our research program with a statistical-experimental paradigm, we found, because of the nature of the data we collected, that we increasingly came to rely on more naturalistic procedures and the paradigm which undergirded that approach to research. In this process we were able to examine many current assumptions about written language learning which are inherent not in written language learning itself, but in the statistical-experimental paradigm which has dominated the study of literacy. Because our conclusions coincide with what others have already said, there is a tendency to conclude that what we, and others taking this perspective, have found is a new set of truths. More productively, given the nature of science, what we have found is simply a new set of beliefs. These new beliefs constitute our best guess given what we currently know and, as such, provide us a research and curricular frame from which we will proceed until we gather evidence which shows these beliefs faulty.

In addition, we argue that our experience reveals that when research and curriculum development are conducted in functional-language situations, the use of the child as informant can become a self-correcting strategy for the profession.

Based on our experience, we advocate use of open-ended, real language situations in which the child, or language user, becomes the research and curricular informant. By real language situations we mean functional instances of language where all language systems (graphophonemic, syntactic, semantic, pragmatic) in the event are allowed to transact with the other communication systems (i.e., art, music, math, gesture, drama, etc.) which naturally co-occur in the setting. This is in contrast to research settings that isolate a single system of language (e.g., the study of the graphophonemic system of language using nonsense materials), a procedure which distorts not only what language is, but how the very language system works as a component of communication. The methodological result of such a belief about the study of language and language learning is that the roles of researcher and teacher potentially converge. We thus conclude that the traditional gap between researcher and teacher is a function of paradigm and in the end is dysfunctional and fails to serve the profession.

Understanding the relationships between belief, theory, science, curriculum, and methodology is important. We believe that understanding these relationships can be a first step on the road to inquiry, professionalism, and professional unity. Further, when research is conducted in open, functional, language settings, theoretical explicitness and the use of the child as research and curricular informant can provide new written language research a methodological self-correcting strategy.

LANGUAGE ISSUES AND RESEARCH PARADIGMS

There is much debate surrounding the methodological issues we have sketched (Carey, 1980; Guba, 1978; Mishler, 1979). As our own

---

(a)   The parts of the event equal the event itself *(EVENT = PARTS)*

(b)   The parts of the event can be meaningfully isolated:

$$
\begin{array}{l}
A \quad B \\
C \quad D \quad E \quad = Reading \\
\quad\; F
\end{array}
$$

(c)   The parts of the event can be summed or manipulated and still form a whole:

$$A+B+C+D+E+F = Reading$$
$$A+B+C+D+E+[F\ Controlled\,] = Reading$$
$$A+B+C+D+F+[E\ Controlled\,] = Reading$$

Figure 5.1. Assumptions Underlying Reading from an Experimental World View.

research began, we attempted to meld what we felt was the best of an experimental and an ethnographic tradition, but in the course of our studies, it became evident that these research traditions represented different and incompatible world views.

The assumptions underlying an experimental approach assume that the world is made up of identifiable variables which interact to form a language event. A complex event, like language, can be broken down, and each variable can be studied in isolation to find out how it really works. Such a position is positivistic, the assumption being that all phenomena are reducible to component parts. Figure 5.1 illustrates this world view when applied to one language process, namely, reading.

Ethnography embodies an alternative world view. There are no such things as "variables." Rather, the things experimentalists call "vari-

Figure 5.2. Assumptions Underlying Reading from an Ethnographic World View.

(a)   The parts of the event do not *equal the event itself (Event ≠ PARTS)*

(b)   The parts of the event form an irreducible whole:

$$ABCDEF \qquad = Reading$$

(c)   The parts of the event transact to form a whole greater than the sum of parts:

$$A><B><C><D><E><F \qquad = Reading,\ where >< \text{ means in}$$
$$transaction\ with\ all\ the\ other\ parts$$

(d)   If the individual parts are manipulated, the whole is destroyed:

Either:
$$A><B><C><D><E\ but\,[F\ Controlled\,] ≠ Reading$$
$$A><B><C><D><F\ but\,[E\ Controlled\,] ≠ Reading$$

---

ables" in an instance of language transact to form a new phenomenon, the subcomponents of which are not reducible. To "control" a component is to distort the relationships which occur, and in the process, alter the event so that it is no longer an instance of what one is studying. This position is semiotic (Eco, 1976). Figure 5.2 illustrates this world view when applied to the process of reading.

To say we started as positivists and ended as semioticians is too dramatic. Given our history and training, the changes were often more ephemeral than that. One of our graduate students probably best captured our dilemma when he said, "By evening, after looking at this data, I'm a true semiotician. The problem is each morning when I wake up I'm a positivist again!"

We found and still find it hard to abandon "variable," "factor," and other such positivistic terminology. Many of our initial analyses were positivistic, a position which, over time, we came to outgrow. Often it took us what in retrospect seems an inordinate amount of time to abandon a term or concept that was theoretically inconsistent with the position we had come to hold.

Even writing up our findings caused us problems. An ethnographic perspective assumes that all aspects of the context of situation, including the researcher, are an integral part of the process and hence an integral part of the phenomena one is attempting to explain. An experimental approach assumes that, through certain controls, the effect of the researcher is equally distributed and hence ignorable. Since the researcher has been removed, the researcher can write as if he or she did not exist. An ethnographic approach assumes that the researcher's presence will be part of that process and that such involvement must be recorded and studied. To write impersonally and abstractly is to be theoretically inconsistent with a position which holds that the researcher is inevitably "in the text" (Herzfeld, 1982).

Entwined with this issue is the issue of generalizability. From a semiotic perspective experimental research data are not generalizable because they deal with a distorted sign. How can studying nonlanguage instances, where key aspects of the process (which we have yet to identify) are not allowed to transact, help us understand real language? From an experimental perspective, though, how does one generalize from naturalistic data?

In the end, our approach was to look for patterns within and across language events. To the extent that there are universal processes involved in any instance of language use or language learning, such an approach seems tenable. A good theory of language learning has to explain all instances of language learning, not just those it finds convenient. Thus, all of the instances of language that occur are important and must be explained by one's evolving theory. No data can be ignored.

From a semiotic perspective, being able to explain all observed behaviors of language users during a language event provides a sounder basis on which to generate theory—to generalize—than does explaining a subset of behaviors one finds convenient, while simultaneously acknowledging observed "error" or exceptions even with this set.

EXAMINING MODELS OF LITERACY LEARNING

INTRODUCTION

In this section we will examine three distinct models of literacy learning: (1) behavioral; (2) cognitive; and (3) transactional. These models vary in terms of their underlying assumptions about how language is learned. A behavioral model assumes the environment (E) shapes the learner (L) (E$\longrightarrow$L). A cognitive model assumes the learner determines what is learned from the environment (E$\longleftarrow$L). A transactional model assumes that the coming together of learner and environment affect what is learned (E$\longrightarrow\longleftarrow$L). When reviewing studies we may not find one or the other of these models explicitly stated; yet, the presence of a particular model can often be inferred from the recommendations being made following identification of the assumptions upon which those recommendations rest.

Recently, for example, a National Institute of Education publication appeared announcing the availability of research monies in reading and language. In the area of early literacy the federal government wished to support research in, and we quote:

How we move from simpler forms of reading, such as letter recognition and sounding out words, to a fuller understanding of written materials.
(NIE, undated, but still being distributed in November of 1982)

While this statement seems to pose a rather straightforward agenda, it makes a series of assumptions about language and language learning. By implication, the statement accepts as viable such notions as "developmental stages," "readiness," "emergent reading," and others which rest on these assumptions. Even further, it endorses, in part at least, a behavioral model of language learning by suggesting that a particular instructional environment—a subskills approach—is unquestionably the base from which one begins to study "higher" forms of reading. Also, implicit in the statement is a belief that written language is a second-order abstraction which is built on an oral language base.

Since these notions and the assumptions underlying them have been proposed as useful constructs for understanding literacy by historical fiat, they constitute part of the conceptual context within which we currently work. At best, NIE's request for research reflects only a selected segment of current thought in the field of literacy and literacy learning; in so doing it raises many of the major issues involved in the study of literacy. In the following section, we will briefly identify these issues, examine assumptions, and, based on our research, suggest theoretical alternatives.

ORAL LANGUAGE LEARNING

Alternative Models.   In the sixties there were important changes in our understanding of oral language development in children (see Lindfors, 1980, for an excellent review). Up until this period most studies of child language were dominated by behavioral models. The majority of these studies were concerned with lexicon, the number and variety of words used by a child. These words were classified according to adult language categories (nouns, verbs, adjectives, and so on), and correlated with such factors as age, sex, race, socioeconomic status, and school achievement.

The problem with such studies was that no collection of words—no matter how vast—in itself constitutes a language. Without precise rules for combining and interpreting these elements there is no language. The first critical point at which associationistic models of learning were discovered to fail, Ferreiro and Teberosky (1982) remind us, was in accounting for the development of syntactic rules. "Neither imitation nor selective reinforcement, the key elements of associationistic learning theory, could account for the child's learning of syntax" (p. 11).

Although it is beyond the scope of this discussion to provide a detailed analysis of the advances made by developmental psycholinguistics, it is necessary to present a brief overview indicating some crucial points. The traditional associationistic model of language acquisition is simple: children learn through imprinting and imitation (see Skinner, 1950, 1978). The environment which surrounds the child is organized to reinforce certain responses and eliminate others. For example, when an infant produces a sound (like "dada") which the parent likes to hear, the parent smiles and reinforces the child's response. In this way the environment selects, from the variety of sounds leaving the child's mouth, only those combinations corresponding to the mother tongue. The problem this model has, as Chomsky (1965) was only too happy to point out, was, of course, how words become meaningful.

In a behavioral model the meaning problem is supposedly resolved by repeated exposure. The adult presents an object and pronounces a word which is the name of the object. Because language is arbitrary—the words we use to label an object have no direct tie to that object's meaning—language learning is seen as being an abstract form of learning. Since language is abstract and arbitrary, learning is difficult and essentially unnatural. By reiterated associations of the sound and the object, these problems of unnaturalness are overcome; in the end an associative bond is formed. In this model the language learner is seen as passive, being shaped by his or her environment.

Work in developmental psycholinguistics greatly altered the profession's view of language learning. Instead of passively awaiting external reinforcement, children came to be seen as actively attempting to understand the nature of the language spoken around them, making predictions and testing hypotheses about how language worked (see Chomsky, 1965). During this period children were said "to form their own grammar" (see Brown, 1973). Cognitivists argued that this was not just a deformed copy of the adult model, but the children's own creation based on the rules of language use they had intuited as members of a language community.

Building upon this work we now understand that children do not, in reality, "develop their own grammar." While child language is different from adult language, it is based on the same rules. Our research shows that the interpretive rules of language use—even written language use— are acquired through social interaction at very early ages (Harste, Burke, & Woodward, 1981). This has led us to hold a transactional view of learning based on socio-psycholinguistic principles.

The regularizing of irregular verbs illustrates both the initial observation and our clarification. If the form is "I walked," "I talked," "I climbed," why not "I ated" (LaShell, age 6) or "She rided" (Sally, age 5)? Such patterns of language use are systematic, but because they do not correspond to adult patterns they cannot be said to have been learned through imitation. Nonetheless the rules children use (add *-ed* to verbs to indicate past tense) are not a "new grammar," but are very firmly rooted in rules of language use in the child's interpretive community. Irregular verbs are not regularized through selective reinforcement; they are regularized because children continue to seek the patterns that occur in the language around them.

Children deduce rules and make predictions about how their language works, testing those predictions in the process of using language to get on with living. Both the cognitive model and the transactive model of language learning assume that all language behavior is organized and rule-governed. The problem with a cognitive model of learning, however, is that it fails to explain *why* it is that children tend to develop the cognitive categories of their interpretive community. Because they are not able to explain this, many cognitivists assume the viability of modeling as a learning technique; others posit a black box such as a "language learning device" in the head of the language learner. Many cognitivists, then, like behaviorists, believe that language is a closed system, i.e., the word *tree* means the exact same thing to all speakers of the language. Because both the 3-year-old and the adult can utter the word *tree*, their meaning is the same. The spoken word *tree* has the same meaning to the homeowner who has recently had one fall on his house as it does to the business executive who has recently fled New York for his new life in the Appalachian foothills.

A transactional view of language learning, on the other hand, assumes that meaning resides neither in the environment not totally in the head of the language learner, but rather is the result of ongoing sign interpretation. Language is seen as open, and meaning is seen as triadic, the result of a mental setting actively attempting to make sense of a print setting. When such a triadic relationship is in place, a sign function has been established, and an instance of literacy is said to occur. Word meaning changes by the circumstances of use in transaction with the history of literacy which the language user brings to the setting. The relationship between the "sound-image" of the word *tree* and its "meaning" is open. Because there is no direct linkage between "sound-image" and "meaning," language is open and conservative; one does not have to have a new pronunciation or a word for all meaning variations which occur as the result of experience or socio-historical milieu. From a semiotic perspective, "sound-images" or words are signs which have multiple meanings. The fact that we share some meaning for the word *tree* is a function of the fact that we are members of the same interpretive community and that language and language learning are social processes. Language is thus seen as open, not a perfectable absolute.

Figure 5.3 contrasts these differences in language learning theory in schematic form.

Over time, assumptions about the active role of the language user and the openness of language as a sign system have altered the profession's view of words and word meaning. Some data we collected illustrate the extent to which even the meanings of words with concrete referents are mediated and not just learned by rote. A preschool child's meaning for the word *tree* ("a place to swing in my back yard" [Alison, age 5]) is different from a second grader's ("wood, shade" [Jason, age 7]), and both differ from the historian's ("a major factor in the westward movement" [College Professor, age 42]). Though pronunciations of the word *tree* are the same, meanings are quite different. Language, even when reduced to words, always involves an active interpreter. The difference, Labov (1982) says, "between a parrot and human saying, 'I'll meet you downtown,' is that the human is likely to show up."

Imitation and Modeling.   Regularity in language use (i.e., a child's use of *-ed* to mark past tense) is evidence of linguistic rules in operation which transcend a particular instance of language use. To find such

1. *Environment* → *Learner*

Behavioral View: Learning is the result of an S−R bond. Problems in learning are problems in the delivery system. The learner is passive.

2. *Environment* ← *Learner*

Cognitive View: The learner is central. Learning is dependent on the assimilative schemas available in the head of the language learner.

3. *Environment* → ← *Learner*

Transactional View: Meaning invloves seeing objects as signs which have the potential to signify. Language is an open system. Semiotically this model is often rendered as a triangle with learner being posed as outside the triad; that is, taking the Object as a Sign to infer signification or Meaning which resides above the Object-Sign plane:

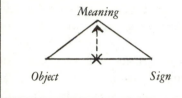

Meaning

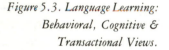

Object   *Sign*

Figure 5.3. Language Learning: Behavioral, Cognitive & Transactional Views.

regularities the child has had to deduce a rule, e.g., make an interpretation above and beyond any particular instance. Such learning is different from modeling, which assumes that there is no abstract rule governing the behavior, but rather only a representative attempt to imitate what has just occurred. In the first instance learning is mediated by cognitive activity over and above what is given; in the second instance no such mediated thought is posited.

Because children grow up in a particular language or interpretive community, the patterns they discover about language inevitably share much in common with the language around them. Some people have mistakenly assumed that this means that some elements of language are acquired through imitation and modeling, while other elements are learned through rule formation and hypothesis testing (a more active mental process).

The problem with such a position is that it accepts the viability of a behavioral model of language learning; that is, it assumes that some of language at least does not involve active interpretation on the part of the language learner. Our own position is that none of language can be explained via an associative or behavioral model of learning. Repeated exposure and modeling explain nothing. In any instance of language there is much to be modeled, yet any two language users elect to "model" quite different things, an act, in itself, requiring "interpretation" and assumptions as to "signification."

Language is not acquired through modeling; it is learned through interpretation. Further, we have found that, upon examination, every literacy event that at first appears to be "rote" or "imitative" is in fact based on the intent to make meaning within the social context. One example should suffice to illustrate this point. As part of our program of research, we and the research associates, graduate students, and teachers with whom we worked, conducted what we called "child-as-informant curricular and research studies." These studies involved selecting a setting and observing young children operating in that setting.

In this instance, the parent-researchers reported observing the following activity in their 2-year-old son, David: It was Sunday morning. The opening and closing of the screen door indicated that the Sunday paper had been delivered. David grabbed the comic section, walked by his toy box and picked up a wooden, cylinder-shaped block. Hopping into his favorite chair, David propped his feet on the ottoman, placed the block—his "play cigar"—in the corner of his mouth, snapped the paper open, and with arms extended announced, "I'm going to read the funnies!"

A behavioral interpretation of this incident would be to say that David was "imitating" what his father had "modeled" on previous Sunday mornings when the paper arrived. This interpretation leaves unanswered the question of whether or not David's actions were deliberately meaningful and why it was that David "imitated" key aspects of the setting and not, for example, the closing of the screen door and other superfluous aspects of the event. This is a most important question. It is at base the difference between our view and a behavioral view of language learning.

From a child-as-informant perspective, if David repeated these or similar actions across language settings, we could infer that his behaviors were intentional and rule-governed, reflective of psycholinguistic and sociolinguistic activity. With only one instance we still suspect this to be true. Clearly, for example, we might infer that David already at age 2 sees reading as a form of social action. Given certain settings, looking at a sheet of newsprint is an acceptable form of social action. David also demonstrates by his actions that he sees newspapers as objects which indicate an activity called "reading." We might suspect that David sees "reading," then, as something one does from things like newspapers. In addition we might surmise that David understands this activity in relation to his world. The newspaper is delivered so that this activity called "reading" can occur. Reading is enjoyable. Funnies are part of the newspaper. Funnies are the things one reads first.

All of these inferences, we might suspect, are part of David's thinking and govern his actions, making them predictable and nonrandom. To dismiss these behaviors by labeling them "imitation" is to miss "the learner" in the event, and what it is that David already intuitively understands about the literacy process. From our perspective, David already has an anticipatory frame for newspapers, which includes what one does with them and why one does it. Newspapers and their arrival are objects which function as signs. David's interpretation of these signs is understandable via a study of his sociolinguistic and psycholinguistic activity and action. Since such anticipatory frames are a central part of the reading process (Smith, 1978; Goodman, 1967), they are much too important to go unnoticed.

It is important to understand that underlying these interpretations of David's actions are radically different conceptions of language and language learning. From a transactional view, language is an open sign system which in operation involves an active interpretation on the part of the language user. From a behavioral view, the language learner is passive, a receptacle, and irregularities in learning are not rule-governed, but random, created by inconsistencies in the delivery system. From a cognitivist view, errors reflect not the environment but the cognitive categories which the learner possesses; the learner is simply duped by his or her own schema. Cognitivists posit biological tendencies and "cognitive dissonance" as the major impetus behind learning; transactionalists posit experience and the search for meaning.

Because of the model of language learning which is the source of the terms "modeling" and "acquistion," we have dropped them from our vocabulary. We recommend that others who see the language learner as active do likewise.

Scaffolding. Some researchers today speak of "scaffolding," a notion much akin to modeling in many respects (see Cazden, 1965, 1966, 1972, 1978). This concept originated from studies of adult-child interaction where it was found that adult-child speech interactions were different from adult-adult speech interaction patterns. Typically, sentences were shorter, children's responses were expanded and elaborated by the adult, and deviations were corrected only when they resulted in loss of meaning. The essential notion underlying scaffolding is that the adult determines the language structures to be used by the child and that such structuring facilitates the child's acquisition of language. The conclusion that is often reached is that natural language settings are far from "natural," thus directly and indirectly supporting the viability of direct instructional models of language teaching and a behavioral model of learning (see Teale, 1982; and Bruner, 1982).

While it is true that child-adult conversations are structured differently than are adult-adult conversations, these differences are predictable and, like any instance of language use, reflect the psycholinguistic and sociolinguistic processes involved in language use. Halliday (1980) argues that what participants do psycholinguistically is to "semantically track" each other; this produces sociolinguistic shifts and moves throughout the language event. In adult-child conversation, the shifts which adults make in adjusting their language to the child—what Halliday calls "tracking"—might be more simply viewed as a case of the adults reacting to "the child as conversational informant"; the shift and moves which the child makes to the adult, as "the adult as conversational informant." Our research suggests that if you put the same child in two different language settings with two different adults, language patterns change. The term "scaffolding" assumes that the adult is in charge, simplifying, manipulating, or structuring the environment for learning. "Scaffolding" as a term thus pulls attention away from the process to the environment and hence implies that language learning is the result of an environment-response bond.

The term "tracking" refers to the psycholinguistic and sociolinguistic processes or strategies engaged in by both participants. Both child and adult are seen as actively structuring the event.

These semantic distinctions between "scaffolding" and "tracking" are significant. When a behavioral perspective is taken, the danger lies in deducing that what children need is simplified language environments and that these are "natural" for language learning. Instructionally this leads to setting up environments where all of the systems of language are not allowed to transact as they normally do (and as, in fact, they were doing in the studies from which "scaffolding" as a concept evolved).

WRITTEN LANGUAGE LEARNING

When one moves from oral language learning to written language learning these issues are accentuated. From a socio-psycholinguistic perspective it seems ludicrous to assume that; given a literate society, young children, while actively attempting to make sense of the rest of their world, would selectively decide not to attend to print. Given everything we know about learners and our print-oriented society, several researchers (Goodman & Goodman, 1979; Smith, 1980; Ferreiro & Teberosky, 1982; King & Rentel, undated) have argued that a more viable theoretical position would be to assume that young children have attended to print prior to schooling and that formal literacy programs should build from this knowledge.

The Oral Language Supremacy Assumption.   Part of the reason so few persons have studied literacy before schooling lies in the assumptions embedded in what we have termed "the oral language supremacy assumption." This assumption is that oral language must be in place before written language can be learned.

The pervasiveness of these premises became apparent to us in conducting our research. We found that more often than not little was being done at the preschool and kindergarten level in the name of reading and writing. When something was being done, that something was usually letter-name knowledge and letter-sound pattern drills. In addition, oral language instructional activities of all kinds typically preceded reading and writing activities throughout the curriculum.

The assumption is that, since oral language is a prerequisite to written language learning, special emphasis should be placed on it in preschool and kindergarten programs. "Reading" and "writing" are not supposed to happen at this level. Many preschool teachers whom we approached thought our requests to have preschool children read and write inappropriate, often feeling obliged to inform us that their children didn't read or write yet. One preschool teacher concluded from the unconventional script her 3-year-old children used to "sign in" in her classroom (a procedure we developed to collect name writing data over time) that she was right; children can't write at this age, and we were unrealistic.

In interviewing preschool and kindergarten teachers in our study, we discovered that reading books and going to the library were seen by the teachers only as activities which were enjoyable and broke up the day. The teachers did not see these activities as part of the reading and writing curriculum. The language arts curriculum in these classrooms consisted of teaching letter-name knowledge and of developing oral language skills. While children did experience other written language events, they were not helped by the teachers to value these experiences and the mental activities in which they engaged as real instances of literacy.

The assumption that one must begin literacy learning with letter and sound matching is so pervasive that many otherwise excellent early childhood educators are not interested in highlighting reading and writing activities in the preschool. Often these are humanistic teachers who take a broader approach to teaching and learning in all other curricular areas. With "new" materials advocating a skills and drills approach to beginning reading and writing, their observations of the written language concepts "Sesame Street" teaches, and their past experience with formal literacy programs, these teachers believe that to stress literacy they must abandon their humanistic learning model. By not being aware of either their assumptions or theoretical alternatives, they permit their children to miss many significant and natural encounters with print.

Even within the formal reading program, oral instructional activities typically precede reading and writing activities. Some teachers delay writing until the second half of first grade (Hill, 1980b). Almost all introduce new words orally, have the children use them in oral sentences, and carry on extensive discussions before permitting the child to read. The assumption is that reading is not a language learning opportunity; all concepts must be in place in oral language before the reading process can work.

A further assumption here is that oral language maps directly onto written language. A semiotic view would suggest that while oral and written language share much in common, both of these systems have their own semiotic potential which must be experienced directly. This is why, in fact, we might hypothesize why written language developed. Certain forms of psycholinguistic and sociolinguistic activities were not possible without written language. In order to value written language, children must experience the social, cognitive, and linguistic potentials written language as a system itself holds.

Even the language experience approach, in which children and teachers construct their own reading materials based on the experiences they have together, assumes an oral-language-to-written-language correspondence based on a serial notion about how the expressions of language are learned. In classrooms using the language experience approach, children rarely were given paper and pencil and permitted or encouraged to write their own messages. Failing to note the difference between an integrated language curriculum (where reading and writing are juxtaposed because of an assumption of a shared language process) and a fused one (where reading and writing are juxtaposed because it is a convenient way to teach the same skills through parallel play) only clouds important conceptual issues which need clarification.

Print as Decontextualized Language.   We also found that teachers can assume a broader position on how children learn and have learned oral language, and yet assume a behavioral position when it comes to how written language is learned. The psycholinguistic argument underlying these beliefs is that oral language is more contextualized than written language (Mattingly, 1972, 1979; Emig, 1971; Olson, 1977). The process of learning to handle written language is a process of learning to handle "decontextualized" print.

In its expanded form the argument runs something like this: Cognitively, in order for comprehension to occur, the language user must assimilate what is being perceived into his or her existing framework. If the prerequisite concepts are not in place, the learner is said not to be "ready," or the material being taught is said to be too "abstract." Oral language situations provide more contextual cues which the language user can use to access assimilative schemas. Written language settings have few if any contextual cues and hence are more "abstract," more "decontextualized." Since contextual cues are not available, a different set of cues must operate in written language use. The trick in teaching children to read and write is thus to teach them print cues upon which they can depend rather than the contextual cues they use in oral language.

Given its popularity in recent literature, this view obviously appeals to many members of the profession. Yet much of our data argue against this view. From a socio-psycholinguistic perspective, reading and writing do not involve less concern for context than do speaking and listening. If particular content or process information cannot be assimilated, it can be said to be "abstract," but this is as true of certain oral language activities and experiences as it is of written language.

All language—both oral and written—indicates its context (Halliday & Hasan, 1980). That is why one can infer by whom or for whom it is produced, whether it is oral or written language, and where it is likely to be found. Consider how much context we can infer from each of the following examples: "On your marks," "Railroad strike averted," "Raise your hands please," "This is to certify that. . . . " Context isn't something added onto language. It's part and parcel of the thing we verbocentrically call the "linguistic sign." The systems of language do not exist in isolation. When the systems seem to be isolated, as happens in some classrooms where phonics is taught in "isolation," the code is just read differently by the participants and as such, indicates a context in which the rules of language use are quite different from the ones that operate in language use outside of this classroom. From a socio-psycholinguistic perspective, the ongoing challenge in writing is learning how to indicate an interpretive context so that readers might construct a successful text world. Rather than written language being decontextualized, context remains central. Language and language learning are contextually dependent activities for all language users. Context plays as much of a role in our first language response as in our last language response. This is as true of our oral language responses as it is of our written language responses. Brandt (1983) highlights the key issue in conceptualizing successful adult writing as transactions between and among contexts, involving orchestrating the context of situation, the context of the text world, and the context of the evolving surface text.

Developmental Stages.   Maturationists hold that much of a child's cognitive development can be explained biologically. As children get older and bigger, they are capable of doing things they were not previously capable of doing.

While clearly not the first maturationists, Montessori (1912) and later Havighurst (1952) popularized this position by weaving biology and psychology into their theories of learning. Earlier, and trained as a biologist, Piaget (1969, 1970, 1973) too began his explorations of children's thinking using a biological lens, and similarly ended up posing a "developmental stage" theory of cognitive development which wove biology and psychology into an interesting and appealing mix.

Essentially what Piaget did was to confront children of various ages with a set of problem-solving tasks. By observing the thinking that led the children to their solutions, Piaget mapped out a set of cognitive processing strategies which children at certain ages were likely to use. Before later forms of thinking were possible, children had to have progressed through earlier stages of thought. Piaget demonstrated that young children's thinking abilities were qualitatively different from those of older children, and that both of these patterns were different from the formal thought of most adults. Among other concepts, he introduced the notion of "centrism" to explain why children were not as flexible in their thinking as were their older and more logical peers.

Given these prestigious advocates, it should surprise no one to find the notion of developmental stages deeply embedded in learning theory, including written language learning theory. But, it should also surprise no one that eventually the biological residue of an essentially cognitive position on learning would increasingly come under attack and question.

The work of Margaret Donaldson and her colleagues (1978), for example, seriously questioned Piaget's notion of "centrism." Their studies demonstrated that when tasks were constructed that dealt with the experiences of the child, children's performance on Piagetian "conversation" tasks improved dramatically. Similarly, when the rules of language use in experimental conditions were explained to children (so that they understood that "the same question" was "the same question" and not an indirect speech act, as it typically is when the same question is repeated by an adult to a child), significant numbers of children were suddenly able to provide correct solutions to otherwise insoluable Piagetian tasks.

Piaget's misjudgment, our research program slowly helped us come to understand, was in assuming that language and thought were separated. For Piaget, language reflected thought, but did not affect it. Since language was not an integral part of thinking, what and how one used language (even with children in research settings), was of no cognitive consequence. Language, for Piaget, was an output of thought, not a generator of the basic process itself.

This is not to diminish the contributions of Piagetians. Piagetian research is theoretically based and its theory of learning is explicitly stated. Further, rather than focus on product, Piaget shifted attention to process and the cognitive operations involved. These are significant contributions which we build upon in our own work.

We do suggest, however, that Piaget's approach to research fails to examine certain assumptions about language, cognition, and the relationship between the two, which we now see as central to understanding literacy. Vygotsky (1962, 1978) in particular helped us to see that thought and language transact and together become more than their individual and independent selves.

Since our work bears much similarity to Piagetian research, some further explanation of our position seems warranted. Built into Piagetian tasks is a conception of how the problem-solving process works and the key cognitive operations which are involved in that process. The assumption is that cognitive ability is a "state" which transcends and affects any particular instance of thinking. In contrast, our research demonstrates that experience affects the kinds and quality of thinking children are capable of doing; thinking ability, like language ability, is thus context dependent. Children are at different "cognitive stages" given their familiarity with the context of situation. From a socio-psycholinguistic view, one should be able to demonstrate that adult thought in unfamiliar settings shares much in common with child thought in such situations. We would make this prediction for settings where experiential backgrounds were similar. Conversely, some literacy settings—like computer literacy—might allow some children to have a cognitively strategic advantage over adults. Studying the child's and the adult's psycholinguistic flexibility in these settings would give us further insight into this issue.

Piaget began with a set of assumptions about the cognitive operations involved in formal thought and designed a set of artificial tasks which he felt would test his theory. He made no attempt to watch language users solve real world problems of personal importance. While his approach may appear logical from a methodological perspective, it is not without its own set of faulty premises.

An example from recent literacy research will help to clarify this point. In written language there are potentially many things to attend to. A partial list might include how oral language maps onto written language, how phonemes and graphemes correspond, how language is written and formatted, how language structure varies by context, how one uses language to mean, how language functions across various contexts, how perceptual information is coded into language, and many more. If tasks are designed to explore any one of these aspects of language use, rule-governed behaviors can be identified. The problem is, of course, that one would never know whether or not the thing identified really operated that way or had much, if anything, to do with evolution of literacy. It may be that when all of the other things to be attended to in language are operating, the particular pattern identified by the task pales to insignificance.

Like Piaget, Ferreiro and Teberosky (1982) begin with certain assumptions about the domain they are studying. One of their implicit assumptions is that children must sort out orthographic subcodes prior to learning to read. Thus they design a task with varying amounts of print on various cards (English equivalents for the Spanish print they used being *duck, mmm, pp, a, cat*), and ask the child to identify which of these cards are readable and which are not. They found that children perceived cards having less than three letters on them as unreadable and that readable print must contain a variety of letters, not simply the same letter repeated. They then argue that since most beginning reading programs assume that little words are easy (a, the, see) there is a problem caused by the discrepancy between the child's concept of print and the adult's.

Although we do not question their findings, we cannot accept Ferreiro and Teberosky's interpretations. Clearly, if a researcher asked you to sort a stack of cards as readable or unreadable, you would assume there were indeed two sets. Why else ask the question? In other contexts, language users might make other assumptions, and the question of readable versus not readable might never arise.

In our research we asked children to read or pretend to read a book. Under these conditions, children never once pointed out that certain print was not readable. What we did find was that children as young as 3 expected print to be meaningful and to sound like language; they also adjusted the length of their response to the amount of print available in particular settings. Further, we found that children younger than those studied by Ferreiro and Tebersoky demonstrated graphophonemic awareness, often long before they had sorted out the distinctive features of letters. The graphophonemic system, however, never operates independently of the other systems available in the setting. When all systems are permitted to operate, as they do in natural language settings, the amount of graphophonemic information needed is significantly less than that necessary if this system is presented in isolation. In addition, the multimodal nature of the linguistic sign has been changed. In an experimental setting one has at best a partial sign; at worst, a distorted sign. Thus, even when functional literacy tasks are selected for experimental purposes, the results may tell us less than we expect about natural language processes. Hunt (1983) terms the result a "textoid":

If we separate words out from the contexts by which they are determined, if we pull sentences out of discourses, if we disengage discourse from a context of use and human purpose, we tend to produce something I call "textoids," synthetic fragments of language which exhibit none of the complex richness of natural language. It is precisely this richness which enables us to navigate as effortlessly and unselfconsciously around the hermeneutic circle of understanding as we all have to do in order to understand any system of signs. (p. 5)

The hard lesson we learned from our research program was that when the rules of language use have changed—even when functional literacy tasks are selected for experimental purposes—the cue complexes normally functioning as signs are changed. Both a theory of learning and a theory of language have methodological implications for conducting literacy research and developing curriculum theory.

Examining Readiness.   The notion of "readiness" (see Gesell, 1925, 1940; Hilgard & Bower, 1975; Bigge, 1982) is closely related to the notion of "developmental stages." Both evolve from a maturational view of learning. Both suffer from faulty premises about the nature of language and thought. Both positions have a content and a process dimension to their argument.

From a content perspective, the notion of readiness presumes that one must have certain information before other information can be meaningfully learned. From a process perspective, readiness presumes one must be performing a certain way cognitively before one can expect new forms of cognitive activity to be able to develop. These assumptions are related in their belief that language is a perfectable absolute. There is one and only one true meaning to be obtained from the author; there is one and only one careful route to this meaning. Language is a closed system.

No concept has been more difficult for the profession to abandon than this notion of language as a perfectable absolute. The notion persists despite tomes of research showing that language variation, including variation in comprehension and comprehending, is the norm rather than the exception. Implicit in the notion of "readiness" is a concern with outcome. If one expects everyone to be the same—arrive at the same meaning, take the same careful path to reconstruct that meaning—then and only then is readiness a language learning issue.

In contrast, our research forces us to assume sociological and psychological variation in language. The same surface experience for two different language users will result in two different events and two different experiences. If one accepts language variation and with it variation in what was learned, one can appreciate a language learner's current achievements and language experiences for what they are, not for how closely they parallel the decisions our set of experiences would lead us to make.

The criteria we hold for what makes a literacy experience good for us cannot be used to judge the value of a literacy experience for another. This must be done by each language learner on his or her own terms. Children, our research shows, get out of an experience what they are personally ready for. And this is enough. One does not have to look at every mountain in the Rockies to appreciate their majesty and grandeur. In literacy, whetting the appetite is better than satiating it. If you explore every nook and cranny of the Rockies, why the need ever to go back? It is essentially our mistrust of the child as a learner, and our misunderstanding of language as an open sign system, which has made readiness the issue, the excuse, and the theoretical subterfuge it often is.

We do not have to wait until every mountain is in place before inviting them to enjoy the view. Under such conditions we would never experience the view ourselves.

Emergent Reading.   The term "emergent reading," currently growing in popularity among many researchers studying the evolution of literacy (see Clay, 1972, 1975, 1982; Holdaway, 1979; Sulzby, 1981), embodies the same assumptions we have criticized in discussing the notions of readiness and of developmental stages. Like the terms "beginning reading" and "beginning writing," emergent reading assumes the process used by proficient language users to be psycholinguistically different from the process young children engage in. Implicitly, the notion of "emergent reading" assumes there are no universals in language processing. At a process level, we find no compelling evidence that the behavior of young readers and writers is a function of different psycholinguistic and sociolinguistic activity. Literacy is neither a monolithic skill nor a "now-you-have-it/now-you-don't" affair. This is as true of us as it is of the young.

CONCLUDING THOUGHTS

Unless we examine the assumptions underlying our work, it is difficult to ensure that these will be tested in our research and teaching. Given our program of research, we believe the notions of "developmental stages," "readiness," and more recently, "emergent reading" need more careful examination. We are, of course, not the only ones to question the usefulness of many of these terms (King, 1982; Goodman, 1982; Graves 1983).

We do not wish to say that reading or writing is idiosyncratic. To do so would be to suggest there are no discernible psycholinguistic and sociolinguistic universals in the processes involved in language use and language learning. We have no evidence that children's psycholinguistic and sociolinguistic strategies are qualitatively different from the kinds of decisions which more experienced language users make. On the contrary, we see many common principles emerging across recent studies of children and adults (Atwell. 1980; Brandt, 1983; Calkins, 1983; Graves, 1983; Kucer, 1982; Siegel, 1983; Shanklin, 1982). These results suggest that the process children engage in is not a pseudo form of the "real" process; it *is* that process.

Instructionally, the problem with many of our current terms— "developmental stages," "readiness," "emergent reading"—is the same problem we have with the term "scaffolding." At its most demeaning level the argument runs: If "little children" have "little thoughts" and attend to "easy cues" in written language, then structured environments need to be designed which recognize these differences and facilitate literacy learning. In more sophisticated form the instructional assumption runs: Complex processes, like written language and written language learning, must be simplified in order to be learned.

This position, in whatever form, inevitably leads to a distortion of the linguistic context and, if we are right, of the multimodal nature of the linguistic sign. Further, the position fails to explore, acknowledge, or appreciate what the young child has learned about written language use prior to formal instruction.

We went into our program of research assuming the young child had much to teach us about written language and the written language learning process. By reflecting our beliefs through the prism of the children we studied, we came to identify some of our assumptions and to challenge existing dogma. We learned that methodology does not stand outside of theory. The assumptions we make limit what can be learned. Alter those assumptions and the potential for learning expands.

Section Two

Literacy Lessons

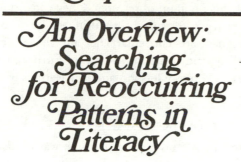

Chapter 6

An Overview: Searching for Reoccurring Patterns in Literacy

The authors describe their research program with its focus on the child as informant.

Both the teaching and researching of literacy is theoretically based. What teachers and researchers believe about literacy is important. Because beliefs affect what child behaviors we value and encourage in our classrooms, our assumptions affect curriculum. The "real" curriculum is the mental trip which the language learner takes. By passing on our conventional notions about the reading and writing process, we can short-circuit the trip. Until we understand the characteristics of the successful trip as well as what conditions make the successful trip possible, we are in a poor position, as language educators, to create a supportive environment in which language learners might encounter quality language learning experiences.

We believe, with Herbert Kohl (1983) that the teacher must be an intellectual as well as a practitioner.

An intellectual is someone who knows his or her field, has a wide breadth of knowledge about other aspects of the world, who uses experience to develop theory on the basis of further experience. An intellectual is also someone who has the courage to question authority and who refuses to act counter to his or her own experience and judgment. (p. 30)

This section explains the rationale underlying our program of research as well as key patterns we see involved in literacy and literacy learning. Our objective is to interpret the process from the point of view of the learner on the basis of the observations we made of preschool and elementary school children—the majority of whom were 3 to 6 years of age—over a six-year period.

We do not attempt to simplify theoretical issues or the complexity of the language learning process. In the end we believe language teachers and teaching are not well served by simplicity. The insights we share represent our current set of beliefs about language and language learning as a function of this program of research. They constitute a new set of beliefs upon which we are currently willing to act in designing new research and language arts curricula. They are, then, our current "best guess," and will remain so up until we gain further insight from the language stories and literacy lessons language learners have to teach us.

THE YOUNG CHILD AS INFORMANT

Since our interest in this program of research was in discovering what construction processes were involved in literacy and literacy learning, the role we as researchers played during data collection and analysis was an issue of conceptual and methodological importance. The position we took was that our role should be one which permitted the child to be our linguistic informant. We did not wish to push the child through our questioning into a state of cognitive dissonance, a procedure which would necessitate our taking ownership of the literacy process away from the child. We were, rather, interested in what problems the child might perceive and what strategies he or she would use to circumvent or solve these problems. This meant a low-key role, taking our cues from the language user during data collection. All questions which the children asked, and all problems which they identified, were turned back to them to solve. Often this meant that assurance had to be given so that children would continue their involvement in the literacy setting. The role we selected, then, was one of support rather than of intervention. We attempted to maintain this role across all data collection settings.

In retrospect this decision was at best a compromise. In natural language settings outside of a school and research setting, children do interact and discuss things with adults and others who share a literacy experience. Such interactions are not outside the literacy process, but an integral part of the literacy event. While such interactions do affect the event and even change its direction, this too is natural.

From watching our behavior on videotape, we can now say our noninvolvement affected the event as much as did our involvement, but in different ways. While we now accept this as true, we believe that, over the long haul, our policy of allowing the child to follow his or her own lead, rather than ours, was a good one. While children did not always address the issue we thought most compelling from our perspective, what they did address proved more interesting and more insightful.

We also believed a position of support rather than intervention within the course of the literacy event would allow for more consistent data to be collected and facilitate generalizing our findings. Over time, however, we have begun to reconceive this issue too. What consistency in a research setting allows is consistency in data. When process and product literacy analyses are done, such consistency only misguidedly appears important. Without variation in research settings within and across language users, one can never be sure that the patterns one sees are a true part of the process or an artifact of the research task, setting, or research procedures used. Even such things, we would now argue, as how young children handle cohesion, are best studied in individual settings, since the ability to write cohesive texts is not a monolithic skill but a function of the task, the setting, and the experience of the language user, and of other transactions in language use. Built into a study of cohesion in children's stories, for example, are aspects which assure that any conclusions reached are extremely limited and not generalizable to the process one is supposedly studying in a broader context.

When research is designed to study the processes involved in literacy and literacy learning, a variety of contrastive settings are one way to insure that any processes identified are indeed involved in, and applicable to, literacy and literacy learning more generally. It is only under such conditions that we can be comfortable that the patterns or configurations we identified are indeed real and not a function of a particular task of or another constraint operating in the setting. Nor does such a procedure diminish the value of any particular set of data. If a particular constraint is operating in a particular way, such patterns are in themselves important to understand. Without the study of this phenomenon in contrastive settings, however, such configurations cannot be identified. Equally important from this perspective, a research report based on one consistent set of data does not increase its generalizability, but rather, because it represents a half-truth, decreases it.

No pattern we discuss occurred in one and only one setting. Because of constraints we saw operating in our original videotape data, follow-up studies were conducted to assure ourselves that the patterns we had identified were reoccurring patterns in literacy and not artifacts of the particular research contexts we had created.

Our position that the child should be the research informant also had implications for data analysis. Rather than examine any data with a preconceived or existing analytic system, our first step was to watch all videotapes and note things of interest and patterns in the data which we saw as evolving. This does not mean that all categories we developed were unique only to us; rather, it means that some of the patterns we saw were patterns other researchers had also observed. In these instances their taxonomic categories were used. Various members of the research team were assigned the task of watching the videotapes and studying our other collections of data for purposes of identifying patterns which they thought interesting and important. Once an initial set of categories evolved from the data, the entire research team rewatched all tapes in order to generate new categories as well as to have patterns already identified clarified.

When taxonomies were used for coding data, categories were developed and enough examples of the phenomena identified so that coders trained on the coding instrument could do so with an interrater reliability of .80 or better. Until such reliability was established, the procedures of adding examples to categories was continued. In retrospect, the research team's interactions during these data analysis and coding sessions proved very interesting and meritorious of a study in their own right, as we are convinced research serves its own informant role. In this sense, the taxonomies we developed for analyzing data were seen as heuristic devices to explore both our thinking and that of our informants. There is

Figure 6.1. Name Writing Across Ages.

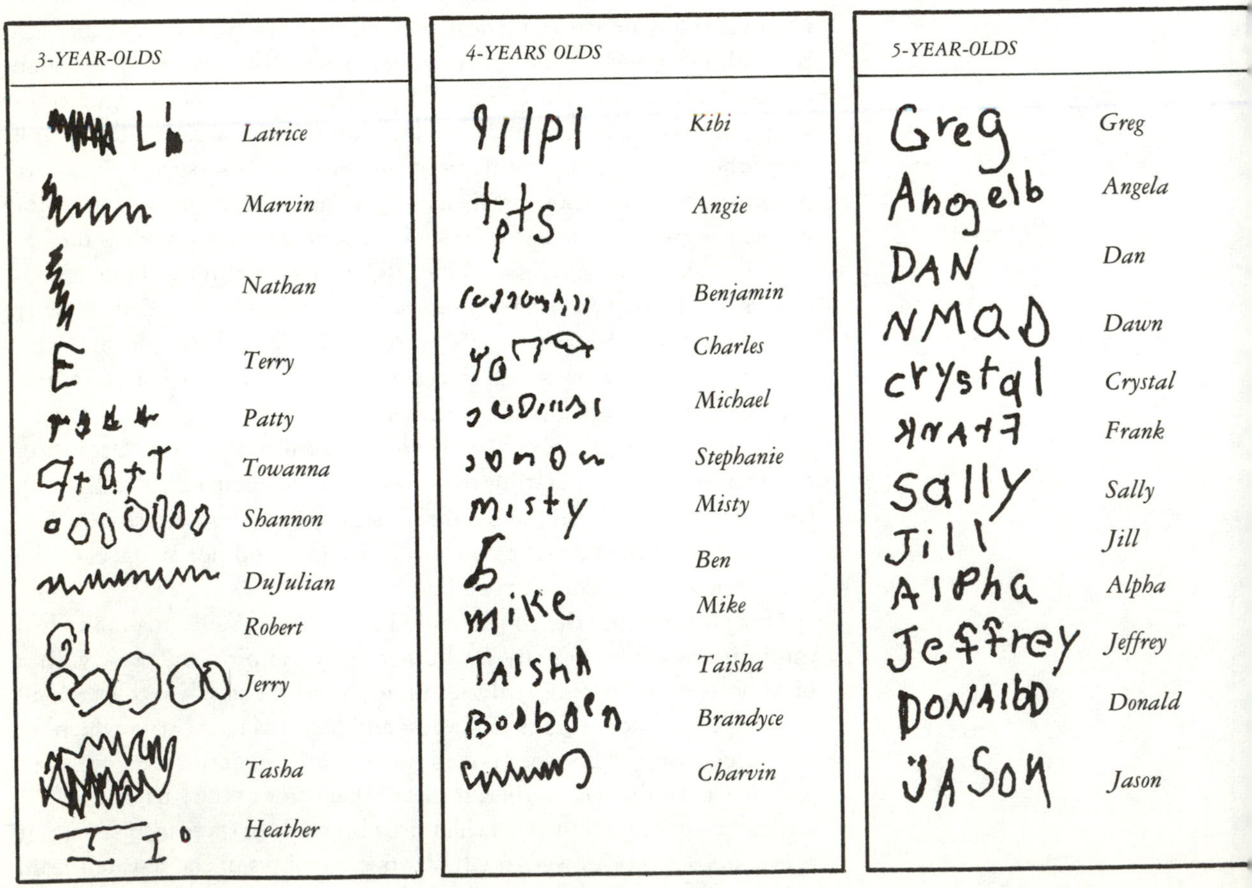

3-YEAR-OLDS		4-YEARS OLDS		5-YEAR-OLDS	
	Latrice		Kibi		Greg
	Marvin		Angie		Angela
	Nathan		Benjamin		Dan
	Terry		Charles		Dawn
	Patty		Michael		Crystal
	Towanna		Stephanie		Frank
	Shannon		Misty		Sally
	DuJulian		Ben		Jill
	Robert		Mike		Alpha
	Jerry		Taisha		Jeffrey
	Tasha		Brandyce		Donald
	Heather		Charvin		Jason

no attempt here to explore all of the analyses we performed on various portions of the data we collected over the course of this research program. Our decision about what to report was to select those patterns and analyses which we believed proved particularly valuable for extending current notions of literacy and literacy learning.

At this point it seems appropriate to say that preestablished factors which supposedly affect literacy such as socioeconomic status, which we could not see as a pattern in our data, were not studied. To correlate these factors against patterns identified by other criteria is to take an essentially antitheoretical stance (see Figure 6.1). Anyone able to identify responses by the socioeconomic status of these children's parents, or on the basis of the race of the informant, is asked to contact us immediately since we have been unable to identify any reoccurring processing patterns which fall out along these factors. The model of literacy we propose, therefore, does not include these as useful constructs for the study of literacy and literacy learning. Unless such constructs have a viable base in theory, one must seriously ask why hair color, shoe size, or other theoretically unrelated concepts are not also studied. To the extent that socioeconomic status, race, and sex are viable constructs for the study of literacy in schooling, but not before schooling, the key theoretical variables are not these, but other more significant attitudes and interaction patterns. To focus on these factors diverts rather than illuminates.

Once a pattern had been identified in the data, existing literature was reviewed to see if others had observed this phenomenon. Whenever possible existing terms from sociolinguistics, psycholinguistics, semiotics, linguistics, and related fields were used to label the pattern identified.

STUDIES WITHIN OUR RESEARCH PROGRAM

Based on a study of early readers in kindergarten (Woodward, 1977) and observations of preschool and first-grade classrooms (Harste & Burke, 1977), we began this program of research assuming that what the young child knew about reading and writing prior to first grade far exceeded what teachers and beginning reading and writing programs assumed. Now after six years of research and involvement in a wide variety of analysis, we realize we were not optimistic enough. Children know much more than any of us have ever dared to imagine.

In the summer of 1977 we received funding in the form of a Proffitt Research Grant to study a random sample of twenty 3-, 4-, 5-, and 6-year-old children in Bloomington, Indiana. These children represent a sample of middle- and upper-class white children. The purpose of this study was to identify what literacy and literacy learning looked like

6-YEAR OLDS	
chris	*Chris*
Gerald	*Gerald*
Deshonna	*Deshonna*
Latisha	*Latisha*
Gina	*Gina*
Vincent	*Vincent*
Jake	*Jake*
LaShell	*LaShell*
Eugene	*Eugene*
Natasha	*Natasha*
Marc	*Marc*
Alanna	*Alanna*

under what was considered, given the literature, ideal conditions. Since then we have found that the circumstances of one's birth are a poor basis on which to predict the evolution of literacy. Given the fact that some upper-class children have very poor literacy learning environments, while some lower-class children have very rich literacy learning environments, the best criterion to use is observation, which is what we did after we handed the children: a paper and pencil and allow them to write; and a book and ask them to read.

Throughout the summer of 1977 we worked out task settings and administration as well as videotape data collection procedures. Our first study involved children in four research settings: (1) reading environmental print; (2) dictating a language experience story and reading and rereading it; (3) writing their name and anything else that they could write; and (4) drawing a self-portrait and writing their name. It was from these initial administration experiences that we decided all videotape data must be collected using two remote control cameras in order to reduce the number of individuals present at the data collection site and to insure the collection of usable videotape data. This policy we have followed faithfully, with Virginia Woodward collecting video data in the homes of two children who moved during her longitudinal study. It was also during this period that we decided our going to the children, rather than their coming to us, was an important part of data collection and would do much to reduce the anxiety that some of the children we studied in 1977 seemed to display. As a result of this decision, in subsequent videotape studies we not only met with the children prior to actually attempting to collect data, but physically transported two remote control camera units and a blender to the sites involved.

In the spring of 1978, Dr. Woodward received funding from the National Council of Teachers of English to follow the 3-year-olds in our Bloomington study over a three-year period collecting data on our tasks at regular six-month intervals. Since our previous study assumed the 3-year-olds we studied would look like the 4-year-olds we studied if we could study them one year later, and so on, this study was specifically designed to check the viability of this assumption. In the course of this study, we came to understand, however, that with prior experience in a language setting, the literacy potentials of that setting drastically change for the language user.

In 1979 and 1980 we received funding from the National Institute of Education for a study of a random sample of 3-, 4-, 5-, and 6-year-old inner-city black and white children coming from low and middle socioeconomic circumstances, based on parental income, parental educational level, and residential area. In this study, conducted in Indianapolis, Indiana, additional story and letter writing settings were added to the research design in order to explore story writing across setting and the stability of certain patterns across a larger variety of contexts.

In each of these studies all data were videotaped for data analysis. This decision proved invaluable as it allowed us to go through our data on a number of occasions to look for patterns which we only later came to appreciate. All data in these studies were collected from children in individual settings spanning a four-day period.

During the 1976–81 period, we and several of the graduate students at our institution conducted longitudinal case studies of selected children. These studies included Lynn Rhodes's study of her daughter, Kara, from ages 3 to 5; Marcia Baghban's study of her daughter, Gita, from ages 2 to 5; Mary Hill's study of Alison, Erica, and Megan from ages 3 to 6; and our study of Alison from ages 3 to 8. These children represent an upper-middle-class sample of children coming from homes where literacy was a highly valued activity. Our decision to study this population as intently as we did was based on a belief that we had to have some notion of what was possible in the name of literacy learning before schooling if we were to be able to judge the quality of the experiences of children coming from alternative and supposedly less fortunate environments.

From these initial studies, patterns were identified in our data. During the 1979–82 period we encouraged graduates, students, visiting scholars, and teachers whom we came in contact with to conduct their own child-as-informant research and curricular studies. These studies were conducted in homes, schools, clinics, and other settings to see if patterns and constructs identified were viable explanations of literacy and literacy learning. Because several of the graduate students and teachers we contacted were involved in special education programs and in multicultural settings in Texas, New Mexico, Hawaii, and Alaska, these follow-up studies also provided us a beginning opportunity to explore the viability of the constructs we had identified for discussing literacy among special populations.

It was from these follow-up studies that we reconfirmed the value of functional language settings for the collection of quality reading and writing data. Subsequent studies, when we attempted to set situations up, have involved extended time periods (e.g., pen pal writing to a group of first graders over the course of a semester); or when not set up, have involved either collecting all writing samples children naturally produce over the period of a week at home, or observing other self-selected literacy events.

During the 1977–82 period: (1) one member of our research team had the opportunity to work with a group of 3-year-olds one morning each week for a three-year period; (2) another member of our research team, because of her faculty position, had an opportunity to influence what happened curricularly at the university-sponsored preschool program; and (3) a third member directed a special summer reading and writing program for elementary age children. Because of these opportunities, curricular studies were conducted to determine how the insights from our initial studies of literacy and literacy learning might translate into instructional practice. During this same time period, one of the current graduate students at our institution, Heidi Mills, was given the opportunity to set up, conduct, and work as a language arts coordinator and resource teacher in a preschool Head Start program in Michigan. The advances in literacy which occurred among this population during the three-year program will form the basis of her dissertation.

During this same period several doctoral students at our institution picked up on key patterns and concepts which we identified in our study to explore the viability of these patterns and constructs at other ages and with other populations. Because their research inevitably proceeded faster than ours, they often ended up pushing our thinking as much as we theirs. Mary Hill, who used her work and ours to develop a theoretically based instructional program for parents (1980), is currently developing procedures for mapping the social interactions and transactions involved in child-to-child literacy learning settings. Margaret Atwell (1980) refined our local and global cohesive mapping procedures in a study of proficient and less-proficient adult writers. Linda Crafton (1981) refined and extended the taxonomic categories dealing with meaning maintenance and meaning generation within and across language events in a study of fourth-grade and eleventh-grade students reading related concepts materials. Stephen Kucer (1983) developed a reader-based as opposed to a text-based procedure for studying text coherence. His work solves many of the problems we noted but could not solve when mapping semantic growth. Karen Feathers (1983) has developed a procedure for studying the cohesive harmony of a surface text using the propositional text base. Nanci Vargus (1982) has developed and refined procedures for mapping changes in register as a function of involvement in a language event over time. Chrystine Bouffler (1983) has refined and extended our taxonomies for studying psycholinguistic and sociolinguistic strategies in spelling. Marjorie Siegel (1983) has studied the psycholinguistic and sociolinguistic processes involved in transmediation from written language to art using a semiotic perspective as the basis for organizing her ethnographic observations of reading comprehension in a fourth-grade classroom. Other studies are still in progress. Given the collaborative nature of this research, we consider not only these studies but also these persons an integral part of our program of research.

PATTERNS OF LITERACY

Goodman (1980) argues that the study of reading has become multidisciplinary rather than interdisciplinary. By making this distinction,

Goodman calls attention to the fact that while a number of disciplines are involved in studying the reading process, each does so from its own perspective and using its own methodologies. He calls for "bridging the gaps in reading" via interdisciplinary work which integrates and respects multiple perspectives.

While the focus of Goodman's remarks is on the status of reading research, his argument is equally applicable to recent work in writing. The following chapters identify and describe what we perceive to be key concepts in understanding literacy and literacy learning. Eight concepts are identified: organization, intentionality, generation, risk, social action, context, text, and demonstration. These labels serve an organizational function for the patterns we found in children's writing across our program of research. Once we identified a pattern in our protocols we searched the literature in reading, writing, and related fields to identify how others had talked about this phenomenon and what specifically their discussions and our observations meant for understanding literacy and literacy learning.

Each chapter which follows contains two parts. Using protocol materials, we first identify what we see as a significant pattern emerging from our data and why we view it as such. Then we trace the significance of the pattern conceptually in order to rethink literacy via a review of pertinent research and a more in-depth analysis of selected protocols. In the process of looking at the young child as reader and writer, typical data and typical data analysis procedures used in our program of research will be presented. Those wanting access to the taxonomies we developed for studying key processes involved in literacy are referred to our final reports (Harste, Burke, Woodward, 1981, 1983).

Chapter 7
Organization

Language is demonstrated as a social event. The responses of young children to reading and writing experiences are systematic and organized reflections of personal social decisions.

THE YOUNG CHILD AS INFORMANT

By "organization" we refer to patterns in children's reading and writing behaviors which seem to reflect, in their genesis, a common set of cognitive processing decisions on the part of the language user and learner. For example, we found that, when asked to write, young children make markings which reflect the written language of their culture. We interpret these data to mean that the psycholinguistic processes in written language use and learning are sociologically rooted. These data support the notion that young children are written language users and learners long before they receive formal instruction and that they actively attend to written language; in short, there is literacy before schooling.

Dawn, a 4-year-old from the United States, writes in unconventional script using a series of wavy lines. Each line is written from left-to-right. Dawn creates a page of such lines starting at the top of her page and finishing at the bottom of her page.

Najeeba, a 4-year-old from Saudi Arabia, writes in unconventional script using a series of very intricate curlicue formations with lots of "dots" over the script. When she completes her story she says, "Here, but you can't read it, cause I wrote it in Arabic and in Arabic we use a lot more dots than you do in English!"

Ofer, a 4-year-old from Israel, prints, first right-to-left, then left-to-right, using a series of rectangular and triangular shapes to create his story, which his grandmother says, ". . . looks like Hebrew, but it's not." Her concern because he sometimes writes "backwards" sound like the concerns of many parents and teachers in the U.S., with the difference being that left-to-right is "backwards" in Hebrew, and right-to-left "backwards" in English.

82

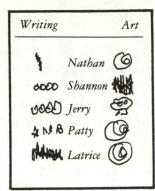

Writing	Art
Nathan	
Shannon	
Jerry	
Patty	
Latrice	

We also found that decisions made for writing are organized and orchestrated beyond language to include and affect assimilative structures across various communication systems.

Nathan, age 3, uses a linear, wavy line for writing but a circular, more globally central set of markings for art.

Shannon, age 3, on the other hand, does just the opposite, using a series of linearly organized circles for writing, but a series of up-and-down lines centrally positioned for art.

Jerry, age 3, like Shannon, uses a series of linearly organized circles for writing, but a series of embedded circles and straight lines to placehold his self-portrait.

Patty, age 3, like Nathan, uses a series of dense up-and-down strokes to placehold her name and a series of open, more circular, forms to placehold her self-portrait.

Latrice, age 3, like both Nathan and Patty, uses a set of dense wavy lines to place hold her name. Her art is more centrally positioned on the page and is created using a broad, circular motion.

The organizational decisions which children make in writing are strongly influenced by the written form of their name. Given information as to what features of the name the child is attending to or has attended to (see below), adults in this society have little or no difficulty

identifying other writing samples which were created by that child, even if we were to present Barbara and Catherine's product randomly.

By the start of first grade the surface texts which children create include a wide variety of organizational structures which clearly mark their genre to literate adult members of the child's interpretive community. When the organizational structures which children use are also found in the surface texts created by successful readers and writers in the child's interpretive community, we assume the child's use of these structures reflects intentionality and a real access to literacy. Further, we assume that in use, "organizational structures" function as "signifying structures." By "signifying structures" we mean text features which are perceived as signs by members of an interpretive community. By studying how and when members of an interpretive community use such features and what they make of them, we can gain insight into the psycholinguistic and sociolinguistic processes involved in literacy and literacy learning.

Stephanie, in a two-day period the summer prior to entrance into first grade, created a birthday list, a letter, a map, and a story. Adult members of her

BIRTHDAY LIST
*Melisa
Laura Guests
Tic-Tac-Toe
(Game to be
played)
White Cake
Balloons*

LETTER
*Dear Mom
I
hope you
come back
Love
Steph
(Note:
Stephanie
decorated her
paper to look
like stationery.)*

MAP FOR
BIRTHDAY
GUESTS TO
GET TO HER
BEDROOM
*My Bedroom
Hallway
Door to
come in*

STORY PAGE
*My dad and me
was swinging
(Note: Quite
different
functions for
art in story
as opposed to
letter and
map.)*

interpretive community have no difficulty identifying which document is which since function and context are clearly signed in the surface texts of each document. Stephanie's decisions as to which information to explicitly include and explicitly exclude, how to allocate such information to art as opposed to writing, as well as how one syntactically and semantically formats and organizes various texts, closely parallel writing decisions made in the adult community for texts of these types.

Robin, in a one-week period prior to first grade, wrote several notes, a story, and a letter. Each of these documents is readily identifiable as to genre and reflects Robin's attention to and understanding of key signifying structures which mark the surface texts that adult members of the interpretive community create for various contexts.

NOTE

Patty in the morning come in my room

PATTY
IN THE
MA OR NPNG
CAM
IM MY
ROOM

STORY

The World's Greatest
My dog   Dog
*   Tina*
and my friends
*   dog Ruby*
*   are very nice*
*   dogs. One day*
*   a little girl*
*   fell in the*
*   water. Ruby and*
*   Tina saved her.*
*   The end.*

THE WRLDS GRAJTS
MY doG   DOG
TEENA
AND MY FENDS
doG RooBE   by
AER VARY NIS   Robin
doGS OAN DaY
A LTL GRIL
FAL IN THE
WOTR RooBY AND
TEENA SAUTARE
THE END

NOTE

Carolyn you are a nice person Ro (begin-ning of signa-ture)

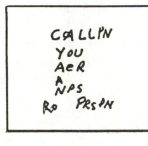

CALLPN
YOU
AER
A
NPS
RO PRSPN

LETTER

Dear Dad
I love you. Is the
cat okay? The puppies
already have their
eyes open. Tina
had 7 puppies. Grandma's
puppies are 1 month
old. Willy said
Hi. My mom painted
my room. We got
an apple tree.
Oops, it's a pear tree.
Marcie said Hi.
I went to see
Gulliver and The
Great Muppet
Caper. Love Robin.

DAY DAD
I LOVE YOU. PS THE
CAT OK THE PAPES
ALL 2 ATE HAV TAR
EIS OPEN TEENA
HAD 7 PAPOS GADMAS
PAPES AET 1 MATH
OLD WILLY SAD
HP MY MOM PATDE
MY RooM WE GAT
A APULL TREE
OPS PSS A PAR TREE
MARIAH SAD HP
I WETTO SEE

GULLVD AND THE
GRAT MAPET
CADPR LUV ROBPN

The structural variations in the oral responses which even children as young as 3 years old give when presented with various written documents and asked to read suggest that attending to the salient signifying structures in various written texts is a key element in written language learning. Attention to these features has obviously, given what the 6-year-old already knows, provided the child a basis for making predictions and testing hypotheses about how written language and oral language differ, as well as how written language operates in various settings.

Latrice, age 3, gave the following oral responses in reading environmental print, "A thing, a cup, eggs, a cup, toothbrush, a Burger King cup." The oral language she used in dictating a story is structured differently, reflecting her understanding that a differing set of signifying structures operates in the written language of stories as opposed to environmental print: "A spoon. A spoon to eat. There's a string. You put it round your neck like this." When asked to read a letter she received, Latrice's response reflects an alternate set of predictions about how written language would be organized in a letter setting: "Linda. My like it."

Charvin, age 4, gave the following responses when asked to read various items of environmental print: "Don't know, eggs, Ronald McDonald's, Coke, toothpaste, Burger Chef." When writing a language experience story Charvin dictated, "It's a horn. It's a baseball bat. This is my choo-choo train. It blows up." When asked to read a letter he received from Linda, a research associate on the project, Charvin read, "Linda, Linda, Linda. I like you."

Children's semantic decisions in responding to print and in creating an extended surface text show a concern for unity and the use of strategies common to their interpretive community.

Sally, age 5, ignores the items she selected for use in telling her story and relies instead upon a story structure she evidently has abstracted out of past story encounters: "Once upon a time there was a little girl and she was seventeen. And she rided a car. And she saw a statue."

Alanna, age 6, selected a Play School person, a toy car, and a toy elephant (which she calls a "pet") with which to tell her story. The unity she creates through a variety of syntactic forms reflects her sophisticated understanding of cohesion and her ability to orchestrate such factors given the constraints on story writing this setting posed: "People walk. Cars drive. People drive cars too. People live in houses. The pets live in houses too."

The range of decisions children make in an attempt to capture in writing what they perceive as key conceptual and perceptual features in

their world is not unlike that which the originators of our language faced and had to solve.

Lisa, age 3, was asked to write her name. She did so using a series of five 1's. When asked to read what she had written, Lisa pointed to the first 1 and said, "My"; then pointing to the second 1, she said, "name", the third, "is", the fourth, "Li", the fifth, "sa". Lisa's "My name is Lisa" response demonstrates her active testing of the hypothesis that oral language maps onto written language following a one mark per one syllable rule. Lisa's decision to use 1's as opposed to some other marking is no doubt influenced by the physical form of her written name and demonstrates the orchestrated complexity of the child's hypothesis testing in writing.

Michelle, age 4, was asked to write her name and anything else she could write. Using English letter forms, Michelle wrote her name M-Y-J-A-E. Underneath this she wrote her father's name, Jay, spelling it, J-Y-A. Underneath her Jay she wrote her mother's name, Nancy, spelling it N-A-N-N. In rereading what she wrote, Michelle read, "Michelle, Jay, Nancy," paused, and then, snatching the pen, drew a circle around the three names and announced, "Now that says Morrison," which was in this instance the family's last name.

Erica, age 4, wrote a letter to Hugh, addressing the envelope H−U−H. Thinking these letters had to be kept together, Erica solved the problem by drawing a circle around them to mark their wordness.

Matt, age 7, was asked to write a story. He elected to write a rendition of "The Three Little Pigs" instead of creating an entirely new story. Matt wrote multiple words on a line but meticulously drew squares which he blackened in to separate each of his word units.

Jennifer, Ranee, David, Aaliya, Ariel, Redzuen, and Saul, all age 9, wrote Thank You *as one word (*THANKYOU*) in unedited set of Thank-you letters they were asked to write by their fourth grade teacher to the researchers for having come into their room to work with them on writing. Since* Thank You *operates as a single conceptual unit, their decision is not an unreasonable one and nicely demonstrates that the problems younger children face are not unique to that age level.*

The organizational decisions which children demonstrate in spelling reflect sensitivity, concern, and an attempt to orchestrate the multiple organizational structures and principles on which our written systems are based.

Jason, age 7, said the character in his story "tried again," a concept which he placeheld by spelling it C-H-R-I-D-A-G-E-N. In reading his text, his C-H-R-I-D-A-G-E-N momentarily stopped him, a problem he resolved by attending to the meaning he was trying to convey at this point in the story. Thinking his spelling was at least a part of why he couldn't immediately retrieve his text, he decided to fix it up by crossing out his first spelling and correcting it. The result of his new effort was C-H-R-I-D-A-G-E-N, the exact same spelling as his original effort. This single spelling demonstrates Jason's attempts to orchestrate his intuititve understandings of the English orthographic system. He attempts to write the way it means ("tried again" being perceived as a single concept); he maps sounds to graphemes (/t/ and /ch/ are formed orally by the tongue being at the same point in the mouth at the time of articulation); he represents sounds by their letter name (/i/ sound at the end of "try"); he placeholds syllables in oral language with a single or double grapheme; and he uses the knowledge he has gained from reading to visually get the word to look right. Even the most phonetic spellings are written in letter forms available only to the child through reading. Notice that Jason's distribution of vowels reflects the English pattern, but that it was his concern for the visual appearance of the word which triggered his revision. It is important to note that Jason's understandings are not random, but rule-governed, so much so that in rethinking and rewriting the idea "try again" he is led to the same conclusions.

Kammi, age 6, wrote a story in which the words their *and* burying *occurred. In writing* their, *Kammi wrote T-H, then paused, pronounced the word, and wrote A-I-R. She wrote* burying *by sounding it out and referring back to her spelling of* their *when she realized it contained the same internal sound. The result was B + A-I-R + I-N-G. Kammi's behavior demonstrates not only her deep understanding of how oral language is mapped onto written language in English, but, like Jason, the value and role visual memory plays in the process. Kammi's assumption that her solutions to problems posed in the past were available as data which she could use in figuring out a new spelling, reflects her access to this strategy and is one decision which the inventors of our orthographic system clearly worked from.*

Rebecca, age 6, wrote when, *spelling it Y-H-E-N. In producing this spelling Rebecca first audibly said "when" and "why," thus attempting to associate the word with others she knew. Since the word* why *says the letter name* y *Rebecca writes* Y *as the first sound. Having gone this far she again audibly says "when" and writes H-E-N to finish her spelling for this word. Having solved this spelling once, whenever she needs the word again in her text she refers back to this spelling and simply copies it.*

Marvin, age 3, in responding to various pieces of environmental print and being asked what they said, responded by giving generic labels ("cottage cheese," "milk"), related concepts ("toothbrush" for Crest; "U.S. Army" for U.S. Mail), attributes ("Hot" for Dynamints), functional descriptions ("Stop" for a Stop sign; "Eat it" for Burger Chef), brand names ("McDonald's," "Lego"), situational descriptions ("cup" for Wendy's, "A box with sugar in it" for Jell-o) and associations ("Rubber-Band" for Band-Aid). His responses, like 98 percent of all reading responses of children 3, 4, 5, and 6 years old, fell within the semantic field and decision matrix our society uses in labeling environmental print, i.e., generic labels (cotton balls), related concepts (Mars for candy bars), attributes (Efferdent), functional descriptions (Mop & Glo), brand names (Johnson & Johnson), situational descriptions (7-11 grocery stores), and associative chaining (S.O.S. soap pads). The importance of these data is that they illustrate how accessible our organizational system is, and how attentive and diligent young children are in understanding the rules which semantically operate in the written language settings with which they are familiar.

Given these observations about organizational patterns in the reading and writing data we collected, in the following section we trace the significance of these patterns in order to rethink literacy via a review of pertinent research and a more in-depth analysis of selected protocols. Specifically, we will attempt to apply and relate recent theoretical research, typically conducted with much older language users, to our findings in order to synthesize and update our understanding of the psycholinguistic and sociolinguistic processes involved in literacy and literacy learning.

INTERDISCIPLINARY PERSPECTIVES

As if to demonstrate that there is nothing so practical as theory, one of the major contributions of cognitive psychologists has been schema theory and its demonstrated applicability to understanding psycholinguistic processes in literacy (Neisser, 1976; Smith, 1978; Spiro, 1977; Adams & Collins, 1978; Rumelhart & Ortony, 1977; Anderson, Reynolds, Schallert & Goetz, 1977). There is presently no single accepted statement of schema theory, though the broad outline is fairly well defined. Generally, schema theorists are interested in how the mind processes, stores, and retrieves input. There are several theoreticians and researchers in this area whose positions are generally similar but specifically different (Neisser, 1976; Rumelhart & Ortony, 1977; Spiro, 1977; Bobrow & Norman, 1975; Minsky, 1975; Schank & Abelson, 1977).

Schema theorists postulate that the human memory system is made up of interacting knowledge structures called schema. Neisser (1976) defines a schema this way:

*A schema is that portion of the entire perceptual cycle which is internal to
the perceiver, modifiable by experience, and somehow specific to what is being
perceived. The schema accepts information as it becomes available at sensory
surfaces and is changed by that information; it directs movements and
exploratory activities that make more information available, by which it
is further modified. (p. 54)*

Put simply, schema theory posits the mind as a highly complex set of
cognitive structures which govern not only perception but also comprehension. Whereas earlier theories had separated perception and cognition, schema theory joined the two and in so doing moved the language
user center stage.

From the perspective of schema theory, reading comprehension specifically, but comprehension generally, was predictable in that what was
brought to the process strongly affected what was gotten out of the
process. From a schema-theoretic perspective, *comprehension* is seen as a
process of sense-making in light of or through assimilation and accommodation of cognitive structures; *learning* is seen as the binding, building,
and reorganization of cognitive structures. A vital component in both
comprehension and learning is inferencing which, from a schema-
theoretic viewpoint, involves the filling in of necessary "default values"
or "slots" based on background information in order that what is being
perceived makes sense.

Because of a tendency to think of schema as static hierarchial mental
structures, Smith (1978) reconceptualized schema theory and began
talking about it in terms of a "theory of the world in the head." Smith's
reconceptualization was a significant contribution since it highlighted
the dynamic, ever-changing nature of schema as well as the power and
significance of this conceptualization as a process perspective for motivating and driving comprehension and learning. Smith's use of *theory* as
opposed to *structure* suggested not only higher, more complex levels of
mental organization, but also an ordered set of relationships between
cognitive structures such that to alter one necessitated reformulation of
the others.

A common thread which runs through all of the work in schema theory
is an assumption of nonrandomness. For comprehension and learning to
be maximally useful and something other than rote, they must be
embedded or tied to existing cognitive frameworks or structures.

It should be obvious from this discussion that there are many parallels
between schema theory and the work of Piaget (see Ginsburg & Opper,
1979). Both schema theorists and Piagetians believe schema are hier-
archially arranged mental structures and that learning takes place
through changes in them. Piaget refers to these changes as assimilation,

accommodation, and equilibration. While schema theorists believe in these processes generally, Neisser (1976) for one does not believe accommodation is possible and that all learning must therefore be assimilative. Shanklin (1982), in making a comparison between schema theory and Piaget, says of both theories:

Schematas are thought to grow from the general to the precise, the personal to the impersonal, and the context dependent to the context independent.
In both theories experience and manipulation of objects is thought to play an important role in such growth. Children come into the world, not as blank slates, but wired with capacities for thought and language. The learning process, according to both theories, is continual and what is learned at one stage must necessarily be carried on to the next. (p. 35)

Important differences between schema theorists and Piagetians do exist. Piaget's view of growth and development, for instance, is much more biologically and genetically based than is the view held by schema theorists. According to Piaget, children develop the capacity for certain kinds of mental operations at certain ages on a more or less fixed biological timetable. This does not mean that experience is unimportant, only that biology takes precedence. Schema theorists, on the other hand, do not tie cognitive maturation so closely to biology, but rather, see experience, particularly accumulated prior knowledge, as central to explaining differences between child and adult thought. They would argue that the cognitive operation underlying child and adult thought is the same and that differences are in content and not so much in process per se. Schema theorists would argue that when faced with a new phenomenon, process distinctions between child and adult thought dissolve; the learning process for all ages looks much the same.

Our own position, while not inimical to schema theory, is more like that of Halliday (1974) and Vygotsky (1978) in that we see language learning as first and foremost a social event. From our perspective, schema are sociocognitive phenomena and specific both to culture and to context. The strongest evidence we have in support of our view is the writing of young children across cultures (see Figure 7.1). In contrast to Najeeba's and Ofer's scribbles, Dawn's looks decidedly like English. Najeeba said as she completed her piece, "Here, but you can't read it. . . . I wrote it in Arabic and in Arabic we use a lot more dots than you do in English." Ofer is an Israeli child whose writing looks decidedly Hebrew.

What these data demonstrate is that long before formal instruction the young child is actively making sense of the world, including the

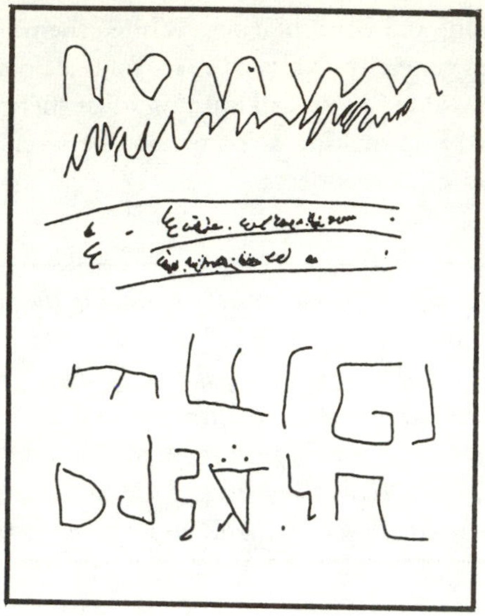

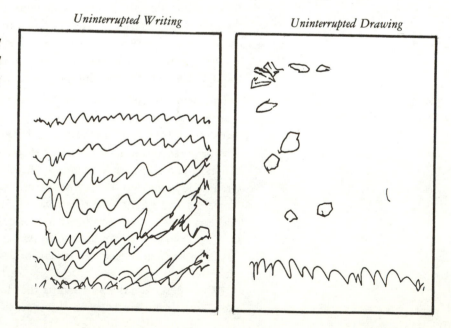

Dawn
United States

Nageeba
Saudi Arabia

Ofer
Israel

Figure 7.1. Multicultural Writing
Samples (Composite).

world of print. Importantly, however, these samples substantiate that not only are the language decisions which children make organized, but also that such organizational decisions are sociologically and contextually rooted. This insight, of course, does not deny a schema-theoretic perspective, but rather sharpens it. Practically what this distinction means is that if we and Piaget were to draw our models of learning in graphic form, they would look quite different from each other, even though they may have the same major components. Let's say, for

Figure 7.2. Uninterrupted
Writing and
Uninterrupted Drawing
Samples (DuJulian, Age 3).

Uninterrupted Writing　　　　*Uninterrupted Drawing*

example, that both we and Piaget would decide to use three overlapping circles to represent the interplay of biological, psychological, and sociological influences in literacy learning. The amount of influence each factor has would determine the size of the circle: a small circle, a small influence; a large circle, a large influence. Which factors were seen as key would determine the order of the circles and their arrangement. While we and Piaget might start with the same components in our models, the size, order, and arrangement of our three circles would be quite different.

Early Organizational Patterns. Although not as immediately evident in the surface structure texts as in those of more experienced written language users, the organizational decisions underlying the writing of children as young as 3 years old are discernible with study. Theoretically this discovery is important since it suggests that scribbling is not scribbling in the sense of being unorganized and random, but bears much similarity at a process level to the activity we have called writing.

Figure 7.2 presents DuJulian's (age 3) uninterrupted drawing and writing samples. Given the fact that DuJulian organizes his writing using a linear, up-down stroke (see Uninterrupted Writing Sample, Figure 7.2); it is readily apparent which marks were made to placehold the picture of himself (see top section of Uninterrupted Drawing Sample, Figure 7.2) and which were made to placehold his name (see bottom section of Uninterrupted Drawing Sample, Figure 7.2). Art for DuJulian involves circular markings; writing involves linear strokes with up-down markings.

If the decisions which 3-year-olds make for art and for writing are indeed different, then it follows that an examination of the sets of scribbles constituting the product of a task which asks them to draw a picture of themselves and sign their name should reflect these alternate decisions; in short, scribbling in art should look different from scribbling in writing. That this is, indeed, the case is readily apparent when we examine the samples in Figure 7.3. Not only can scribble writing be differentiated from scribbles drawing, but we have found that adults have little difficulty, given the linearity of writing and the global cohesiveness of art, in differentiating which is which, even when the markings have not been labeled and categorized as in Figure 7.3.

These data demonstrate the organization present in the products of art and writing scribbles. The unity of the child's decisions across art and writing, as well as the support such unity provides in motivating and driving literacy learning, needs further elaboration. In searching for the process principles underlying the decisions made for art as opposed to writing, one of the things to be noticed is that some children reserved up-down strokes for writing and circular markings for art; other children did just the opposite, i.e., used circular markings for writing and

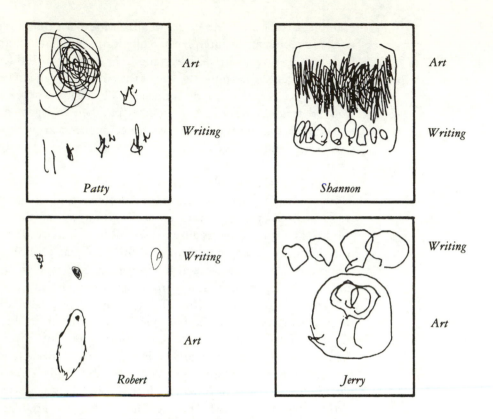

Art

Writing

Patty

Art

Writing

Shannon

Writing

Art

Robert

Writing

Art

Jerry

Figure 7.3. Uninterrupted Drawing Samples (Self-Portrait and Name, Age 3).

up-down strokes for art. For example, Robert (see Figure 7.3) used an up-down stroke for writing and a circular stroke for art. Shannon, on the other hand (see Figure 7.3), used a circular stroke for writing and an up-down stroke for art.

In studying this phenomenon we discovered that if the child's name begins with a letter which is made up of linear elements, such as the *L* in Latrice's name which is made up of two straight lines, the odds that the child's scribble writing is composed of up-down strokes is high. Similarly, if the child's name starts with a letter which is composed of curved elements, such as the *S* in Shannon, the odds are high that the child's scribble writing is circular. Among the 3-year-old sample, using this simple formulaic relationship, prediction as to the organization of writing and hence art for any individual child is 0.91. When all of the letters of the name are used and a proportion of linear letters to circular letters is calculated, the prediction made from the proportion which results rises to 0.93. While it appears to be largely irrelevant which organizational form is selected for art as opposed to writing for any given child regardless of the form of his or her name, the point is that a relationship exists between decisions made in writing and decisions made in art, and vice versa. These data, then, support Smith's clarification of schema theory in that they show that the complex of decisions a child makes in writing, in contrast to the complex of decisions made in art, are orchestrated and organized at levels beyond the particular cognitive structure of the system itself.

Later Organizational Patterns. Language is, of course, laced with organization. The reason age correlated with language is that three additional years allow the language learner twice the number of opportunities not only to encounter, but to discover more and more of these organizational features. Figure 7.4 outlines some of the organizational perspectives available in looking at young children's writing. In the sections that follow, two texts will be used for an extended discussion of some of the organizational features which are present in the written products of children two and three years older than those we have been examining.

Testing Your Child-As-Informant Skills. Because many adults assume children are in a state of "cognitive confusion" when, in fact, this label better describes their own present level of understanding, they miss much of the organization displayed by children. Before reading the translations for Sara's and Matt's texts (Figures 7.5 and 7.6), one must assume, as we have trained ourselves to do in this project, that the decisions which these young writers have made are organized. (Readers can test their child-as-informant skills by attempting to read these children's written efforts.) The pictures Sara and Matt include in their stories are an integral part of their texts. It should be kept in mind that children two and three years younger than Matt and Sara, when reading what they have written—long before their surface texts become as "conventional" as are Matt's and Sara's—demonstrate that their writing shares many of these same organizational features.

Surface Text Organization: A Pragmatic Perspective. A pragmatic perspective means asking what function the piece of writing was designed to serve. Knowing that Sara's surface text ("Once upon a time there was a loveable bunny who picked a rose for his mommy") was a Mother's Day card, we have to say that the product served as the expression of love, thoughtfulness, appreciation—in short, "mother's-dayness"—quite well.

This observation does not resolve all of the pragmatic issues surrounding Sara's text, however. While the surface text functions as a Mother's Day card, "Once upon a time" is more suggestive of a fairy tale than a greeting card. Sara's use of one genre in service of another adds to the intrigue of the piece and is a text strategy which will be discussed more fully later.

Pragmatically, Matt's surface text is easily recognized as having been produced after a trip to the zoo with his first-grade class. The fact that

TEXT PERSPECTIVES

- *Pragmatic
  function*

- *Graphophonemic
  spelling the way it sounds
  spelling the way it looks
  spelling the way it means*

- *Syntactic
  flow
  structure*

- *Semantics
  semantic field
  semantics of syntax
  (transitivity)
  syntax of semantics
  (i.e., case grammar)*

*Figure 7.4. Text Organizational
Perspectives.*

*Figure 7.5. Uninterrupted
Writing Sample (Sara, Age 5).*

*Figure 7.6. Uninterrupted
Writing Sample (Matt, Age 6).*

Matt's text is appropriate for this context would be evident if he asked adults to tell us where they might find such a piece of writing. In workshops we have conducted, almost without exception teachers can identify what events led up to the creation of Matt's text.

Pragmatically, it is also important to note that Matt's text has no title. Some educators and linguists would take this as evidence that the young child has not developed the ability to produce a "decontextualized" text. The context of situation, however, makes entitling this piece "My Trip to the Zoo" unnecessary, since this was an assumption which was shared by all of the language users in this setting.

Surface Text Organization: Graphophonemic Perspectives. As suggested in Figure 7.4, we might look at Sara's and Matt's surface texts with graphophonemic eyes, noting the regularities which appear. For purposes of discussion we have divided this section into strategies which involve the phonemic, the graphemic, and morphemic systems of language; namely, spelling the way it sounds, spelling the way it looks, and spelling the way it means.

Spelling the way it sounds. Much work has been done in this area (Marcel, 1980; Read, 1975; Baron, 1980; Marsh, Friedman, Welch & Desberg, 1980; Henderson & Beers, 1979, 1980; Zutell, 1978, 1979; Bissex, 1980; Chomsky, 1979). Our own analysis of the products which young children produce would suggest that there are essentially three sound-to-letter strategies employed: (1) spelling the way it sounds; (2) spelling the way it articulates; and (3) spelling the way it sounds out. Often more than one of these spelling strategies is involved in the single spelling of a word, i.e., JRESS for "dress" (Jeff, age 6) where the J is produced because *j*'s and *d*'s are formed at the same spot in the mouth (the point of articulation), and RES is produced on the basis of letter-sound correspondence. A fourth sound-to-print strategy is really a subtle instance of the first strategy, but has been termed "the letter-name strategy": the name of the letter coincides with a desired sound unit, as in R for "our," or in Sara's case, A as in "a loveable bunny." Sara's three uses of A's in *A LOVE A BAL BONE* demonstrate that the same marking can occur for entirely different sound-to-letter rules. Sara's first A is produced via a letter-name strategy; her second and third A's (LOVE *A* BAL) are produced via a letter-sound strategy.

Spelling the Way It Looks. Letter-sound observations are only a small portion of the spelling organizations and orchestrations which can be studied, and are probably the portion that has had the most intense observation by researchers to date. From the perspective of the young child as reader we might ask ourselves, "What evidence exists that past encounters with print have influenced the child's spellings?" We would then be looking for spelling which involves fine-tuning written language with written language itself, or which involves aspects of visual memory (Tenny, 1980). Since both of these surface texts are written using English letterlike forms, the thing we immediately know is that reading is involved in the spelling process and that no matter how phonetic a spelling may appear (R or "our"), just by virtue of the fact that it is placeheld with a recognizable letter of our alphabet, the spelling involves visual memory. Where else would these forms and this information come from? Those who suggest that children write first and read later and use "invented spelling" as their evidence, have failed to appreciate key transactions between reading and writing in literacy learning.

In Sara's text she writes FRO for "for." While we might wish to assume that the F and the R are produced on the basis of some sound-to-letter strategy, the very fact that these forms are recognizable as letters of our alphabet means that visual memory is inherently involved in what appears to be a phonetic act. Sara's inclusion of the O at the end of her FR is also motivated by visual memory. Having been a reader, Sara obviously recalls that there is an O in there somewhere and so tags it on at the end. Whether this piece of information was accessed because the FR didn't look long enough we don't know, though if this were the explanation offered, we might have a tendency to want to conclude that the child was spelling by using a phonetic strategy and confirming by using a visual memory strategy. The fact that both phonics and visual memory are involved in the production of even a single letter like the F just means that such efforts at bifurcation and order are misguided.

This point is important since many persons working in the area of "invented spelling" seem to believe that children initially spell using a phonetic strategy and that only later do they employ visual memory. We have shown that no such tidiness is possible, nor, we would argue, is it desired. The redundancy of cues across strategies sets up "tensions," permits reading experiences to transmit and support writing, and allows spelling systems to be mastered, if desired, via orchestration.

Spelling the Way It Means. In addition to looking at spelling organization in terms of sound and visual memory, we might also look at spelling organization based on meaning. In Sara's and Matt's surface texts we have several excellent examples. In these instances we would be looking for spellings which have morphemic and higher levels of semantic organization. LOVE A BAL ("loveable") in Sara's surface text is probably a spelling arrived at through a combination of syllabic and morphemic decisions. Sara's WASAPANATAEM ("Once upon a time") is an even better example, in which she demonstrates that for her, this spelling is one conceptual unit. Semantically, "once upon a time" is a unit which signals fairy tales. The meaning of each individual word adds up to be quite different from the meaning of the phrase itself. From a psychological processing perspective it makes more sense to write "once upon a time" as a single unit than to break it up into units unrelated to its meaning or psychological significance.

Sara's LOVE A BAL ("loveable") in contrast to her WASAPAN-ATAEM ("Once upon a time") is a nice instance of how various ways to organize writing are not only conceptually possible, but are simultaneously being explored in a single setting by the young child. Think of how much less language confusion there might be in the profession if the originators of our language had decided to write in chunks of meaning (like Sara's WASAPANATAEM) rather than in words. An interesting feature of Sara's surface text is the fact that she simultaneously tests at least three optional writing systems in a single setting: chunk writing by meaning (WASAPANATAEM); chunk writing by syllables (LOVE A BAL); chunk writing by words (BONE).

Matt's text has as many clear examples of his testing hypotheses relative to meaning in his spelling. Matt's refusal to divide the word LUNCH, which he squeezes on the line, suggests that for him LUNCH is a single conceptual unit and therefore not easily divided. Once children discover that in writing they can divide what previously had been a single conceptual unit by using a hyphen, they often divide everything and everywhere.

Alison, at 6.5 years of age, discovered the hyphen while reading a book. In this instance she asked what the "little mark" meant. For the next several weeks, hyphens appeared throughout her writing. In making her best friend Jennifer a birthday card, she began writing Jennifer's name on the left-hand side of the page, but then suddenly realized that if she continued in that fashion she wouldn't be able to apply her latest language discovery. She decided to erase and begin writing Jennifer well toward the right of the page, thereby running out of space and getting to use the hyphen.

The realization that concepts can be divided in writing when they are not able to be divided in real life comes late for most children—well after their early markings demonstrate application of a one-mark per one-concept rule. In fact this one-mark per one-concept notion is so natural that it is literally impossible to decide when children first develop a notion of "wordness." Our own frustrated attempts led us to conclude that when the child makes one blob for "a dog," another for "a tree," and a third for "a bear," the basic notion of "wordness" is evidenced. When one thinks about "wordness" from this perspective, the notion has so little power to explain growth in literacy that violations, "nonwordness" decisions like Sara's WASAPANATAEM, are more significant in understanding the evolution of literacy than are instances of the concept.

Other Spelling Strategies. There are, of course, other decisions which can be examined in spellings, even of those words which we have already looked at in Sara's and Matt's texts. In spelling "loveable"

(LOVE A BAL) Sara, at least in part, may be resolving this spelling on the basis of how she has resolved similar spellings in the past. As reported in our earlier volume (Harste, Burke, Woodward, 1981), we have some evidence that children consciously spell by their own or someone else's rules, often adding silent *e*'s and the like after they have applied other initial strategies.

A final strategy which we have found enters into children's spelling decisions is one we entitle, "Knowing One Doesn't Know." Often in these instances language users select a different word, or put down some rendition of the word they want which placeholds the item until they have time to check on the spelling later. Which of these strategies they use—choosing another word or placeholding the word they want using the best spelling they can muster on the spot—is seemingly a function of present and past writing contexts and the child's sense of the risk involved. Nonetheless, "knowing one doesn't know" is a very complex strategy. The language user is saying that, after having tried all of the spelling rules which seem applicable, the only thing he knows is that application of known rules doesn't solve this spelling problem. Because realizing one doesn't know is a significant step in knowing, this is clearly a strategy worthy of further study. Currently Chrystine Bouffler (1983), one of the graduate associates on this project, is completing a dissertation in the area of spelling, building from and extending the work which we have discussed here. Some of the issues she explores are that spelling ability varies by context of situation, that "invented spelling" is but a component of a more general and universal strategy which all writers use, and that development in writing ability involves the flexible use of and even tentative setting aside of spelling information.

Evidence of Graphophonemic Orchestration in Reading. As a further measure of the young child's attention to the graphophonemic systems of language, we compared the graphemic units in their language experience stories to the phonemic units they produced during reading in terms of the relationship which existed between them. The categories which emerged from our data were (1) items which were *Unavailable in the Surface Text* read; (2) items which represented a *Minimal Textual Signal* (this could include attempts at sounding out); (3) items which were *Available in the Text* read; and (4) items which represented a *Mixed Response* combination of available and unavailable items.

In analyzing the children's first reading of their stories only categories three and four proved useful, with 45.9 percent of all units read being available in the story and 54.1 percent of all units read representing a mixture of available and unavailable items. The trend in terms of *Available in Text* to *Mixed Response* was 28.6 to 71.4 for 3-year-olds, 40.0 to 60.0 for 4-year-olds, 45.5 to 54.5 for 5-year-olds, and 66.7 to 33.3 for 6-year-olds.

In rereading their language experience stories one day later we found that 5.4 percent of all units produced were either *Unavailable in the Text* or represented a *Minimal Textual Signal*; 45.9 percent of all units read were *Available in the Text* read; 48.6 percent of all units read represented *Mixed Response* types involving what was in the text and what was new or unavailable in the surface text. The trend in terms of *Available in Text* to *Mixed Response* was 57.1 to 28.6 for 3-year-olds, 27.3 to 72.7 for 4-year-olds, 40.0 to 60.0 for 5-year-olds, and 66.7 to 22.2 for 6-year-olds. While 3-year-olds look more constrained in reading by the graphemic system than do 4- and 5-year-olds, this phenomenon is largely a function of the relatively shorter stories they dictated and hence were asked to read and reread. Nonetheless, these data do suggest that when 3-year-olds engage in reading they do so with some understanding of the graphemic constraints which are operating in this literacy event.

Overall, what these data show is that children are monitoring their early reading in light of available graphophonemic information, and that from ages 3 to 6 an ever-conventional orchestration and use of the graphophonemic system occurs.

Surface Text Organization: Syntactic Perspectives. At another organizational level we can look for syntactic organization in the surface texts which young children produce. From this perspective we can ask questions about how the messages in these surface texts flow and whether or not there is inflectional agreement within and across sentences in the surface text.

From a socio-psycholinguistic perspective syntax is a text-context transaction. While many, for example, might not perceive environmental print to have a true syntax, such a perception ignores pragmatics. The syntax of environmental print is expressed in rules about how print functions and operates in this context.

At one syntactic level we can ask, "Do these texts sound like oral or written language?" Since not many of us run around saying, "Once upon a time there was a loveable bunny who picked a rose for his mommy," except under special settings such as storytelling, we intuitively know that Sara's surface text is written language. Oral language, according to Halliday (1980), is syntactically complex, but conceptually not very dense ("Well, you see, there was this mouse . . . and this mouse was walking along . . . "). Written language is conceptually dense, but syntactically elegant ("Once upon a time there was a loveable bunny who picked a rose for his mommy").

Matt's text, because it is composed of several syntactic units, allows us to explore intersentential grammar more fully. Matt begins with an I LIKE statement which is followed by an Activity statement (I LIKE) + (GO TO THE ZOO). This format is used in the next sentence, becoming almost formulaic: (I LIKE) + (TO HAVE LUNCH THERE). His final statement is an I LIKE + Object statement, which breaks the pattern. What is particularly interesting is that together, his choices constitute a highly organized set of syntactic and semantic decisions which greatly add to the coherence of the piece. His ordering decisions here are so good that even if one gives adults each of Matt's statements separately and asks them to put these statements into a surface text, they almost inevitably put them in the order in which Matt has put them.

Matt also seems to know that one way to signal the end of the text is by altering the syntactic patterns that have been set up. Here we have evidence of the interrelationship between reading and writing in language learning. From Matt's past encounters with written language as a reader, he has abstracted out how written language differs from oral language, and how authors alter syntax in an effort to terminate the text. While Matt may not be consciously aware of this understanding about language, he demonstrates that successful language use and metalinguistic awareness are two different things and ought not—indeed, should not—be confused.

There are, of course, other things we might look at syntactically, e.g., the density and complexity of ideas; but because syntax and semantics are not independent language systems these seem best discussed using more semantic perspectives, especially since the one thing we have learned in the last ten years is that semantics is not a single language system, and the syntax and semantics transact to form several systems (De Beaugrande, 1980).

Evidence of Syntactic Orchestration in Reading. As a further measure of the young child's attention to the syntactic systems of language, we compared the syntactic units in the language experience story dictated to the syntactic units produced during the child's reading of the story and described the relationship which existed in terms of syntactic coordination. Four categories emerged from our data: (1) *No Apparent Coordination*; (2) *Generalized Coordination* (TEXT: *Fall Down. A Block*; READING: "Grey Block. Fall Block"); (3) *Available in Text* (One-to-one syntactic correspondence between text and reading); and (4) *Mixed* (TEXT: *And we read a book*; READING: "And we read books"). This last category accepted minimal changes in meaning such as that illustrated above.

For purposes of analyzing the children's first reading of their language experience stories, only categories two, three, and four proved useful, with 18.9 percent of all units representing a *Generalized Coordination* between the text and what was read; 51.4 percent *Available in Text* or a one-to-one correspondence between syntactic units; and 29.7 percent a *Mixed* syntactic correspondence. The trend in terms of the percent of one-to-one syntactic correspondences between text units and what was read, the *Available in Text* category, was 28.6 for 3-year-olds, 40.0

for 4-year-olds, 54.5 for 5-year-olds, and 77.8 for 6-year-olds.

Because we suspected that some of what the child had dictated was not meant to be part of his or her story even though we had originally written it down as one, for purposes of analyzing rereading behaviors, we used the child's first reading as the text base. In rereading the language experience stories one day later and comparing these syntactically to the surface text of the first reading, 5.4 percent of all units showed *No Apparent Coordination,* 16.2 percent showed a *Generalized Coordination,* 48.6 percent represented a one-to-one correspondence (the *Available in Text* category), and 29.7 percent showed a *Mixed* correspondence. The trend in terms of age for the *Available in Text* category (one-to-one syntactic correspondence) was: 42.9 percent for 3-year-olds; 45.5 percent for 4-year-olds; 40.0 percent for 5-year-olds; and 66.7 percent for 6-year-olds.

Overall, what these data show is that even 3-year-old children are very cognizant of the syntactic constraints operating in written language. The reason this effect is more pronounced in the rereading data than in the data from the first reading is that asides which the child made to us during story dictation were no longer being considered part of the child's text. In this sense, the set of figures quoted for rereading represent the degree of predictability of the child's second reading given his or her first reading. As can be seen syntactically, this is universally high across all age levels. Theoretically, these data suggest that children are cognizant of the fact that syntactic constraints are very much a part of the "text world" created during reading. Access and reaccess to this "text world," and with it to the constraints which operate within it, allow them both to predict and to generate a syntactically quite successful text when reading, and, given our previous analyses, when writing.

Surface Text Organization: Semantic Perspectives. From a semantic perspective several features of the surface text may be studied and noted. There is the semantic field of meaning set up in the text which is partly identifiable through the lexical chains that run through the surface text to establish parameters of meaning within which the text world resides (Pratt, 1977). In Matt's surface text one such chain is formed by the lexical items ZOO and ZEBRA; another is formed by the repetition of LIKE. Recently King and Rental (1981) completed an extensive study of cohesion as a perspective from which to study written language growth and development. Their study demonstrates that all children have a fundamental understanding of various cohesive devices by the time they enter first grade, that such knowledge varies by story mode, and that it is best affected by quality story encounters over time.

How larger chunks of meaning are ordered in the text is called the "syntax of semantics." Knowing the setting in Sara's text, "Once upon a time there was a bunny," sets a stage in which we expect an initiating event ("who picked a rose for his mommy"); the initiating event sets the stage for us to want to hear an attempt; an attempt, a consequence, and so on. While the "syntax of semantics" in some genres of text is better known than in others, the reality of story superstructures in reading and writing seems to have psychological validity. When children's opening story lines from our uninterrupted story-writing task are examined, for example, all children who elected to write stories began with the introduction of a setting or an antagonist. Story beginnings ranged qualitatively from "A Halloween ghost" (Terry, age 3); to "This is the boogyman house" (Towanna, age 3); to "Once there was a large forest with a house . . . The little girl lived there" (Jill, age 5). Additionally several children under this condition wrote informational stories about themselves which they introduced as: "I like candy" (Vincent, age 6); "We have a cat" (Latisha, age 6): "Chris is in first grade" (Chris, age 6). Often because the process of physically producing a surface text was so all-consuming, children never finished their "stories"; yet, what they did produce supports the concept that mental story structures schematically operate in writing.

In many ways several of the newer issues in reading and writing involve current attempts to further understand the complexity of the semantic systems of language. Meaning is orchestrated through mood, intonation pattern, rheme-theme, cohesion, transitivity relationships, given-new contracts, and more (Halliday & Hasan, 1976, 1980; Fries, 1980; Christensen, 1979). Cohesive harmony (Hasan, 1979, 1980), propositional analysis (Kintsch & van Dijk, 1978; Fredericksen, 1977), macrostructural analysis (van Dijk, 1977, 1979), semantic negotiation across art, writing, and context (Harste, Burke, Woodward, 1981), and others are attempts to describe and understand the semantic system of language is use.

Studying Semantic Features in Children's Writing. To be coherent a text must have unity; that is, the units of meaning in the text must cohere or hang together. Coherence resides, however, not only in the linguistic surface structure of the text (this element of coherence is called cohesion), but in the mind of the beholder (Tierney & Mosenthal, 1982). Coherence simply defined is a measure of how unified the idea units of a text are. Part of coherence is directly expressed in the surface structure of the text, including art work (see for example Sara's and Matt's use of pictures to support their written surface texts); the rest lies outside the surface text in the "text" we create in our heads as readers.

To study the coherence in the linguistic surface texts which young children produce we developed a semantic mapping procedure which assumes that the expression of coherence in surface text is important. From the writer's vantage point, the expression of coherence insures that the reader will be able to follow, or track semantically, the ideas being presented. From a schema-theoretic perspective, such an expression of coherence insures that the units of meaning are organized and are not just bits of isolated information.

If we take Sara's text, the first thing we need to do is to identify the mainline units of meaning which reside in the surface text. Once we have identified the mainline units of meaning we can then look across them in order to see what relationships exist between them. The system we use for this purpose is propositional analysis (Kintsch & van Dijk, 1978). Using this system the first thing that a reader does is to attempt to identify mainline units of meaning, or what van Dijk has called "basic facts." Acknowledging that the text we create as readers may in fact be different from the text Sara wanted to placehold in the surface text she produced but that they probably will share features in common because we are members of the same interpretive community, what we find in the first part of her first sentence is one basic fact: namely, *that there exists a bunny*. We write that in propositional form as follows where P1 stands for Proposition 1:P1 (EXIST, BUNNY).

Once upon a time tells us the circumstances of when the bunny existed. The second proposition modifies the first proposition. It is not a new basic fact, but a condition modifying the first basic fact. We write this proposition P2→(CIRCUMSTANCES: (1), ONCE UPON A TIME). We draw an arrow through the P2 to indicate that this is a modification of a basic fact since all we need to deal with at this level are the basic facts themselves. We do this under the assumption that modifications (propositions which modify basic facts) are by definition already coherent.

Sara's text reads, "Once upon a time there was a loveable bunny." To this point, we have everything mapped except the concept *loveable*. Our third proposition, then, is: P3→(QUALITY OF, BUNNY, LOVEABLE). This, too, is a modification of a basic fact and so it too receives an arrow.

The next part of the sentence reads: " . . . who picked a rose for his mommy." Here we find another basic fact: P4 (PICK FOR, BUNNY, ROSE, G: MOMMY), where G stands for goal, or to what end the motion was performed.

We now have two basic facts: P1 (EXIST, BUNNY) and P4 (PICK FOR, BUNNY, ROSE, G: MOMMY). Since Proposition 1 (P1) and Proposition 4 (P4) share a common case, namely, BUNNY, we map them as tied. To show this we can draw a line connecting them: P1 —— P4 .

Sara's text ends here, but before we end this discussion, we will assume three different endings and explore what each of these endings means in terms of the mapping of surface text coherence. For example, assume that the next line of her surface text were, *She was happy*. We could propositionalize that: P5 (HAPPY, E: MOMMY), where E stand for experiencer. Because the case, MOMMY, appears in P4 (PICK FOR, BUNNY, ROSE, G: MOMMY) and P5 (HAPPY, E: MOMMY) we tie these two when we map them: P1 ——— P4 ——— P5 .

For purposes of further illustration, let's assume the text didn't read, *She was happy*, but rather, *Bunny and Mommy were happy*. We would propositionalize this alternative proposition (AP) as: AP5 (HAPPY, E: MOMMY AND BUNNY). Because P4 (PICK FOR, BUNNY, ROSE, G: MOMMY) and the new alternative AP5 (HAPPY, E: MOMMY AND BUNNY) share the case MOMMY, and because P1 (EXIST, BUNNY) and the new alternative AP5 (HAPPY, E: MOMMY, BUNNY) share the case BUNNY, we would have to draw our evolving map such that both elements of coherence could be shown.

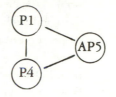

As can be seen, the map changes shape as the coherence in the surface text changes, providing a visual display of surface text coherence.

To carry this even further and for purposes of contrast, let's assume that Sara concluded her text with, *Father threw up*. A propositional analysis of this sentence would render: BP5 (THROW UP, FATHER). Since (THROW UP, FATHER) shares no cases with (PICK FOR, BUNNY, ROSE, G: MOMMY) nor (EXIST, BUNNY), we would have to map it showing no tie: P1———P4 BP5. This does not mean we could not make it coherent or tied to the other text portions, but it does mean that we, the readers, must do the tying mentally and that whatever coherence there may be does not express itself in the transitivity relationships expressed in the surface text.

A coherent text need not be one that has all of its mainline propositions tied to each other, but Margaret Atwell (1980) has found that surface texts which are judged by readers as being well-written have a higher degree of local coherence (.90 + or −) than do texts which readers perceive as less well written (.76 + or −). Mapping texts in this fashion, then, gives us a look at the local coherence expressed in a surface text.

When we examined the language experience stories which 3-, 4-, 5-, and 6-year-olds produced for us, we found that the older the child the more likely he was to produce a story consisting of multiple propositions. Twenty-five percent of our 3-year-olds produced such stories, 50 percent of our 4-year-olds, and 75 percent of our 5- and 6-year-olds. When we mapped these stories we found that all children were addressing issues of local coherence in their texts. By examining the proportion of mainline propositions which were tied to each other in the text base we found this ranged from .17 to .46 for 3-year-olds to .25 to 1.00 for 4-, 5-, and 6-year-olds. In looking at a child's ability to handle coherence across story tasks, we further found that this ability was context specific depending upon the task and story writing conditions.

By looking at the maps produced one can tell whether global coherence is expressed in the surface text or whether it must be inferred. Expressed global coherence means that there is a proposition in the text to which all other propositions are somehow tied. Inferred global coherence means that there is no single proposition which is expressed to which all others tie, but that one can easily create a proposition which might serve this function. In Matt's text, the title "My Trip to the Zoo" would be such a unit. It must be remembered, however, that because of the conditions surrounding the production of Matt's text, no such proposition needs to be expressed in the surface text. For this reason its absence cannot be taken as indicative of a lack of surface text organization. In fact, what appears to be lack of organization from one theoretical position is evidence of orchestration and growth from another.

Sometimes when one asks young children to dictate a story, they decide not to do so, electing instead to have a conversation, to play, or to do other things. Of the forty-eight children we asked to dictate a story in our Indianapolis study, forty-six engaged in story dictation at some point during the event. When we looked at how global coherence was handled by the children in their language experience stories, we found that only four stories contained an explicit macroproposition to which all other main line propositions tied. For twelve of the stories one could infer a macroproposition. This proposition was implicit rather than explicit, much like the proposition one can infer for Matt's text. Thirty of these stories were contextually dependent, meaning that in order to make sense of the surface text created, a reader would have to be familiar with the context of story dictation in terms of the objects used or the actions and antics of the language user. Further, when we looked at the global coherence of the texts children created across story composition conditions in both reading and writing (dictate and read a language experience story, write a story, read a story), any individual child's ability to handle global coherence was found to be a function of the story condition and the topic selected.

While this procedure for studying coherence is not without its conceptual faults, we have found it useful for studying variation among the surface texts produced by young writers across a variety of contexts. Generally, what we have found is that coherence is not a monolithic skill in writing. It is not true that language users either have it or don't have it. Under certain conditions the surface texts which children produce express more or less coherence. Even more importantly, our data suggest that young children are dealing with these issues and, in the process of using language, discovering what coherence means for texts within a variety of contexts.

Recently, Stephen Kucer (1982), in a study of college students' writing, also demonstrated that the amount and kind of coherence expressed in the surface text is more a function of the conditions under which the text is produced than it is an expression of linguistic capability. Certain settings not only allow, but also encourage children and obviously adults to test other language hypotheses. These hypotheses range from pragmatics, to graphophonemics, to syntax, to other dimensions of semantics, and seem affected by topic choice, background information, and task conditions. In its specific detail, then, the amount of coherence expressed in a surface text is a function of the setting in which the writing takes place and the intentions and assumptions of the language users involved. These aspects of textual organization will be discussed in subsequent chapters.

From an organizational perspective these data demonstrate both the schematic complexity and the schematic sophistication which young children bring with them to writing at the age when most formal writing programs begin in this country. These data question many current instructional assumptions about the young child's writing ability, as well as the theoretical grounds on which these assumptions rest.

From an interdisciplinary perspective, the decisions which children make in reading and writing from age 3 through age 6 are not only organized, but are laced with both personal and social organization. This interplay between personal and social organization in the evolution of literacy is universal. Randomness and language are inimical concepts. It should not surprise us to find that it neither characterizes our writing nor that of the 3-year-old.

Chapter 8
Intentionality

Intentionality is shown to be more complex than just 'thinking ahead.' Language users' attempts to make sense are predicated upon their contextually-based conceptualizations of potential texts. This whole process is central to the development of a transactive view of literacy.

By "intentionality" we refer to an expectation on the part of language users and learners that written marks are cultural objects, or signs, which signify. Even before children have determined what a particular written mark may signify, their responses reflect a basic understanding of written marks as cultural objects which have a sign potential.

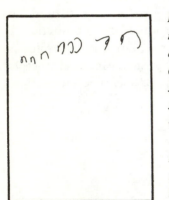

Kibi, age 4, when asked to write, made a series of marks on the paper. Kibi looked up quite pleased with her performance and asked, "What did I write?" Kibi's question suggests that she sees written marks as signs which signify meaning to other language users. While she does not have a knowledge of how one produces specific marks to sign specific meanings, she does understand that these objects are signs which signify. In other words, she has accessed the deep structure of literacy without controlling in any precise way the surface structure.

Frank, age 5, was shown various pieces of environmental print and asked what they said. Frank's responses included, "mints" for Dynamints, "Kroger" for Kroger Eggs, "blocks" for Lego, "street" for Indianapolis, and "Don't know" for For Sale. What is important to understand is that all of these responses are governed by an assumption of intentionality, even his "Don't know." What "Don't know" means is that Frank, having studied the cue complexes available in this setting, does not recognize them as immediately identifiable. For example, when shown the Evil Knievel Chopper box and asked what it says, Frank initially responded, "Don't know." By our asking, "What things do you see that help you know what this says?" Frank buys himself more time to pursue our first question, and responds, "I think it says 'motorcycle'."

Greg, age 5, received a letter from Linda and was asked to read it. Greg initially responded, "I forgot what it said." After a pause he read: "Dear Greg, I want to go back to school with Greg Winston and come and work with you again too."

Megan, age 4, wrote a personal letter and a story on two separate sheets of paper using a wavy up-and-down script to placehold her texts. When asked to read her letter she read, "Dear Mary, I hope you bring me here every day, The end. Megan." When asked to read her story Megan read: "Once upon a time there was a ghost. Three ghost family. One day they went out for a walk. They honked the horn cause they saw Mrs. Wood and said 'Hi,' then they went back to Mrs. Corners and they honked the horn and sa-said 'Hi.' The End." While the physical products which Megan produced do not look like a letter or a story to our conventional eyes it's important to understand that for Megan, these sets of markings had particular meanings which closely correspond to our conventions for how the print in letters, as opposed to the print in stories, operates.

While language users and learners may not know what a written mark may specifically signify, for us to suspect that it is a sign purposely created in order to communicate something to somebody is to hypothesize intentionality. Intentionality is such a pervasive assumption reflected in children's responses that instances which may initially appear to violate this premise merit special examination.

Boyd, age 3, was asked to draw a picture of himself. During the completion of this request, Boyd turned to the researcher and asked, "Do you like Boyd's picture?" The researcher assured him she did, but given his question and the nature of his markings, decided she had best clarify the task indirectly and so said matter-of-factly, "That's a picture of Boyd." Boyd responded, "Yep. This is Boyd's picture." What is significant about this instance is that it demonstrates that our intentionality (draw a picture of Boyd) and Boyd's intentionality (here is Boyd's picture) are often quite different and correspondence cannot simply be assumed.

To say that written language users and learners approach print with an expectation of intentionality is to say more than that they see it as purposeful or even meaningful, however. Embedded in this notion also is the expectation that combinations of these written marks, as well as the relationship these written marks have to the context of situation in which they are found, will contribute to the attainment of a unified meaning. Intentionality governs the responses of all written language users and sets into motion cognitive search strategies by which literacy and literacy learning are propelled.

Chris, age 3, along with his father and aunt, was on a camping trip. As they were going back to the cottage to put Chris down for a nap, Chris's aunt spotted a *snake. Trying not to sound alarmed and thereby excite Chris so he couldn't sleep, the aunt calmly said, "Tom, do you see the S-N-A-K-E?" while continuing to walk with Chris to the cottage. Two hours later, after his nap, Chris bounded out of the cottage and said he wanted to see "the A-B-C." "What do you think an A-B-C is?" his aunt questioned. "A snake," Chris replied.*

Alison, age 4, when shown the phrase Kroger Cottage Cheese *typed out in primary type on a 3" × 5" card and asked what she thought it said, responded: "Well, it should be the alphabet, but it doesn't start with A." Alison assumed here not only intentionality, but also that what was shown her would be personally meaningful. The cognitive operations she engages in are universals which undergird both successful and unsuccessful instances of the process.*

Kara, age 6.5, brought home a basal reading story from school to read. The text read, "I want to hide here. I want to stop here. I want to eat and eat . . ." At this point Kara stopped reading and turned to her mother and said, "Does this make sense to you!?!"

Language users assume that the various signs in a literacy event are intentional, nonrandom, and together operate to convey a unified meaning. Further, language learners seemingly operate under the assumption that it is not beneficial to them over the long haul to ignore or disregard objects perceived as signs. Together these assumptions cause the language user to actively search for unity and propel the active testing of language hypotheses by language users and learners.

Charles, age 4, was shown a box of Jell-O pudding and asked what it says. Charles responded, "Jell-O," but then asked, "What's that little mark mean?" pointing to the registered trademark beside the word Jell-O. *While neither we nor Charles pursued his question, implicit in it is an assumption that this mark is a sign which signifies. Later when shown the Johnson & Johnson Band-Aid box and asked what it says, Charles responded, "Band-Aid." Then seeing the registered trademark beside the word* Band-Aid *he reflected, "There it is again."*

Once again while neither we nor Charles pursued his observation, the fact that he made it suggests that, having once recognized a sign, and having assumed it was intentful, Charles is actively searching for its meaning. By collecting instances of its appearance, he will make an inference and test a hypothesis. Two related observations are important. Language learners, like Charles, always seem more interested in what they haven't sorted out than what they have. It does not surprise us that Charles focuses on the trademark symbol, this being his latest language discovery. Second, when we began this study we were concerned that the print in the print setting be big enough for young children to see. Experiences such as this led us to realize the eyesight of young children is never as serious an issue as beginning reading and writing programs assume. In fact, we have some evidence that lined school paper, which forces the child to write with a certain size print, actually distracts the child's attention from the real issues in literacy learning.

Jill, age 5, was asked to read or pretend to read the book, The Ten Little Bears. *In this book a predictable structure is set up whereby page by page another of the bears leaves home to participate in an adventure. This structure is also conveyed in the pictures, which show fewer bears on each page. Jill began her reading by making up a story about a group of bears who go on various trips. As she created her story she noticed the repeated at-home pictures and visibly counted the bears. Having thus discovered this structure Jill is led to building it into the text she creates. This decision leads her very close to the surface text structure. Her line: "Then five little bears stayed home." The actual story line: "Then five little bears were at home."*

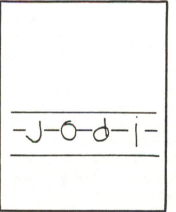

Jodi, age 6, was asked to write her name "between the lines" on some hand drawn school paper as part of a test given to judge reading readiness in first grade. Noting the horizontal dotted line running down the center of the line she was to write her name on, Jodi assumed its role must be to separate the letters of her name. Ever so carefully, she wrote J in the space between the first two dashes, O in the second, D in the third, and I in the fourth space.

Jodi was an extremely competent young writer, having had three years in Heidi Mills's preschool program in which she had had extended opportunities to interact with books and select from a writing center paper appropriate to whatever writing she wished to do. Encountering school paper for the first time, she rightfully assumed the markings down the center of each line were intentional and decided they must be to separate the letters in writing.

The assumption of intentionality characterizes our current written language discoveries just as much as it does our very first explorations with print. It is this assumption of nonrandomness about context and about any and all markings encountered which drives literacy and makes written language learning sometimes appear effortless. Understanding intentionality is fundamental to understanding the sociolinguistic and psycholinguistic activities involved in literacy and literacy learning.

We are not the first to see intentionality as a universal pattern reflected in all instances of literacy learning, although we may be the first to see unconventional responses as instances of the phenomenon. Every protocol example in this volume reflects this assumption on the part of the language user. If it were not so fundamental to understanding literacy, its pervasiveness alone would in itself be boring. The review of literature, discussion of selected protocols, and description of analysis procedures which follow look more closely at some of these patterns of intentionality in our data in order to trace the conceptual and historical roots of this notion and discuss its significance to the understanding of and rethinking of literacy. To illustrate that the concepts we discuss in this report, like "organization" and now, "intentionality," are applicable to any piece of reading and writing data, we will reference organizational patterns present in the new protocols we introduce in the following section for the reader's benefit.

INTERDISCIPLINARY PERSPECTIVES

The past fifteen years have been heralded as a period in which phenomenal advancement has been made in understanding the reading and language process (Pollock, 1979; Shuy, 1979). To the extent that this advancement is real, it may well be attributable to discovery of the centrality of the semantic system not only in reading (Goodman, 1967; Rumelhart, 1977; Smith, 1971, 1978; Adams & Collins, 1978; Kintsch & van Dijk, 1978; Fredericksen, 1977), but in language and language learning (Brown, 1973; Halliday, 1973, 1975; Hymes, 1967; Shuy, 1979). Given a perspective which only the passing of time can offer, we might well see the past period of research in reading and related fields as that of the discovery of the centrality and the complexity of the semantic systems of language. To date seven semantic systems have been identified (Halliday & Hasan, 1980), of which transitivity relationships (Fillmore, 1976) and cohesion (Halliday & Hasan, 1976) have received the most study by cognitive psychologists and others.

The importance of intentionality in understanding the cognitive processing operations involved in reading comprehension has only very recently been reemphasized by Schank (1980). In attempting to get a computer to simulate human comprehension, Schank's programming of the computer to perform advanced operations on the semantic base proved insufficient. Frustrated in this effort, Schank reported that he and his colleagues needed to develop a special program called "What's Your Point?" in order to get the computer to prioritize propositions and reach conclusions similar to those made by language users when reading.

The net result of work in this area across disciplines has led to the articulation of a functional perspective on language and language learning (Bates, 1976, 1977, 1981; Grice, 1975, 1978; Searle, 1969, 1975, 1979). Functionalists argue that the very essence of language is meaning (Bates, 1976, 1981; Halliday, 1973, 1975; Goodman & Goodman, 1979). They argue that language did not develop because of one language user, but because of two, who had as their purpose communication. Halliday (1973), as a result of a longitudinal study of his son, describes the whole of growth and development in language as "a saga in learning how to mean."

Vygotsky (1978) sees one of the crucial points in written language learning as that moment when the child intends, and then makes marks on the paper to placehold that intention. He characterizes this crucial period in literacy by a formula which reads "meaning over object" (meaning/object), and contrasts it to an earlier state, which he characterizes as "object over meaning" (object/meaning). This latter formula is illustrated by a child's making a squiggle on a paper (object) and only later deciding to name the mark something (meaning), for example, "a snake." Vygotsky's formula necessitates the naming of the representation before it is written for it to be considered an instance of literacy. If naming is not done before production begins, then Vygotsky assumes that intentionality is missing. The young child's question, "What did I write?" after putting marks on the paper signals that he or she has inferred that the marks made should mean. Vygotsky's insights, while important, need extension.

Given two sets of corroborative data—the children's reading of what they have written in comparison to what they have been requested to write, and the in-process verbalizations children make during the process of writing in comparison to the responses they make when asked to read what they have written—*all* children studied in this program of research wrote with the intent to mean. The complexity of this finding as well as its significance for the study of literacy are best seen when one analyzes the in-process behaviors and verbalization of our young language users involved in written language encounters.

Beth's uninterrupted story writing behaviors will be analyzed to demonstrate her "intentionality" in writing. Beth's final product is shown in Figure 8.1. The step-by-step process data in Figure 8.2, which correspond to the verbalizations involved in the creation of this product, are made possible by stopping the videotape and reproducing, using a light table, the product produced at each of these points. The correspondence between the demands of the task, the in-process verbalizations, and the child's subsequent reading of her story, constitute what was considered evidence of intentionality in this study.

Beth begins by drawing a picture of a sun and a house (Figure 8.2: Sample A). Beth writes her name (Figure 8.2: Sample B) and then announces "I can write my name another way," producing the second spelling with an altered *E* form (located in center of page). After this, Beth writes *David Dansberger*, announcing it to be her brother's name. She decides also to write *Jeff*, her other brother's name, but decides her *J* doesn't look right and says, "That doesn't look right!" After this announcement she tries to erase her *J* with her finger. Next she draws a

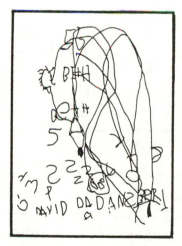

Figure 8.1. Uninterrupted Story Writing (Beth, Age 5).

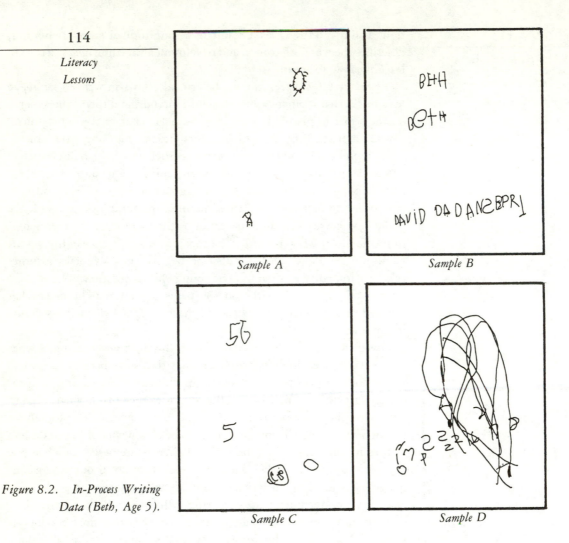

*Figure 8.2.   In-Process Writing
Data (Beth, Age 5).*

Sample A

Sample B

Sample C

Sample D

picture of David and announces as she does so, "This is David." She begins to draw Jeff but remembers she didn't finish his name and so decides not to finish his picture, correcting herself at this point by saying, "Oops!"

Beth next decides to write her age, "5" (Figure 8.2: Sample C). Not pleased with her product she immediately tries again (see 5 in middle of page). Beth pauses for a moment at this point. She then begins saying and writing her numbers in backward order: "8, 7, 6, 5." Not pleased with her 5 she makes several attempts to make an improved one, saying "5, 5, 5, 5," and produces the array of forms shown here (Figure 8.2: Sample D). Finally shrugging her shoulders she continues by saying and writing "4, 3, 2, 1, Zero, BLAST OFF!"

At this point Beth hastily sketches the rocket you see in the middle of the page. She terminates her picture story complete with sound effects by adding the streamers coming out of the top of the rocket and flowing down the page, saying as she does so, "VAROOM!! VAROOM!! VA-ROOM!! VAROOM!"

At this point Beth announces that she is done and the researcher asks her to read what she has written. Beth says, "Well, this is a story about what me and my brothers do at home, play rockets and things like that." While this "reading" has the psychological distance characterizing a retelling, it is important to note that in light of her intent as she expresses it, each and every mark has as its function the placeholding of components of her story. While the surface level organization of the product may look random (see Figure 8.1), the semantic features of her markings at a deep-structure level are intentional. Not only are her markings intentional, but these markings were organized during production in story structure form. We notice, for example, that Beth begins with a setting (sun and house), introduces characters (herself and her brothers), and relates an organizing event (play rockets and things like that) around which her story coheres. Despite surface-structure form, her story clearly contains a recognizable story grammar (Propp, 1928; Stein & Glenn, 1978; Applebee, 1978; Thorndyke, 1977; van Dijk, 1977) which, we can only conclude given the available data, was intentionally orchestrated and placeheld via a highly ordered set of in-process markings.

Beth, the youngest of six children, is a 5-year-old without preschool experience. Although her behavior and her story are particularly good examples to illustrate the complexity and sophistication with which children orchestrate intentionality in their written products, all children, as stated earlier, demonstrate intentionality in their writing.

Latrice, age 3, who produced what from a conventional perspective might be viewed as the most primitive markings of all the children studied, began by saying she was going to "make a dog," attempted to do so, but said she couldn't and decided to make "a Mickey Mouse." Later, when asked to read what she had written, she said she had written a "dog and a Mickey Mouse," responses which fall nicely within the semantic field of the intent signaled by her speech during writing.

As a related aside, it is interesting to note that oral speech during writing not only signaled intentionality, but acted almost as a plan of writing action. In this regard, we, like Vygotsky (1978), noted that almost inevitably speech produced in the process of writing signaled a plan of action either in abatement or in initiation. Speech, then, seemingly served an organizational function in writing. The hand seemed to follow speech as if subservient to decrees of oral intent. Rather than being a tool for thought, speech in the process of writing acted metaphorically as an "intention director."

As a further related aside, one cannot help but note that speech during writing served as its own sign in a semiotic sense, which seemingly triggered the writing of the next semantic unit. In part this is evident in the nonrandom and often ordered semantic field in the written product. Rarely does one find it difficult to infer the class around which specific elements in the written products of preschool children cohere. Latrice is a noticeable exception. More typical of the data we collected is that from Shannon, age 3, who said, for example, as she produced the respective lines in the product shown in Figure 8.3, "This is Anita. This is Shannon. This is Robin. This is Angel. This is Daddy. This is Mommy." In analyzing her product, the cohering elements are initially "playmates" and logically, given the bridge of her sisters, "family members." The interesting process feature of this list, however, is that once Shannon had come up with the first item, that item acted as a sign which seemingly stimulated the production of remaining coherent elements in this set. To the extent that this is a viable theoretical formulation for the phenomenon observed, these data suggest that intentionality signs intentionality and that decisions as to intention are not isomorphic but orchestrated through a process of unlimited semiosis (Eco, 1976, 1979). Given the recent cognitive processing model of Flower (1981) and Flower and Hayes (1980) for writing, this phenomenon merits further study since it may explain the process by which plans come to be embedded within text production, and why the dominant product

Figure 8.3. Uninterrupted Writing (Shannon, Age 3).

characteristic of such a process is not only intentionality embedded in intentionality, but unity across plans and subplans.

The model of language which this research has compelled us to hold shows that intentionality is as much a part of written language production as it is of oral language production. This statement assumes a common language process undergirding all expressions in language—reading, writing, speaking, listening—as well as a common linguistic data pool (Burke, 1977, 1980) created and made available regardless of the language expression through which a particular linguistic insight is made.

In art as in the literature on written language growth and development, intentionality and conventionality are often confused, the assumption being that in order for written language to be intentional it must be conventional. From our data, nonconventional markings on paper could not be construed as unintentional in meaning.

One of the definitions of "scribble" offered in *A Dictionary of Reading and Related Terms* (Harris & Hodges, 1981) reads, "to produce meaningless written marks" (p. 287). When we take a functional look at the written efforts of children, such a definition falls far short of reality, and seems to confuse conventionality with intentionality. To the extent that more successful writers may not always write what they intend, although what they elect to write is written in conventional form, this confusion may prove as problematic in our attempts to understand proficiency as it is in our attempts to understand the evolution of literacy.

Chapter 9

Generativeness

Language serves a cognitive as well as a communicative function. Our interests ought to be focused on how the inventive aspects of language generate conventions.

THE YOUNG CHILD AS INFORMANT

In use, language is an open system which permits the maintenance and generation of meaning. To say that written language is an object which functions as a sign is to suggest that the system is infinitely open. What the language user takes the sign to mean is a function of his or her purpose and background of experience. Language as a sign can sign different things to different people, or even different things to the same person on different occasions.

Ben, age 4, was shown a Crest toothpaste carton and asked what it said. He responded, "Toothpaste." Later when asked, "What else can you tell me about this?" Ben responded, "Well . . . we use Crest at our house."

For Ben the letters C-R-E-S-T signed not only "toothpaste," but, we find out later, also "Crest," the response we might have expected to our initial question. For Ben as for us the letters C-R-E-S-T sign many things simultaneously, including "cavities," or the lack of such (as it did for Tyler, age 3), "fluoride" (Heather, age 3), and "toothbrush" (Shannon, age 3). To say that Ben's and these other responses are "wrong" is to fail to understand of the generativeness of language as an open sign system.

Nathan, age 3, was shown a box of Jell-O pudding and asked what it said. His response, "It's got sugar in it," indicates to us what J-E-L-L-O signs to him given the nutrition lessons he has obviously learned at his mother's knee. While General Foods might not be pleased to know that J-E-L-L-O signs "sugar product," it is the openness of language which keeps it alive and ever pertinent. The amount of time an object like J-E-L-L-O has been around and the amount of effort General Foods has devoted to establishing a better meaning is, in itself, no guarantee that

118

language users will give the interpretation that General Foods desires. Despite our or their desire to close language, it remains an open sign system.

The generativeness of language does not stop once convention is understood. It is the generativeness of language which propels our learning of language, about language, and through language and makes reading and writing real and educative experiences in their own rights.

From a cognitive processing perspective, engagement and reengagement in the language process increases the opportunities language users have to discover for themselves the generativeness and self-educative aspects of language in use. In this sense not only language, but the process of language use, are in themselves generative, buying the language user time, allowing him or her to shift stances psychologically, permitting orchestration of what is already known, and allowing him or her to organize the evolving text. This process occurs during both reading and writing and involves all communication systems.

Charvin, age 4, was asked to dictate a story using the objects he had selected from a box of toys. He dictated, "It's a horn. It's a baseball bat. This is my choo-choo train. It blows up." When asked to read what he had written, Charvin read, "This is my baseball bat. This is my horn. It blows up. This is my choo-choo train. This is my base-. . . a . . . I don't know." At this point the researcher commented, "You're reading your story very nicely." Given encouragement, Charvin began reading again, "This is my baseball bat and it hits balls. And this is my choo-choo train and it . . . (pauses) . . . I don't know how to read."

While complex, this example illustrates that Charvin simultaneously explores both the maintenance and generative functions of written language during this event. His initial reading includes all of the original propositions in his dictated text. In rereading, he not only builds off of these propositions, but discovers he has more to say about each and adds descriptive statements; "This is my baseball bat and it hits balls." While this process scares him into concluding that he doesn't know how to read, his very behavior belies this fact and indeed, demonstrates engagement in and exploration of the key cognitive processes and benefits of literacy.

Charvin begins by inventorying what he sees as available to him in this setting. This act is in itself generative in that it sets up implicit contrasts which lead Charvin to the discovery of what he might say about this concept as opposed to another. When he rereads, this process continues with the result that he adds descriptive statements for items inventoried. In our study we found this pattern of inventory-description operating not only in writing but also in reading with the result that, once descriptive statements were generated, a narrative or expository text more in line with our expectation of such texts resulted. It's important to

*understand that repeated opportunities to engage in the process with this text—
first as a writer, then as a reader—offered Charvin the chance both to work
through the process and simultaneously to discover its generative and self-educative
benefits. Also illustrated is the importance of a supportive environment for this
engagement and growth.*

*Jason, age 5, selected a spoon, a toy suitcase, and some play money to use in telling
a story for dictation. Jason began by dictating, "Dollar. Spoon. Case." Then as
much to himself as to the researcher, Jason asked, "Do you know what you do with
these?" Without waiting for a reply, Jason continued his dictation, "You take the
spoon and you dip it in chili and cereal and you eat it. You take it (suitcase) for
some money to go to the store. Boy. Girl. Money. Case. Spoon." Like Charvin,
Jason mentally begins by inventorying concepts he sees as available to him in this
instance. His inventorying activities serve as a heuristic for comparison and
contrast which leads him to discover that one of the things he knows is that you do
different things with each of these objects. From here he begins to generate
descriptive statements and is led in the process to tying and weaving these concepts
together into a "story." Jason's reading and rereading contain all of the
propositions in his original story, the only difference being that his "story" is now
much tidier: "Spoon. Case. Dollar. Take a dollar to the bank. Take a case to
Chicago. Dip the spoon in chili. Eat the chili."*

*It's important to note the various psychological stances Jason takes during the
course of this event. During dictation he's initially a participant using language
to get on with dictation; then, by asking his rhetorical question, he is suddenly a monitor looking at what he has dictated in light of what he knows; and
finally, he's a participant again. Just as asking his rhetorical question allowed
him to switch stances during dictation, so asking him to read affords the same
opportunity, and he again takes advantage of it, only this time as an editor. His
final text, the result of the generative process itself, while probably not much of a
story by our definitions of well-formedness, has parallel syntactic and semantic
structures.*

*Eugene, age 6, dictated a story much like that of Jason's: "Money. I like money.
Ice cream have a spoon. Doctors have a suitcase." Like Charvin and Jason,
Eugene also mentally follows an inventory-descriptive text generating process. In
rereading, Eugene maintains most of his text, but edits his last two lines to read,
"Ice cream goes with a spoon. A doctor needs an suitcase."*

*Heather, age 3, followed a strategy similar to that of Misty and picked several
objects with which to tell her story, but saw these objects as candy, and more
generally as "food." She dictates: "Candy. Mints. Trick or Treat. They go
driving. They go hunting. They going to drive down the spoon. I like milk. I like
cottage cheese . . ."*

While Heather's "story" seems to go nowhere in particular, it shows the inventory-descriptive generative sequence. As Heather dictates she acts out her story by manipulating the objects she has selected. Play in this instance seems to serve Heather the same way Jason's rhetorical oral question did him. Psychologically these moves allowed the language user, in both instances, to take a new or alternate stance resulting in the generation of text.

Latrice, age 3, was asked to read or pretend to read the book, The Ten Little Bears. *She began by identifying items in the pictures she recognized, "There's a table . . . a chair." From here she moved to simple description, "He's driving," and proceeded in this fashion throughout her reading of the book. Here, again, we see this inventory-descriptive pattern reappearing.*

Brandyce, age 4, also began with an inventorying sort of behavior but rapidly moved to descriptive statements as the basis of her story. She began, "Bears. These bears sitting—laying down. Going to be that . . . And he's going there to the roller coaster . . . and he's going there to the swimming pool . . ."

Alpha, age 5, began with descriptive statements and continued this pattern throughout her reading. What is particularly interesting is that in this process she arrived at a syntactic and semantic parallel structure for her story and a final statement that ties her story together semantically. "A bear sailing in the ocean. Bears playing around. Bears driving a jeep. There's a bear riding on a roller coaster. Bears swimming. Bears jumping rope. Bears taking a haircut. Bears get candy. Bears at airport. Bears at the fire station. Bears having fun!"

Focusing on the generativeness of language in use is not meant to deny the value or importance of the meaning maintenance functions of language, but rather, to suggest that language psychologically and sociologically is a tool by which we clarify our thinking and collaboratively explore our world. The protocols, analysis procedures, and discussion of related literature which follow are meant to demonstrate the importance of understanding language and language use as generative processes in order to rethink what's involved in literacy.

INTERDISCIPLINARY PERSPECTIVES

One of the advantages of written language over spoken language is that written language supposedly affords a more precise memorability and retrievability of ideas over time and space (Goodman & Goodman, 1979). Vygotsky (1978) argues that yet another index in literacy growth and development is not only when the child intends to mean, but later when he encounters that marking anew and retrieves the original intention. From the perspective of psychology this literacy feat entails an individual's retrieval and maintenance of ideas from Time 1 to Time 2.

The maintenance of ideas across language users in a society, that is, from one language user to another, given the previous distinction, might be thought of as "sociological language maintenance." It is, of course, at the level of sociological maintenance that convention becomes important. Convention is defined as a set of social rules of language use and form which have as their purpose facilitating communication (Freedle, 1972, 1977, 1980).

One's own particular rules, which may well serve a "psychological maintenance function" in that, despite their nonconventional form, they serve personal memorability as well as retrievability (and must, therefore, be standardized enough to function across time for the individual at least), might best be thought of as personal convention. Understanding not only language change but the processes involved in this change is important. Language, whether on a psychological or a sociological level, serves a maintenance as well as a generative function (Goodman, 1980). Recent work in cognitive psychology has not only explicated the generative nature of reading, but in so doing it has explicated the maintenance and generative function of language more generally.

These insights into language are most evident when newer models of reading comprehension are contrasted with their historical counterparts. Historically, reading has been viewed as a process of information transfer and the reader seen more or less as a faulty vessel. A proficient reader under the historical view was someone who acquired all textually implicit and explicit units of meaning and did so without distortion or intrusion.

Newer models of comprehension have challenged this view (Adams & Collins, 1978; Goodman, 1967; Rosenblatt, 1938, 1969, 1978, 1980; Eco, 1979) and have demonstrated that readers construct a text in their heads given their reading of available signs in the graphic display (Eco, 1979; Iser, 1978; De Beaugrande, 1979, 1980; Culler, 1980). Under this view, comprehension is much less precise; what a reader makes of a text is dependent upon his knowledge of, familiarity with, and interpretation of, available signs. While all readers in a given culture will come to have a good amount of shared meaning simply by virtue of the fact that they share a history of language encounters in a given interpretive community (Fish, 1980), each reading, because of the individual reader's unique experience, will also be slightly different. What a reader reads may mean more to that reader than it did to the author. The same process which leads to "less," leads to "more." It is, in fact, the generative function of language which keeps it psychologically and sociologically alive. It is the maintenance function of language which gives language psychological and sociological continuity.

Within any retelling there is not only a maintenance, but a generation of ideas (Crafton, 1981). In part this is true because of the nature of comprehension, but in part it is also true because a reading and a retelling is not a linguistic act but a linguistic event with each component—both the reading and the retelling—being a language encounter in its own right. Carey, et al. (1982) argue that one cannot parse a retelling in terms of whether the source was author or reader, but rather suggest that a retelling is a new event, the result of a transaction rather than a simple interaction between author and reader.

Using recent research in reading comprehension, Shanklin (1982), Smith (1982), and Kucer (1982) have developed models of the writing process which capture not only its maintenance but its generative functions. Writing, like reading, has historically been viewed as a process of recording one's ideas on paper. The generative function which writing serves for the writer (Smith, 1982), while frequently discussed by writing theorists (Berthoff, 1975; Young, Becker & Pike, 1970), was noticeably absent in most formal models of writing and hence in research and instruction.

Recent work in metaphor and the cognitive processing operations involved in understanding metaphors (Altwerger, 1980; Altwerger & Strauss, 1983) may prove to be viable models for understanding the maintenance and generative function of language processing generally. Altwerger's work (1980, 1981) moves in this direction by studying metaphors and how readers process them in more natural reading situations. She finds, given the processing behaviors of readers, that not only do traditional definitions of metaphor break down, but that the process underlying how readers understand metaphor is similar to how they understand portions of text not previously thought to be metaphoric. From a child-as-informant perspective, what the reader processes metaphorically fails to coincide with what a linguist might code as metaphor in the surface text itself.

We will attempt to clarify these understandings by following a written language event through time. As part of our study of written language growth and development, we asked 3-, 4-, 5-, and 6-year-old children to select from a box of toys three objects with which they might tell a story. The story as dictated by the child was transcribed by the researcher. Immediately following transcription, the child was asked to read the story. One day later the child was again asked to read the story. Analysis of the child's first and second readings illustrate the maintenance and generative aspects of language both within and across encounters.

Dawn's dictated story, both in its original and propositional form, is found in Figure 9.1 (for propositionalizing the children's stories, Kintsch's propositional system as explicated by Turner & Greene, 1977,

I'm going to buy a book of jingle bells.
1. (BUY, DAWN, BOOK)
2. (QUALIFY (1), POTENTIAL)
3. (SUBJECT OF, BOOK, JINGLE BELLS)

I'm going to buy a paint brush.
4. (BUY, DAWN, PAINT BRUSH)
5. (QUALIFY, (4), POTENTIAL)

I'm going to buy a elephants.
6. (BUY, DAWN, ELEPHANT)
    (NUMBER OF, ELEPHANTS, TWO OR MORE)
7. (QUALIFY, (6), POTENTIAL)

I'm going to buy a car.
8. (BUY, DAWN, CAR)
9. (QUALIFY, (8), POTENTIAL)

Figure 9.1. Dictated Language Experience Story (Dawn, Age 4.3).

with adaptations by Harste & Feathers, 1979, was used). When we compared the dictated story to Dawn's first reading of that story (Figure 9.2) we noted certain modifications in the propositional base. A portion of these modifications served a cleaning-up function. For example, that

Figure 9.2. First Reading of Language Experience Story (Dawn, Age 4.3).

I'm going to buy a book of jingle bells.
M   1.   (BUY, DAWN, BOOK)
M   2.   (QUALIFY (1), POTENTIAL)
M   3.   (SUBJECT OF, BOOK, JINGLE BELLS)

I'm going to buy a paint brush.
M   4.   (BUY, DAWN, PAINT BRUSH)
M   5.   (QUALIFY, (4), POTENTIAL)

I'm going to buy an elephant.
M   6.   (BUY, DAWN, ELEPHANT)
PG   (NUMBER OF, ELEPHANTS, ONE)
M   7.   (QUALIFY, (6), POTENTIAL)

I'm going to buy a car.
M   8.   (BUY, DAWN, CAR)
M   9.   (QUALIFY, (8), POTENTIAL)

Dawn was going to buy one or more elephants, now becomes clearly just one elephant. Modifications of this sort were classified as partially generative (PG) in that two of the original three cases making up the proposition remained intact ([Number of, elephants, two or more] [Number of, elephants, one]).

When one compares the original story (Figure 9.1) with Dawn's second reading of the story (Figure 9.3) one sees even further modification of the propositional base. Rather than continue with her structure, "I'm going to buy . . ." she now writes, "I'm going out to buy . . ." thus clearly indicating that the text world to be created is one which puts the author physically at home or at some site not nearby where the shopping is to be done. These modifications add a whole generative level

I'm going out to buy a book of jingle bells.

M	1.	*(BUY, DAWN, BOOK)*
M	2.	*(SUBJECT OF, BOOK, JINGLE BELLS)*
G	3.	*(GO OUT, DAWN, HOUSE)*
G	4.	*(PURPOSE OF, (3), (1))*

I'm going out to buy an elephant.

M	5.	*(BUY, DAWN, ELEPHANT)*
G	6.	*(GO OUT, DAWN, HOUSE)*
G	7.	*(PURPOSE OF, (6), (5))*

I'm going out to buy a car.

M	8.	*(BUY, DAWN, CAR)*
G	9.	*(GO OUT, DAWN, HOUSE)*
G	10.	*(PURPOSE OF, (9), (8))*

Figure 9.3. Second Reading of Language Experience Story (Dawn, Age 4.3).

of propositions (G), the meaning potential of which was not very clearly signed prior to this revision (GO OUT, DAWN).

When Dawn's readings are systematically studied and coded on a proposition by proposition basis and marked M for proposition maintenance, PG for a proposition which is partially generative, and G for the new proposition which is generated, one has clear evidence of both the generative and maintenance functions of individual language encounters.

Dawn's story and her readings of it illustrate one of the patterns we observed in watching young children read their language experience stories on our videotapes. This was that, while often their readings were unconventional by our standards, they inevitably fell within the semantic ball park of the dictated story. Because the oral reading often did not neatly map onto the surface text of the dictated story, we needed to develop a procedure by which we could study what was happening semantically. The procedure we turned to was propositional analysis. By propositionalizing the language experience story which had been dictated, and by comparing these propositions to the child's first and second reading of the story, we found we could semantically track changes over the language event.

Three functional categories evolved from our comparison of propositions across the surface texts available from dictation, the child's first reading, and the child's second reading: (1) *Maintenance*, or propositions in which all agent categories matched (*TEXT*: ISA, $ [unspecified something], BASEBALL BAT; *READING*: ISA, $, BASEBALL BAT); (2) *Partially Generative*, or propositions which maintained the dictated propositional meaning but did so in slightly altered deep structure form through a change in one agent category of the proposition (*TEXT*: EAT, DOG, FOOD; *READING*: GET, DOG, FOOD); (3) *Generative*, or new propositions which expanded the original semantic base and involved two or three new agent categories in the proposition itself (*TEXT*: ISA, $, BASEBALL BAT; *READING*: ISA, $, BASEBALL BAT and POSSESS, CHARVIN, BASEBALL BAT where the latter proposition is completely new to the story). Taxonomic categories were worked on until a .80 level of interrater reliability was reached.

When a formal propositional analysis of the language experience stories which children dictated was made, we found that the stories contained, on the average, 14.81 propositions per story. A study of the distribution of propositional types—predicate propositions (GET, DOG, FOOD) to modifications (POSSESS, CHARVIN, BASEBALL BAT) to connectives (CAUSALITY: BECAUSE [GET, DOG, FOOD], [EAT, DOG, FOOD])—revealed no significant differences by stories across ages. Overall, of these 14.81 propositions in the dictated story, 8.2 were *Maintained* in the first reading. Additionally, the first reading contained 3.62 propositions which were *Partially Generative* and 3.3 propositions which were *Generative*. These data are based on our analysis of all story reading in which language users maintained the communication contract, that is, read when we asked them to read. They include eight stories by 3-year-olds, ten stories by 4-year-olds, ten stories by 5-year-olds, and nine stories by 6-year-olds. The maintenance as well as generative aspects of reading are clearly shown and hold across all age groups.

Rereadings (second readings) on the average contained 14 propositions. Of these, 7.032 served a *Maintenance* role, 2.687 were coded as *Partially Generative*, and 4.375 as *Generative*. These data show the ongoing maintenance and generative aspects of the language event for all age groups.

Semantically these data suggest that each opportunity to engage in the language process provides the language user an opportunity not only to maintain meaning, but to generate new meanings. Reading is in its own right a language experience. What engagement and reengagement in the reading process afforded the story author were opportunities to maintain meaning, clear up meaning, and generate new meaning, the net result being that the final reading or text was a much improved document.

Further, these data suggest that young children understand and are cognizant of the semantic constraints and opportunities which exist in engagement. Theoretically, these data suggest that young children are cognizant of the fact that semantic constraints are very much a part of the "text world" created during reading. Access and reaccess to this "text world" and within it, the constraints which operate, allow them not only to both predict and generate a text which a reader might judge as quite successful, but to reap the generative and self-educative benefits of literacy which can only come through engagement in the event.

Crafton (1981), building from our work, used this procedure to study the retellings of fourth- and eleventh-grade students and demonstrated that the phenomenon observed here is found in all retellings. As a result she not only argues that both reading and retelling are language experiences in their own right, but begins to explicate under what reading conditions more or less maintenance and generation are likely.

The applicability of this perspective to the study of writing is apparent when one looks at Dawn's second reading, marked using standard miscue marking procedures (Goodman & Burke, 1972). As if Dawn's original text had been written, the changes Dawn makes in her second reading would look distinctively like those a writer might make in editing a first draft (see Figure 9.4). Even Dawn's deciding that there are

Figure 9.4. Miscue Markings of Language Experience Story (Dawn, Age 4.3).

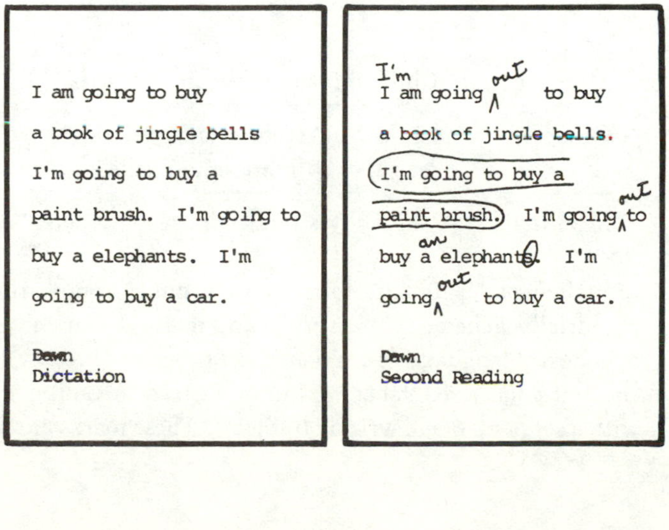

Key: I'm
I am = substitution
elephants = omission
going out to = insertion

more event sequences than needed and therefore her getting rid of one, would not surprise us if this were editing being done on a piece of writing.

Given what we know about the way the initial drafts of our manuscripts take form, we are not surprised by the generative and self-educative benefits of continued engagement in the process which Dawn and the other children we studied displayed. Of course, it is parallels like this, between reading and writing and between what children do and what we do, that lead us to look not only at reading behavior as scribbling, but at the processes involved in scribbling as universally applicable to the study of written language growth and development at all ages.

While this generative process is less trackable in the writing which 3-year-olds do, given their nonconventional script, it is nonetheless discernible through propositional analysis of the text read. Often children at 3, but not nearly so often as some would lead us to believe, wrote one thing at Time 1, but at Time 2, when asked to read what they had written, renegotiated the markings to be something else. Often these renegotiations in reading, as has already been illustrated in previous sections of this chapter, fell within the semantic field of the original text. While Vygotsky (1978) would argue that renegotiation is evidence of the child's lack of understanding of how written language functions, his argument ignores the generativeness of language and instead, falls into the trap of looking at written language as serving only a maintenance function.

For Vygotsky, literacy only occurs when language users demonstrate that the original meaning has been maintained from conception in the head (meaning[1]), through writing or invention of a mark (object[1]), through reading or reconstruction of the original meaning. We might represent Vygotsky's thinking formulaically as:

Meaning[1]	Child thinks "snake"
Object[1]	Child makes mark (swiggly line) on paper to represent "snake"
Meaning[1]	Child reads mark and reconstructs "snake"

In lieu of Vygotsky's formula we would propose that language is potentially generative at every point in the event, and that it is the openness of language which makes the process of literacy both generative and self-educative. What we initially mean (Meaning[1]) gets placeheld with a set of marks in writing (Object). These marks are signs which can trigger our original meaning (Meaning^1) or a new meaning (Meaning^2). We could represent our thinking formulaically as:

Meaning^1	Child thinks "snake"
Object	Child makes mark (swiggly line) on paper to represent "snake"
Meaning^2	Child reads mark and constructs "the path the snake took"

More accurately, the formula might read: Meaning^1 over Object$^{1 \text{ or } 2...N}$ over Meaning^2, where the Object as a sign can signify different meanings.

Further, our data suggest that the generativeness of language is not something laid on literacy after one first knows and understands its maintenance function. Both the maintenance and generative functions of written language are there and being explored from the start. It is the openness of language which leads to growth. What I write can mean more to me later than what it meant to me when I wrote it. What others write can mean more to me than it did to them. The openness of language leads to both creativity and error. That the process which leads to creativity is also the process which leads to error is something we must accept; but clearly, since we cannot have one without the other, then we cannot ignore, confine, or fail to appreciate or to encourage this process.

Chapter 10
Risk-Taking

The thesis is developed that risk-taking is central to cognitive processing. In order to learn we must allow ourselves to be vulnerable to the situation, to others' perceptions, and to our own past experiences. The sharing of half-baked ideas is an integral part of language, learning, and teaching.

THE YOUNG CHILD AS INFORMANT

Language is inherently social. Because the trail of marks we leave during the writing process makes language users vulnerable, engagement in the process can scare both participants and observers. When this happens withdrawal from the process can occur. Since access to the process can only be gained through involvement in the process, strategies which allow language users to set aside perceived or real constraints and which permit engagement on the language user's terms are central to growth in literacy.

Benjamin, age 4, when handed the book The Ten Little Bears *and asked to read, questioned, "You mean pretend to read?" "Yes," the researcher responded, "just do the best you can." Given this assurance, Benjamin was able to proceed.*

Benjamin's question shows a concern for the constraints he perceived as operating in this context. Having abstracted out of past encounters with reading some notion of what is involved, he decides that if this is the kind of reading we are talking about, he can't read. If, however, he can "pretend," that is, set his own constraints, he can proceed on his own terms. Since access to the process can only be attained through engagement in the process, Benjamin's strategy is significant. Though "pretend," constraints can be set aside; a new set of rules operates.

Boyd, age 3, was asked to write his name and anything else that he could write. He began by writing a B which came out backward. Saying "I can't" as he tried to erase his mark with his finger, he quickly announced, "I'm going to make a monster," and then proceeded to do so using art instead of writing. While his monster was not placeheld with any more of a conventionalized set of markings

130

than was his aborted name, Boyd evidently saw art as not imposing a set of constraints as writing did, which made his efforts inadequate. By age 4, most children are very aware of the constraints involved in writing. When the management of these constraints appears overwhelming, children often elect not to participate.

Leslie, age 6, when asked to write, initially responded, "But I can't spell." When we assured her that we were not interested in her spelling, but in her writing, she was able to proceed. The perception that when one writes one must spell correctly appears to be the single biggest constraint which 5- and 6-year-old children see as the reason why they can't engage in the process. Given the attention spelling is given by teachers and parents, this perception is understandable, but nonetheless dysfunctional to growth in literacy.

David, age 4, was handed a sheet of paper and asked to write his name and anything else he wanted to write. David looked at the researcher in dismay and responded, "I don't write! You learn to write in kindergarten!"

While David's response appears "cute," given all that the other 4-year-old children in our sample had learned and continued to learn about literacy through involvement in the process, dysfunctional notions such as this fail in the end to serve the language learner.

Bill, age 4, was shown a variety of logos from selected pieces of environmental print and was asked what they said. When shown the Kroger Eggs logo, Bill responded, "Milk." When shown the Kroger Milk logo, Bill responded, "Mil— . . . no . . . I don't know." When shown the Kroger Cottage Cheese logo, Bill paused and responded, "I don't know." Bill had similar problems with Jell-O, Coca-Cola, and Band-Aid, in that having once said, "Coke" to Band-Aid he felt this option used up and so missed Coca-Cola too. One day later we laid all six items out in front of Bill and said, "Give me the one that says 'Kroger Milk'." Bill scanned the set and handed us the Kroger Milk logo. "Give me the one that says 'Kroger Cottage Cheese'." Bill handed us the Kroger Cottage Cheese logo. "Give me the one that says 'Kroger Eggs' . . . 'Jell-O' . . . 'Band-Aid' . . ." until the one remaining was Coca-Cola. When we asked, "What does this one say," Bill proudly said, "Coke."

Knowing what items we had used in our product condition of this task, Bill was familiar with the options he was likely to face. Since he was trying to work within this set of options, his previous experience with our task operated as a constraint on his current decisions. Once he had used an option it was no longer available. When we altered the task the range of options available was clearer; hence, the quality of his decisions improved. Under this later condition with optional constraints clear, the task became manageable.

Constraints operate in all language settings. These constraints are both perceived and real. Alter the constraints operating in a context of situation and a new set of linguistic resources suddenly appears.

Because language is an open sign system, risk is necessarily a central feature of the process involved in its use. Without risk there can be no discovery of the generative potentials of literacy. Overemphasis on the maintenance aspects of language discourages risk.

ThcISA DUrAnt

TSr DUrANTS

Bradley, age 4, was shown first a picture of one dinosaur and then a second picture of two dinosaurs and asked what each was, in a replication of Emilia Ferreiro's and Ana Teberosky's tasks (1981) designed to observe whether or not children have strategies for coping with plurality. Bradley said of the first picture, "This is a dinosaur" and of the second, "There are dinosaurs." When asked to write, "This is a dinosaur," Bradley wrote: T-H-S I-S A D-U-R-A-N-T." When asked to write, "These are dinosaurs," Bradley wrote: "T-S R D-U-R-A-N-T-S." While Bradley clearly understands plurality and how to sign it in writing, what is more interesting is the hypothesis he tests relative to the spelling of dinosaur. Knowing that his last name is Dryant clarifies his strategy. He begins, however, by sounding out the word dinosaur and at this point writes the d. Then, pausing and running through all the "d-words" he knows, he comes upon his last name, Dryant, and decides to give it a try. While his strategy "doesn't work" in this instance by our standards, it was the hypothesizing and testing that such relationships were possible which have led to the written language growth Bradley currently demonstrates.

Carol, age 3, was asked to sign her name as part of a "sign-in" procedure instituted in her preschool whereby children keep their own attendance. Since this provided a functional writing setting and allowed us to collect name writing data over time, both we and the children were pleased with the activity. Carol's signatures consisted of c's, o's, and l's in a variety of upside-down and back-ward forms. One day as Carol nonchalantly signed in, she said to the teacher, "I tricked you last Friday, I signed in Carlos's name!"

In searching all of the signatures we had collected from Carol no discernible Carlos signature was to be found. Having sorted out what constraints were operating, Carol, being the confident writer she was, was off testing more hypotheses about language. Carol's new hypotheses had a lot to do with us, but were not the set we thought we were interested in when we designed the study. In comparison with Carol's subtle understanding of tenor relationships in language, our interests pale to insignificance.

Alison, age 5.5, purchased a fill-in autobiography book during her visit to a school book fair with her brother. Since functional spelling had not only been

*accepted, but was encouraged, she knew asking for spellings was something others did; she must rely on her own resources. In completing the page on favorite clothes she began one of the sentence starters, "My favorite shoes are _____."
Alison completed the sentence by writing "my Sunday shoes" spelling it M-I S-N-D (backward)-A S-H-O-E-S (a correct spelling she got by copying the word* shoes *from the sentence starter stem in the book). Pointing to her correct spelling of* shoes *she showed her mother the book page, saying, "Boy, is Dad going to be mad. . . . I got this one right!"*

This story, like those of Carol's, Leslie's, and others in this section all illustrate the insightfulness of children and their cognizance of the constraints that operate in particular language settings.

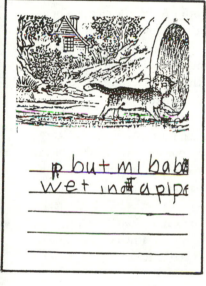

Jason, age 8, had stopped writing as a result of too much emphasis on correctness in his first-grade reading program. His parents sent him for remedial help. When asked to write, Jason refused and elected to draw pictures instead. After much encouragement and assurance that we could read anything he wrote, Jason began writing and elected to write a twenty-eight-page story to a wordless book he particularly liked. His story demonstrates an extensive knowledge of language, and few teachers whom we have worked with can understand how a child with this written language knowledge could possibly have been "in trouble" in first grade.

Given that all that we know cannot be attended to at once, and that our latest language discoveries are always more fun to think about than those which we already think we have sorted out, we find written language an almost perfect medium for the mind to work with. The process leaves a revisitable trail. In doing so, writing allows the mind an opportunity to do what it considers exciting—to think about, attend to, and record the new—while simultaneously permitting, via the convenience of another literacy (reading, speaking art, etc.) the opportunity to revisit, reflect, and orchestrate these latest discoveries with the old or known. Given the make-up of human cognition, this arrangement metaphorically allows us to have our cake and eat it too.

Since there is no good way nor is there any good reason to alter these penchants about how the mind naturally works, understanding this process and the psychological centrality which risk plays in it is important. The role risk plays in literacy needs to be supported, facilitated, and reflected sociologically in the supportive environments we create for literacy learning.

The discussion of risk in relation to written language learning which follows further expands this position by tracing its origins and by demonstrating that this concept is as applicable to the understanding of our writing behavior as it is to the writing behavior of young children.

If one very carefully sits down to analyze how reading cognitively differs from writing, almost all of the initial differences one might propose dissolve (Goodman & Emig, 1979). Both the reader and the writer must identify appropriate background information, create a text, make inferences, plan, search for unity, self-correct, and so on. Clearly one process is not more generative than another. It takes both the reader and the writer to create a revolution.

After this sort of analysis, about the only difference between reading and writing that remains is that under normal conditions, writing is more public than reading. Even this difference, of course, disappears in oral reading.

Generally this difference holds, however, and it is, we believe, an important one. Oral reading and writing both involve the creation of a potentially misusable private record of one's process decisions. Every false start, every misguided hypothesis, every mispronunciation or misspelling, every incoherent thought, every missed transaction (Shanklin, 1982) is available for analysis for both the language user and any would-be language teacher in the immediate environs.

This is an important understanding, since the implication is that the vulnerability which a language user feels under the conditions of writing and oral reading is a "learned" vulnerability, not something inherent in the process itself. While it is the case that reading during the process of writing may heighten the author's own awareness of any false starts or other communication difficulties (Atwell, 1980; Perl, 1979), the feeling that these should not be present in one's first draft constitutes a dysfunctional view of the writing process, and is a learned dysfunctional view at that (Britton, Burgess, Martin, McLeod & Rosen, 1975; Emig, 1971).

The relationship between linguistic constraints and linguistic resources has been clearly established (Hymes, 1967; Halliday, 1975; Harste & Carey, 1979). Social learning theories such as that of Lewin (1935, 1942) suggest that a change in one vector alters the homeostasis which was maintaining the behavior and is the impetus behind behavioral change, a new homeostasis. Language users bring to a language encounter their past readings of the constraints present and some sense of the successfulness or unsuccessfulness of the resource decisions which they have attempted: What worked last time becomes the general frame from within which one might attempt variation this time. Within this personal, but social, history of literacy, a range of choices present themselves. From the standpoint of a social learning theory, risk is a relative, but clearly not an unaltered, attitude. The more evident constraints are to the language user, the less likely that language user will adopt an attitude of risk.

These understandings are crucial, since recent research suggests that reading and writing are risky businesses. Because of the limits of short-term memory, the mind in relation to text leads; the hand and eye follow. Planning is an integral part of both the reading and the writing process. Global intention propels the successful instances of the process and is the frame within which more specific planning takes place (Flower & Hayes, 1980; Kucer, 1982; Atwell, 1980; Shanklin, 1982).

Robert's text is a prime example of this phenomenon in writing (see Figure 10.1). In wanting to write *she could*, Robert wrote instead *should*, demonstrating that when his hand was writing *she*, his mind was running ahead. Because of this "mind-hand span," writing must be functional for all of us at "the point of utterance."

What is true for writing is also true for reading. Smith (1978) and Smith, Goodman, and Meredith (1978) argue quite powerfully that in order to decide what the left-hand portion of a sentence might mean, the reader already has to have decided what the right-hand portion of the sentence is likely to mean. More simply, the function which a word serves in an utterance is not inherent in the word but in its use. *White* is potentially anything: a noun (Mrs. *White*, the *white* of an egg, *whites* as opposed to blacks), an adjective (The *White* House, *white* electricity), a verb (as in *whiten* the picket fence, or *white out* the line of type). The reason not all options need to be explored by a reader in reading is that the context helps to establish intent and limit the available options.

Having established that: (1) risk is an integral part of the language process; (2) the process of risk-taking is constrained by the language

Figure 10.1. Story Writing (Robert, Age 9).

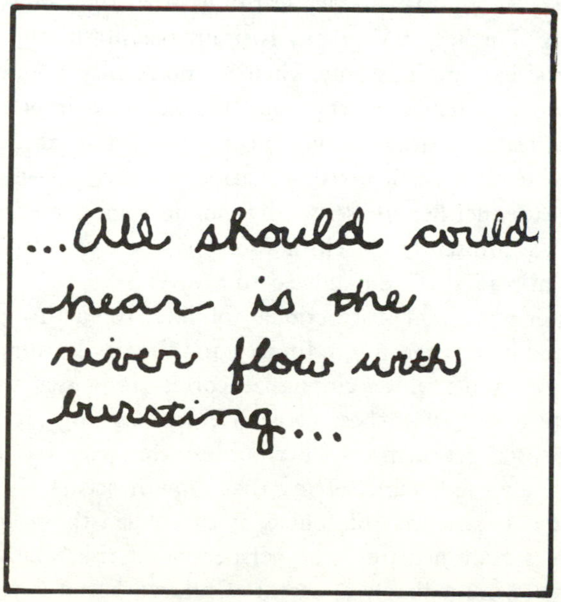

...All should could hear is the river flow with bursting...

user's personal-social history of literacy; and (3) there is nothing inherent in the process itself that leads language users to perceive writing and oral reading as more risky than other language engagements, what remains is to establish risk-taking as a central and universal strategy in literacy learning. While this insight is similar to the argument which establishes risk-taking as a central feature of the reading and writing process, it is different. The previous insight asserts that it is via the process of risk-taking that language learning and, hence, growth in literacy occurs.

Vygotsky (1978) probably argues this point the most cogently of anyone. He maintains that under known conditions the language user's responses are predictable and hence safe. Under such conditions, rather than learn new rules, what the language user is doing is confirming old rules. Only when things go wrong, that is, when the expected relationships or known rules do not hold, is the language user forced to develop new rules and new responses in order to cope. To live within existing rules and predictable patterns is not to grow. It is only under conditions in which all of the relationships are not known that language users must scamper to outgrow their current selves. In this process they identify new patterns and relationships and, in Vygotsky's terms, "become a head taller than their current selves."

The importance of these theoretical arguments for literacy learning should not go unnoticed. By penalizing the language user for engaging in risk-taking, teachers or would-be teachers potentially convince the language learner to play it safe or, worse yet, encourage nonengagement. Since one can only access the process through use, such settings mitigate against the very goal—literacy learning—that they are supposedly encouraging. Further, if Vygotsky is right, playing it safe is not an ideal learning situation. It is only when we don't play it safe that we can outgrow our current understanding. It is, then, neither a no-risk nor a high-risk learning situation which constitutes an ideal literacy learning setting, but rather a low-risk situation. In such an environment the language user neither guesses wildly, nor does not guess at all; rather, he or she finds himself or herself in a setting where calculated guesses and "what-I'm-ready-for" are allowed to evolve.

Counter to current instructional folklore, recent insights into risk-taking and its relationship to literacy and literacy learning suggest that literacy programs which emphasize correct responses and attempt to eliminate error fail to best serve literacy learning. It is only when language users get themselves in trouble within what was perceived to be a moderately predictable setting that growth occurs.

What is fascinating, of course, is that when the writing of young children is examined from the perspective of risk-taking, all of these insights are immediately apparent. Children 5 and 6 years of age are much more cautious about written language than are children 3 and 4 years of age. This is as true in reading as it is in writing.

The response times of 5- and 6-year-olds in reading environmental print, for example, are slower than the response times of 3- and 4-year olds (see Harste, Burke, Woodward, 1981). Figure 10.2 shows these data using three categories of response times: *Immediate*, defined as the normal pause of the language user; *Pause*, the normal rate of the language user plus a count of four to six; *Prolonged Pause*, the normal rate of the language user and a count of six or more. The older the child, the slower the response time. This is not because 5- and 6-year olds know less about written language, but because they know more.

Figure 10.2. Response Time to Environmental Print by Age.

Category Label	Age 3	Age 4	Age 5	Age 6
1. Immediate	98.3	96.6	90.2	87.6
2. Pause	0.9	2.9	6.7	6.9
3. Prolonged Pause	0.9	0.5	3.1	5.6

The more that is known, the more that must be taken into account. As any expert will report, knowing more about a topic than someone else is liberating in one sense, but constraining in another. The "expert" 5- and 6-year-old has had more language encounters and hence more opportunities to observe and note the orchestrated contextual, behavioral, affective, and linguistic demonstrations which constitute successful language use in the literacy event. While such encounters make them more realistic, they also make them more easily intimidated. With better and better clarification of all that must be orchestrated comes cognizance of others' inadequacies as well as one's own.

Nanci Vargus (1982), in reporting ethnographic data on her own children's growth toward literacy, recorded the following interchange between her younger (kindergarten) and older (first-grade) daughter, while the former was reading to the latter:

Becka: Abigail! The word is *fetch* not *get*.

Abigail: Yeah, well, *get* works.

Becka: That kind of reading is okay at home, but it doesn't work in school!

As the interchange between Becka and Abigail shows us, it is as easy to demonstrate and support notions of written language inadequacy as it is notions of written language literacy.

Rarely do language users at any level think of themselves as really prototypically ideal readers or writers. From our observations of readers and writers of all ages we conclude that rarely do language users stop reading a good selection because they feel there is nothing more to learn if they were to reread, nor do they stop rewriting their manuscripts because they believe them done. In both instances, language users stop because they've gone as far as they can and believe that continued engagement isn't worth the effort.

As authors, we will submit this manuscript not because it is done, but because right now it is what we can do. As readers, the more we get out of a book on our first reading, the more we are convinced that rereading the book a second time would be profitable. This poses a dilemma for the language user, a dilemma that can only be solved in a supportive environment—one where our understandings gained from reading are appreciated for what they currently are, not what they could become; one where our written attempts are appreciated for what they currently and boldly attempt to say, not what they might say if they had been better penned.

The hardest thing for any language user to appreciate who has had more opportunities to be present in a literary event than someone less fortunate is the other's literacy achievements. Older informants in our studies were always more sympathetic, more understanding, more impressed with the achievement of their younger siblings than were parents who seemed to be more ready for the next "stage" than for the one the child was currently in. Given the superordinate-subordinate relationship between would-be teacher and would-be learner, this language phenomenon needs to be both understood and anticipated or it results in the creation of settings not conducive to language learning.

When we look at the child's willingness to engage in our writing tasks what becomes clear is that with increasing experience comes an increased awareness of risk and a concomitant reluctance to engage in risk-taking. Three-year-olds never refused to participate in any writing experience we suggested; they were always game, although they discovered more about some writing tasks from their actual engagement in the writing event than they brought with them as stored information.

Four-year-olds were initially more reluctant, often asking, "You mean pretend to write?" This question demonstrates their understanding of the constraints that were operating in real instances of literacy of this sort, as well as their own sense of inadequacy in terms of these perceived demands. Pretending allowed them a way out of this dilemma. It permitted them to set aside the complex of constraints of which they were cognizant, constraints which suggested to them that they were unfit to engage in the event successfully. Pretending for them was an engagement strategy. It afforded them the opportunity to engage in activities they knew they were not ready for and, in the process, to demonstrate to themselves and to others that their sense of nonreadiness was all the readiness needed.

In contrast, the written responses of 5-year-olds and 6-year-olds are more cautious, more "I'll-live-within-your-world" strategic attempts at literacy learning. Whereas 3-year-olds would give us unhesitatingly a page of markings, and 4-year-olds a "pretend" but viable text attempt, 5- and 6-year-olds would give us an acceptable but safe surface text. While this is not immediately apparent in the graphic displays themselves, it is important to understand that 5- and 6-year-olds were orchestrating as many constraints—though a different set—as were 3- and 4-year-olds.

What their experience in school literacy settings had taught them was where to devote their selective attention. Being 5 and 6 they know that in this context—a school setting, working with individuals who look distinctively teacherlike and who were or seemed interested in distinctively teacherlike things, i.e., reading and writing—they were not to experiment, but rather to demonstrate what they had learned. The only thing they were sure they knew was what their teachers had taught them. Under these conditions, the results—a list of known words, a shortened rendition of a famous fairy tale—are not surprising.

From the perspective of risk, the 3- and 4-year-olds look like better, more aggressive language learners. They test much bolder hypotheses about how to make literacy fly (not how to get by), get themselves into more trouble, and in the end, given our measuring stick, are more

Figure 10.3. Axlacutted Story (Robert, Age 8).

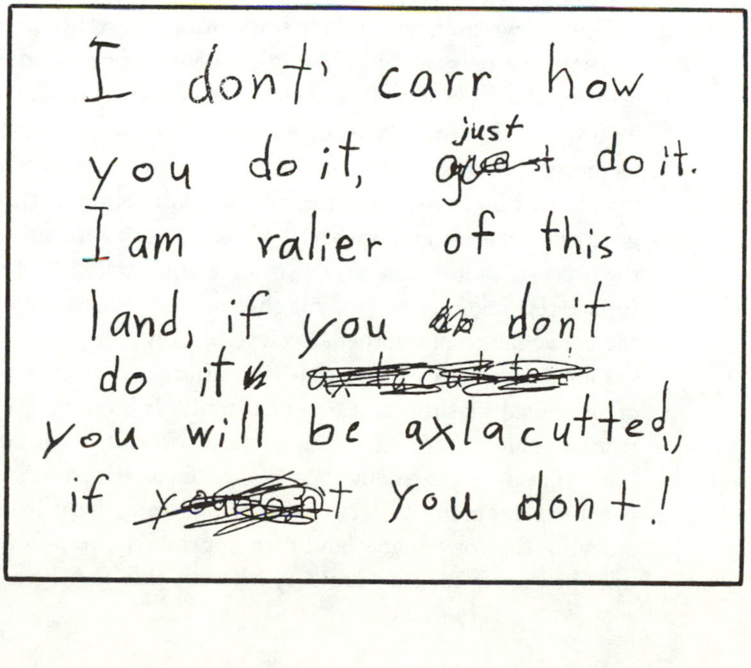

successful than their older, wiser, and more cautious literate friends.

It is important to understand that the vulnerability which 5- and 6-year-olds displayed is a learned vulnerability, not something inherent in the literacy process. If this were not the case, there would be no difference between the response patterns of 3- and 4-year-olds, and 5- and 6-year-olds. While constraints operate in any language setting, what our data confirm is that when awareness of constraints is heightened, the result is a decrease in the very risk-taking behaviors which are essential to literacy.

The centrality of risk-taking to literacy is best exemplified when we look at 8-year-old Robert's writing (see Figure 10.3). Robert has the king in his story talking: "I don't care how you do it, just do it. I'm ruler of this land, If you don't do it you will be axlacutted if you don't."

Notice Robert's first use of "axlacutted." Meaning is far out ahead. Robert initially writes "axlacutted" almost a whole line ahead of where he really wants it. The "mind-hand span" in writing is clearly demonstrated here and so, too, why writing at "the point of utterance" is, and must be, functional.

It is the writer's image of a unified "text world" in tension with the discontinuity of the evolving "surface text" (a tension noticed when the writer acts as reader) that causes a shift in the language user's psychological stance. Now the language user must look at language anew: analyze it, revise it, and move on. This "new look" is metalinguistic. In self-correction Robert has to take stock of what went wrong and more consciously apply what he knows about language as a tool. It is in the heat of orchestrating an evolving surface text to placehold an imagined text world that one's consciousness of language as a system is raised.

During writing, the writer's attention must be focused upon the creation of a text world—solving problems of unity and discontinuity between the "text world" and the "real world," creating and searching for unity within this fictionalized world. Given the limits of short-term memory, the writer—short of disengagement—has no other option than to accept a functional transcription. To worry about correct spelling and good grammar is to occupy short-term memory with surface text and, in the process, to lose "text." The more viable strategy is to placehold the surface text, no matter how roughly, and allow refinement to come via the convenience of another literacy, namely, reading.

Our data would suggest that the surface text transcription strategies of functional writing are learned naturally. It is only when dysfunctional strategies are suggested—such as those associated with error-free writing—that disengagement becomes the favored option and the unfortunate mode for many writers. Rather than live with the litter of literacy by enjoying the convenience and by accepting the responsibility for clean up, they never see, nor are they offered, this franchise.

Early Draft	Later Draft	Still Later Draft
Robert's crossed out "axlacutted" is not a pointed instance of *messed up* text but a semantic placeholder.	Robert's crossed out "axlacutted" is not a pointed instance of messed up text but a semantic placeholder.	Robert's revision serves a semantic placeholding function, which, while messing up the surface text, assures textual direction.

Figure 10.4. Writing as a Functional Process.

Equally important is the fact that in crossing out "axlacutted," Robert has placeheld where he wants to go, and can now selectively attend to how he might get there. Robert's revision serves a semantic placeholding function, which, while messing up the surface text, assures textual direction.

For adults under known and well-rehearsed writing conditions, it may be possible to produce what looks like error-free writing. Nonetheless the more unsure the adult is in a writing setting, the more functional will be the resulting written output. For both children and adults, there is simply too much to orchestrate initially to make correct writing the criterion of successful writing.

This position argues against automaticity. It's not the fact that lower, more fundamental processes have been mastered which allows us to selectively attend to text, but rather that having attended to text functionally, we can selectively afford the luxury of attending to essentially textually related matters like linearizing semantics and conventionalizing syntax and spelling.

In equivalently unfamiliar writing territory, the writing of children and adults looks decidedly similar (see Figure 10.4). We note, for example, our initial draft of an earlier portion of this manuscript and subsequent drafts, bearing in mind Robert's "axlacutted" behavior and the similarity involved.

Show us a safe writer and we'll show you someone who doesn't write much, often, or well (English teachers are prime but sensitive examples). By not rooting curriculum in the functional strategies which successful writers use, we convince children to abandon their more functional approach and lament the result, compliment them on writing achievements which do not merit comment, and fail to appreciate that what they have learned to orchestrate are our demands and not the process.

The first definition of "scribble" offered earlier by Harris & Hodges (1981) was "to write carelessly without attention to shape or legibility of letters, accuracy of spelling or grammatical correctness." If this definition holds, then our data suggest that all initial writings by all language users—both young and old—are scribbles. To the extent that scribbling is a strategy which allows language users to search for, find, and placehold text, it is an extremely functional one. To the extent that all initial engagements in literacy events are less than perfect, scribbling is not so much a stage as it is a universal characteristic of any language user's initial response. The only thing any of us can do in any instance of written language use is to scribble; that is, given our current level of understanding, to take our best shot.

Chapter 11
Social Action

It is argued that print in a culture generates alternate cognitive processes which, through use, become available to all members of the culture, including children.

THE YOUNG CHILD AS INFORMANT

Understanding that one stops at a Stop sign, attends very carefully to story details to be successful in the classroom, and eats at McDonald's is not something one learns by abstractly thinking about print, but by inferring relationships between print and the actions of other participating representatives of the culture. While language labels like words are arbitrary and abstract, the psycholinguistic and sociolinguistic actions they sign are concretely referred to a variety of experiences and encounters with language in use.

Alison, age 1.5, was told by her father to "close the door" which had been left open as the family entered the house after coming back from a shopping trip. Alison looked at her father and then at the door and then slowly made her way to the door and closed it. At age 1.5 Alison's productive abilities were very limited (by age 2, Alison's vocabulary contained two hundred words). While she could not have produced this sentence herself, her behavior demonstrates that she was already a language consumer and user.

Nathan, age 3, was shown a carton of Crest toothpaste and asked what it said. Nathan responded, "Brush teeth." To Nathan, C-R-E-S-T was not an abstract symbol, but a concrete index to a particular form of social action; namely, brushing teeth. Language, while arbitrary and abstract at one level, is a direct and concrete sign of psychological and sociological action when in use.

Tasha, age 3, was shown a box of Band-Aids and asked what she thought it said. Tasha responded, "Bandages . . . You're not suppose to stick them on the toilet." In talking with Tasha's mother about this incident we came to find out that Tasha had taken a box of Band-Aids and stuck them all over the stool in the

143

toilet in their bathroom one afternoon six months earlier. While the letters B-A-N-D A-I-D signed "Bandages" to Tasha, it also signed a particular form of social action which had a particular set of meanings to her, given her personal history of literacy regarding this object.

Nora, Saul, and Mara, age 9, were asked to read a selection together and at the end of each paragraph, say something to their neighbor about what they had read. Rather than talk about what the selection meant to them, Nora, Saul, and Mara asked teacherlike questions of each other at the end of each paragraph, checking each other's comprehension. While this strategy had been developed to support children in developing a more functional view of reading, what the opportunity to talk during reading signed to these children was questioning, the focus of their questions being on correct answers. These dysfunctional notions about reading were learned instructionally via the demonstrations which were made available to these children each time they read assigned selections in the classroom. Reading to them signs particular cognitive actions which in the end short-circuit their explorations of what real reading, as it relates to literacy, is all about.

Language is a socio-psycholinguistic process, not just a psycholinguistic one. While in the final analysis each language user must learn how to use language for him or herself, language learners are never psycholinguistically on their own. Psycholinguistic activities are sociologically available to language learners as they participate in a literacy event because they observe other language users engaged in the process. In a literate environment, identification of objects which are considered culturally significant signs (like written language), as well as what these signs signify in terms of psychological and sociological stances and actions, are available in the participatory activities and behaviors of others engaged in the event.

Heather, age 3, when shown various pieces of environmental print and asked what they said, would pick up the item and toss it across her shoulder, or put it to her lips and act like she was eating it, or do any number of things we initially found incomprehensible. In watching and rewatching our videotapes we discovered that, rather than answering our question, "What do you think this says?" Heather answered the question, "What things can you do with this?" From this vantage point her actions were logical and could be successfully read as signs for "throwing," "eating," "drinking," etc. For Heather, as for all of us, written language is something one does something with. An object is a sign signifying certain forms of physical action.

Leslie, age 4, was shown a carton of Crest toothpaste and asked what it said. He responded by chanting the names of the letters in Crest forwards and backwards and then by pronouncing its name:

"C-C-C-R-R-R-E-E-E-S-S-S-T-T-T-T-T-S-S-S-E-E-E-R-R-R-C-C-C, Crest."

Leslie demonstrates here that he can do several things with written language including naming the letters, saying the product's name, and later, when we ask him, "What other things do you know about this thing?" he knows that "You brush teeth with it." The word Crest directly signs a variety of social actions and permits a variety of psychological stances. To say that written language is abstract is to take only one stance in regard to it. In use, written language is concrete, indexing a whole range of certain social and psychological actions.

Alison, age 4, when shown the U.S. Mail logo and asked what it said, responded, "American picture sign."

When a sign function is established, that is, when an object is perceived as a sign which is interpretable as meaning, then an instance of literacy has occurred. Alison's fundamental understanding of literacy is readily apparent in her response as she tells us that she sees this object as a sign—"a picture sign"— signifying American.

Sometimes we seem to forget that language is, by its very nature, social. Not only do writers assume there are readers and speakers assume there are listeners, but interaction with real or supposed social others involving all of the expressions of language is an integral part of any instance of the language and language learning process. This position suggests that how one learns written language is not different from how one learns oral language. Further, it suggests that how we made our most recent written language discovery was not different from how we learned our first. These insights fly in the face of much past thinking in the field. The discussion which follows elaborates this position and the thinking and experiences which have led us to reformulate and challenge how language is conceived of within the structure of knowledge and knowing. We are much indebted to Professor Robert F. Carey for his assistance in helping us think through our data in this way.

INTERDISCIPLINARY VIEWS

Language can be and has been studied in a variety of ways. Linguistically, language is studied as a rule-governed system. Psycholinguistically, language is studied as a form of mediated, rule-governed behavior. Socio-psycholinguistically, language is studied as a form of mediated, rule-governed, social action. Not only does each of these postures give us an alternative perspective on language, but each perspective—moving from a linguistic perspective to a psycholinguistic perspective to a socio-psycholinguistic perspective—is more encompassing than the former.

Socio-psycholinguistically, language is a context specific event. In order to understand the cognitive and linguistic operations that take place in language learning and use, one must study these operations in light of the contexts—situational and cultural—in which that cognitive and linguistic processing occurs.

Language researchers such as Firth (1935) have argued that meaning must not be regarded as either a fixed mental relation or a historical process. In attempting to translate a tribal language into English, Malinowski (1923) found that direct translation was not adequate. In order to really interpret a tribal language, knowledge of the situation in which the language was used was required, as well as of the role language played in the communicative event as opposed to other communication systems; the relationship between the individuals involved and how such individuals responded to each other in that culture; and a sense of the activity being performed. He coined the term "context of situation" to describe the transactions which occur between text and context during the process of languaging. Richards (1925, 1936) extended this notion to the field of rhetoric arguing that writing cannot be arbitrarily judged as good or bad. Such judgments must rest on knowledge of the task and the writer's intent.

More recently Halliday (1975, 1978) has studied children's early oral language development in terms of language use in natural situations. He believes that children "learn how to mean" by learning the functions language serves in use.

When we seated sixty-eight 3- 4- 5- and 6-year-old children, one at a time, in front of paper and pen and asked them to write, it is of significance to note that all of them picked up the pen and made marks on paper when requested to do so. Not a single informant got up and closed the door, stuck the pencil in the knot-hole on the table, or did 101 other things which we might deem behaviors unrelated to the request. All picked up the pen and made marks on paper.

What this observation means socio-psycholinguistically is that all of these children saw writing as a legitimate form of social action. By their performance, children in our study—inner-city as well as suburban— demonstrated that they already understood that given certain kinds of oral requests, the making of little black marks on a piece of paper was not only culturally acceptable, but culturally expected.

Our conclusion is that by the age of 3, children demonstrate a personal as well as a social history of literacy. The single act of putting pen to paper when requested to write, repeated as it was across sixty-eight children in our Bloomington and Indianapolis studies, and within the group of children across various writing tasks, tells any observer—

including a hypothetical man from Mars—that the children being observed came from a culture in which making marks on paper is an accepted and important form of social behavior. Their behavior demonstrates that they had not only been present in language settings where this behavior had occurred, but that, by 3 years of age, they had abstracted out of such experiences some personal significance, and within this frame had gone on to learn their cultural lesson.

To make this observation, however, is not enough since it fails to clarify how this important language learning occurred. Working from the premise that it was the child's presence at past encounters through which such understandings were learned, Mary Hill (1980, 1982), one of the early members of our research team, has recently conducted her own follow-up studies. In her current work she has set up a multiage group situation in which three children, ages 4, 4, and 2-½, are asked to write stories and to engage in written conversation. Watching the 2-½-year-old on the first of these videotapes is fascinating. Initially, the child does not have a very clear notion of what to do. Watching the other children grab paper and pencil, however, she follows suit. From here on, while she makes marks on her paper, her rapt attention is upon the other children. Her stance is as observer, but as active observer. It is not so much her direct physical participation in the experience as her presence at the encounter which allows her to sort out what is happening and its significance. The importance of these data lies in the fact that they begin to help us clarify the difference between a language encounter and a language experience, to appreciate such a difference, and to value both as significant language learning events.

What was demonstrated to Annika, the 2-½-year-old, among other things, was that writing is a culturally acceptable form of social action. Additionally, the setting demonstrated to her not only what one uses pencils for, but also, whether she needed it or not, what pencils do, what purpose paper serves, how one uses both in conjunction with an oral request to write, how such activities allow exploration of the world, how such events allow participants to share their worlds, and how one's presence allows and affords not only social action, but social interaction. From a single quality written language encounter, this videotape demonstrates that the young child learns a great deal. Clearly from this moment on, embedded within her notions of paper and pencil are what paper and pencils do.

Eleanor Gibson (1976) talks about children's perceptions of chairs as affording "sitting," cars as affording "driving," tricycles as affording "riding." While such characteristics are seemingly not inherent in the objects themselves, it is the child's presence in such settings which permits the child to abstract out key social forms of action. Annika teaches us that the same process holds in writing and reading.

Language in one sense is never abstract. Embedded in the concept *dog* is what dogs afford: friendship, petting, messes, puddles, trouble. *McDonald's* is not an abstract set of symbols in one sense, but an iconic potential having features indexical to psychological and social action (Carey & Harste, 1982). Language as a sign does not directly point to inherent qualities, but rather, suggests interesting modes of psychological and social action which might be taken by the language user. The plus (+) and minus (−) signs of mathematics are analogous to how language operates more generally. Looking at a plus or minus sign we know what we are to do—what cognitive operations to perform. While we can say the terms' "names," at this level we miss the psychological and sociological forms of action directly signed by these symbols. When we see M-C-D-O-N-A-L-D-S we can say "McDonald's," but more importantly *McDonald's* indexes as the iconic territory of what we can do there.

*Figure 11.1. A Semiotic Theory
of Content.*

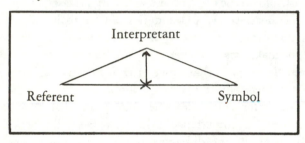

The semiotic study of content (Richards, 1923; Peirce, 1931–58) is often depicted in the form of a triangle in which an arbitrary cultural relationship has been established between the word (symbol), the object (referent), and the meaning (interpretant). The sign is the set of relationships that exist between symbol, referent, and interpretant (see Figure 11.1). When all of the relationships between symbol, referent, and interpretant have been made, that is, when the sign function has been established, literacy can be said to occur. In this chapter we use "sign" to mean "sign function" and all instances of its use should be read as such.

According to the theory of semiotics, there are different kinds of signs. A weather vane is "indexical" as is a knock on the door; one indexes the direction of the wind, the other someone's presence. A map is "iconic" because it represents the actual item it references. Language is "symbolic," meaning arbitrary; "dog" stands for *dog* not indexically or iconically, but by cultural fiat. Because of its grammar, some semioticians refer to language as a "legisign" (Thomas, 1977), though for now we will not concern ourselves with this distinction. The theory of semiotics further suggests that the order of sign development is from index to icon to symbol. Though there can be signs which are symbolic icons and iconic symbols, language in use is conceived of as being symbolic and hence abstract (Carey, 1982).

Semiotics provides us with a powerful perspective, but our data would refute the notion that semiotic order moves from index to icon to symbol. Language, at base, is iconic. While language as a mediated form of behavior allows us to stand back and reflect on it as a system, thus permitting us to perceive language as symbolic, this is a metalinguistic stance; in use, language is iconic and as such indexical to psychological and social forms of action (Carey & Harste, 1982).

Band-Aid signed for one of our informants, "Put it on your owie," and "You're not suppose to stick them on the toilet," two forms of social action. U.S. Mail signed for one of our informants, "American picture sign"; the beauty of the response is that it captures in verbal form the nature of the iconic image which U.S. Mail mentally generated. While often children might have difficulty verbalizing what they thought a given item of print might say, few had difficulty, if they had even encountered the print previously, in telling what one did with it socially. "Brush Teeth" for Crest, "Drink It" for Coca-Cola, "Eat It" for Jell-O, all are early social action response forms made possible through an iconic response to print.

Seeing language—both oral and written—as simultaneously indexical, iconic, and symbolic, depending on psychological stance, explains why written language cannot be seen as some more abstract, second-order kind of cognitive processing which is laid upon oral language. Further, it suggests that sign functions can be established with written language at a personal level as well as at a social level, and that social language artifacts, like convention, cannot be equated with literacy or the literacy process, which by this view entails establishment of the sign function.

The child who repeatedly uses a dot to placehold his name (Hill, 1980), is, in so doing, demonstrating a real access to the literacy process. He has a symbol (the dot), an object (himself), and an interpretant (signification). The fact that over time he moves to represent his name using the symbol H and later the symbol HANK is evidence of cultural refinement of this process but not of cultural access; this was demonstrated much earlier. His election, one day, to write his name as HAK because "the N is giving me too much trouble" may be a fine-tuning of a personal and cultural literacy decision, but even his personal sign, HAK, has a host of cultural entailments.

The child who at 2 uses "du' ba" for "I want toast and jelly" (Halliday, 1975) and the family who semantically track and respond, despite the surface-structure form of what has gone on, are engaged in the real literacy process, not some pseudo form of it.

Access to the mother tongue is a culturally predictable form of social action given the child's presence in what are likely to be available language settings, but such access does not constitute the onset of literacy; that has occurred long before.

Picking up a pen to write when requested to do so is not only a form of social action then, but a form of social action mediated through and with language. The significance of this event is that it provides evidence that the oral request acted as a sign, and that, given the child's written response, a sign function had been established. Literacy is both a product and a process. Since it is product, to focus on surface structure form—be it convention or scribble—is to miss the literacy process, or in this instance, the social and socializing action.

Chapter 12
Context

The language process does not function unless or until a language user imposes context. To fail to contextualize is to fail to understand. There is no such thing as decontextualized print. Linguistic signs exist only in a social cognitive setting.

THE CHILD AS INFORMANT

Situational context is not something one can consider or not consider in language—it is not a "variable," but an integral part of the linguistic sign.

Joe, age 9, was shown a Stop sign with the word Ban *written on it as part of our efforts to further explore the linguistic sign as formed by the relationship of print in context. We had found this particular Stop sign in a magazine advertising* Ban Underarm Deodorant. *In the context of the magazine advertisement the message was clear: "Ban stops wetness." By clever cutting, we were able to remove all other print and so managed to save the octagonal shape with the word* Ban *on it. We showed this print setting to Joe, a neighbor child, who not only knew of our interest in studying young children's growth in reading and writing, but also knew us and our research quite well. Interrupting his play we asked, "Joe, what do you think this says?" Joe paused a moment and said, "I suppose it says 'Stop' in German or something; that's just the kind of junk you'd carry around to pull out and ask unsuspecting kids about!"*

In addition to his humor, Joe taught us more about reading than our assumptive experiment could have rightfully hoped to teach us. Joe's response demonstrates not only his awareness of print, but more specifically, of the relationship of print and context as the signing element in reading. We can speculate that the print in the context of the red octagonal shape suggested that the message should say "Stop." That this print-context relationship is somewhat unpredictable is evident in Joe's response: "I suppose it says 'Stop' in German or something." But this isn't the only print-context relationship which Joe reads. He also reads the print-context that operates between the print in its octagonal shape and us. He tells us

151

that this second print-context relationship confirms his first prediction: "That's just the kind of junk you'd carry around to pull out and ask unsuspecting kids about!" Print clearly played a role in Joe's orchestrated decisions, not, however, as an isolated cue, but as part of a complex of cues which form a sign in a semiotic sense. Print doesn't sign meaning; print in relationship to its context— in this case its contexts—signs meaning. When we remove the road sign from the magazine, we change not only its signing potential, but its meaning potential. In the context of the magazine, this print setting meant one thing; in our hands it meant something quite different.

Ian, age 3, was shown a carton of Crest toothpaste on which we had whited out the print to see if a 3-year-old's reading responses would be different under this condition than they were under the normal condition we had previously used in this research task. To our question, "What do you think this says?" Ian responded, "Well, it should say 'toothpaste,' but you took the print off!"

In contrast to the responses we received when the print was present—"Toothpaste," "Crest," "Cavities," "Aim," "Toothbrush," "Brush Teeth"—Ian's response is qualified, demonstrating that the absence of print in this setting was a sign in itself which was noted and had to be addressed. The linguistic sign is formed by print in context. Even if young children's responses bear no direct phonemic-graphemic match, Ian teaches us that we cannot conclude that print is not involved in the forming of the response. When the print is removed, the nature of the child's response to print changes drastically—from "Toothpaste" to "Well, it should say 'toothpaste,' but you took the print off!"

Embedded in text is context. The contextual rules of language use reflect themselves in the semantic, syntactic, and graphophonemic systems of language. Since context is embedded in language, it is also signed in that part of language we call print. In its function as a contextualized surface text, language signs psycholinguistically a potential range of interpretive procedures which we might employ.

Joshua, age 3, loved to have books read to him. Since we know he is the son of a student studying for the ministry, the "Amen" he said at the end of each and every book read to him is understandable.

Noah, age 6, was asked in his first-grade classroom to complete a series of worksheets designed to give children practice in visual discrimination between the letters of the alphabet. Each line on each worksheet focused on a different letter. The first line on the first worksheet focused on the letter t. *Along with this letter was a picture of a tulip and the word* tulip *written out with the* t *circled. Adjacent to this picture were a series of words like* table, melt, plant, town, tiger, rabbit, *etc.; the children were to look at them, find the* t's *and circle them.*

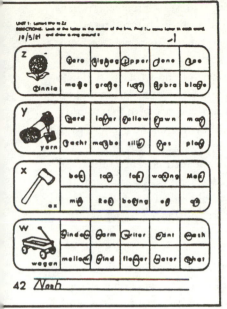

UNIT 1: Lesson the to Zz
DIRECTIONS: Look at the letter in the corner of the box. Find the same letter in each word and draw a ring around it.

10/3/84

z					
zinnia	zero	zigzag	zipper	zone	zoo
	maze	graze	fuzz	zebra	blaze
y					
yarn	yard	layer	yellow	yawn	may
	yacht	maybe	silly	eye	play
x					
ox	box	tax	fox	waxing	Max
	mix	Rex	boxing	ox	ax
w					
wagon	window	warm	writer	want	wash
	mellow	wind	flower	water	what

42 Noah

Deshonna

DeShoNNA Love LioPS
I Like To Do The Thin
for You.

This is Deshonna ~~~~~~
DEShoNNA is jirg roig

Despite the fact that Noah did the first set together with the class, when he went to work on his own, rather than just circle the s's, Noah circled all the s's, c's, i's, o's, and r's he found in the words sister, desk, base, socks, sun, safe, sunset, snow, etc., since all of these letters were used in spelling the word scissors. He followed this procedure for the entire worksheet, and since the teacher never discovered the rule upon which he was operating, his worksheet was graded unsatisfactory. The teacher's written comment on the top of his worksheet, "You weren't concentrating," was more of a reflection on her, than on Noah's performance. One week later, however, Noah, got a new worksheet covering the letters z, y, x, and w (in that order). This time he had no trouble doing the exercise. For zinnia he circled only the z's in the words zero, zigzag, zipper, zone, zoo, maze, graze, fuzz, zebra, glaze, etc.

We must ask ourselves what Noah learned about reading from this experience, however. We must conclude, "nothing," although he learned a great deal about "reading instruction." Given his initial performance, Noah could already visually discriminate between the letters of the alphabet or he wouldn't have made the "mistakes" he did. Rather than expanding his capacity for language, Noah learned how to limit and channel his thinking to be successful in literacy events of this sort. Rather than reflecting his cognitive abilities or literacy potential, Noah's thinking processes are an artifact of the instructional setting in which we find him.

Deshonna, age 6, was asked to write under a number of conditions. When asked to write her name and anything else she could write, Deshonna wrote her name and then drew a picture of herself, a pumpkin, and a Christmas tree. When asked to write a story, Deshonna decided to do a personal narrative piece of writing: "This is Deshonna. Deshonna is jumping rope." In rereading, she decided to cross out her first line, so her final text was a single written line: DESHONNA IS JIRG ROIG. When asked to write a letter, Deshonna wrote, "Deshonna. Love Linda. I like to do things for you," written as DESHONNA LOVE LIODS I LIKE TO DO THE THIR FOR YOU. Under two writing conditions Deshonna elected to write; under one writing condition Deshonna elected to draw. If we had only collected writing data under the write-anything-you-can-write condition, we might have erroneously concluded that the only thing Deshonna could write was her name. We would have missed discovering that Deshonna knows how to produce an appropriate text for an appropriate context (her letter sounds like a letter; her story sounds like a story), knows her communicative options in terms of placeholding her text (the decision to use an alternate communication system is our decision also), and has a growing knowledge of directionality, letter-sound correspondence, wordness, sentenceness, and more.

The word "context" contains the word "text." Psycholinguistically and sociolinguistically language is always whole. This is as true of the language of classrooms as it is of the language of research reports. When a teacher writes the letter *l* on the blackboard and the children respond, "la-, lion, ladder, lady," as they did in one setting in which we were observing, the rules of language use in this setting dictate the semantic rules which allow the children to make sense of the situations. They know enough to make the initial sound of the letter in isolation and to follow this activity by thinking of three words that start with that sound. The context of situation further specifies the syntax of the event. From past experience they know the order of things to do after the teacher has written the isolated letter on the board. Even further, the context of situation specifies what graphophonemic associations they are to make. Despite the surface structure, this is a whole instance of language. Language is always whole in this and other instances in which the syntactic and semantic rules are also embedded in, and hence signed in, oral or written language.

Because of the relationship between text and context, finding a newspaper in a classroom as opposed to finding a newspaper on the steps leading to his house can sign widely different psycholinguistic and sociolinguistic activities to the same language user. Since both language and classrooms are inherently social, classrooms have the potential to be qualitatively natural language learning environments in which quantitatively multiple opportunities for engagements in natural language learning circumstances could be increased. The protocol examples and discussion which follow extend and elaborate these ideas.

INTERDISCIPLINARY VIEWS

Probably no word in the modern history of language is more maligned than the term *context*. We know researchers who say they are "studying context" when what in fact they are studying are three- and four-word syntactic strings. Some of our reading teacher colleagues refer to helping students read by using "context cues," meaning for the most part the syntactic and semantic cues which reside in the immediate line of print. The fact that they have stripped the line of print from its textual and situational support to teach "context cues" never seems to give them a moment of concern.

Just as teaching is too good a term to be reduced to some narrow reductionistic stimulus-response framework, so "context" and "research on context" is too important to our understanding of language and language learning to be lost in reductionistic research and practice.

While some might wish to label researchers and theorists who perceive context beyond four-word syntactic strings as "radical contextualists," recent work in this area would suggest that contextual studies at these levels are eminently more helpful in our attempt to understand literacy than are reductionistic efforts which do more to confuse the issue than to clarify it.

We use the term *context* to refer to the linguistic, situational, and cultural milieu of language in use. Key dimensions of this context have been described by Halliday (1978) as field (what's happening), tenor (the relationship of the parties involved), and mode (the channel of communication used, with specific reference to the role language plays in the overall communicative event).

From past encounters with language in a particular context of situation, language users bring with them an anticipatory frame for how language works in this particular context. This anticipatory frame has been termed *register* by sociolinguistics like Halliday (1978) and Hymes (1967, 1972). While Cicourel (1974) would not deny that on one level register is an anticipatory frame, he would vehemently hold that the specific register of a language event evolves throughout the event via application of interpretive procedures by the language participants involved. Cicourel's insight is an important one as it suggests that register is not totally formulaic, but changing, a construct helpful in understanding how what was supposedly an informal meeting suddenly turned into a formal interchange, sometimes even to the chagrin of the participants involved.

Cicourel's work on interpretive procedures (1974) and Grice's work explicating the cooperative principle of language use (1975) do much to explain general registers which language users bring to a languaging event. While at present researchers do not know what all of these interpretive procedures are, Cicourel's list includes: (1) reciprocity of perspectives (language users assume there is no difference between how they and their participants assign meaning); (2) et cetera assumptions (language users assume their participants will fill in common details); (3) normal forms (language users attempt to interpret anything ambiguous by making restatements of ambiguity congruent with the other forms used); (4) retrospective-prospective sense of occurrence (language users will attempt to see if ambiguities are clarified later on, or if this is not possible, attempt to clarify them in light of previous statements); (5) the reflexive nature of language (language users will use the specialized vocabulary selected by their participants as clues to how something is to be interpreted).

Additionally, Grice (1975) has identified what he calls the "cooperative principle" of language. There are four maxims to the cooperative principle that can be interpreted as underlying assumptions within which language participants operate. These are maxims of (1) *Quantity* (say or write enough but not too much), (2) *Quality* (say or write what you believe is true and provide evidence); (3) *Relation* (say or write what is relevant); and (4) *Ambiguity* (say or write to avoid obscurity, i.e., be logical). Because language users know that other cultural participants understand these maxims, meaning can be and is signed through what Grice calls "implicature," or the deliberate breaking of these rules.

Within these general frames, specific registers for language events develop. Recent work by Hasan (Halliday & Hasan, 1980), for example, begins to explicate the register language participants have in shopping at the "Greengrocer," an equivalent probably to a family-owned neighborhood food store. As Cicourel (1974) and Corsaro (1980) point out, however, not only do language participants bring with them an anticipatory frame relative to their past readings of field, mode, and tenor in this and similar language settings, but refinement of the register takes place via the language user's ongoing reading of field, mode, and tenor during the languaging event itself. Thus register is not a static concept but an ever-evolving one. This notion is theoretically important since it suggests the value experience plays in language learning.

When one examines young children's responses for evidence of context, one is immediately impressed with the young child's sensitivity to language variation and change. An example typical of our data is Zach. In the following dictated story (see Figure 12.1), the corrections that Zach initiated in his rereading indicate an understanding of the functional differences between an oral story (his dictated version) and a written story (his miscued version). "There are *planes*" is an oral language form. "They are *airplanes*" is the more formal written language form and reflects Zach's knowledge of how written language texts differ from oral language texts. "*They're* having a dog fight" is an oral language form; "*They are* having a dog fight," the more formal written language form.

*Figure 12.1. Dictated Language
Experience Story & First
Reading (Zach, Age 6).*

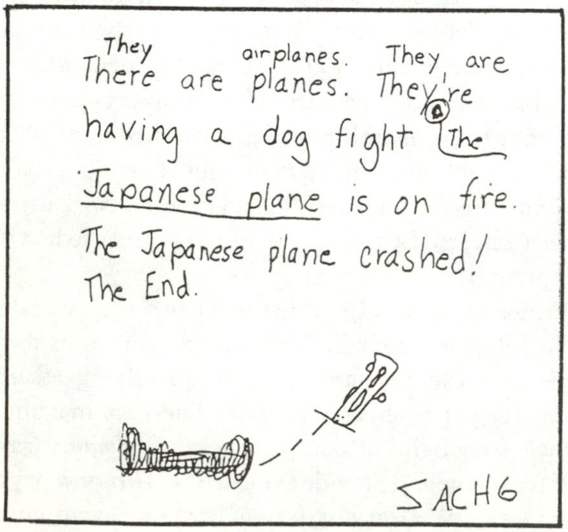

Key:

They

There = substituted *they* for *there* when reading.

a = repeated phrase in reading.

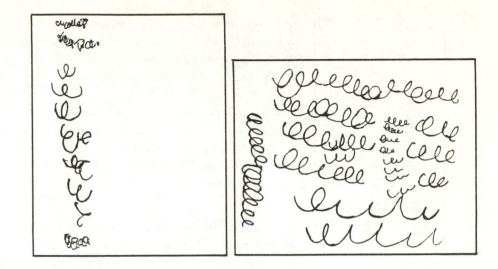

Figure 12.2. Uninterrupted Writing: Shopping List & Story (Hannah, Age 3).

Theoretically we might say that Zach's behavior demonstrates that he had already developed one register for oral story forms and another register for written story forms. In each of these instances, Zach's reading of elements within the context of situation helped him bring to memory past registers which he saw as appropriate. Operating within a general anticipatory frame (which included his understanding of the interpretive procedures of language, the cooperative principle, and these past registers), Zach's particular reading of the field, mode, and tenor of the alternate contexts, which were available under a condition of oral story dictation as opposed to oral reading, allowed him to make particular shifts in register which reflect themselves in text.

Embedded in text is context. The reason all of us can successfully answer questions like: (1) Where are you likely to find this instance of language? (Field); (2) Is it oral or written language? (Mode); and (3) For whom and by whom is it produced? (Tenor), for language fragments such as "On your marks," "From here take the path north," and "Raise your hands please," is that embedded and hence signed in text are the register shifts reflective of and appropriate to context.

Shifts in register allow language users to produce appropriate texts for appropriate contexts. Zach has, via shifts in register, produced an oral language text (his dictated story) and a written language text (his reading). These are not alterations in form so much as different texts. Zach is a kindergarten child about to enter first grade. His subtle understanding of language is truly impressive.

Figure 12.2 presents a shopping list and a story which Hannah, age 3, has produced. We challenge our readers to identify which is which. What Hannah demonstrates is that the linguistic understandings we

Figure 12.3. Uninterrupted Story Writing Samples (Alison, Age 5).

Figure 12.4. Uninterrupted Story Writing Samples (Alison, Age 5.6).

have been discussing are not added onto language after some more elementary forms are learned, but rather are essential understandings underlying access to the literacy process. Nancy Shanklin (1982) expresses this insight more formally:

Thus, language has no real meaning separate from the environment, i.e., the context of situation in which it is used; therefore it would seem that language and the nature of schematas are intrinsically related to the context of situation in which they occur.

Because of the extensiveness of our research program we had ample opportunity to study and discover for ourselves the importance of context and its relation to understanding and to researching the evolution of literacy. Alison's writing at home and at school provides an illuminating first instance.

Mary Hill used Alison as a subject in her longitudinal study of young children's evolution in writing (1978, 1980). At around 5 years of age, Alison's stories took on a familiar pattern, which Mary readily accepted (see Figure 12.3). Alison continued to use this pattern even though at home she wrote using an alphabetic script. At home, on the very day that Alison had produced the second sample in Figure 12.3 for Mary, in response to the suggestion that she write about "What makes you happy," on a finger puppet she had cut out from paper, Alison wrote MN I C FLOMRS ("When I see flowers").

She moved so rapidly from a placeholding script to alphabetic script that we were stunned and forewarned Mary that she was in for a surprise on her next data collection day.

But alas for Mary, Alison continued to write stories as she had in the past (see Figure 12.4). This occurred not once, but over several ensuing weeks. What had worked in the past became the register of the present. For each context Alison had developed an appropriate register. Alison knew and understood the constraints that were operating in both settings. She knew that Mary accepted her stories, and while this did not stop her from messing around with a sure thing, as we'll show later, moving from a placeholding script to an alphabetic script was not one of the things she elected to do in this setting.

During the early years of this research effort, we, like many of our colleagues, became quite fascinated with "invented spelling" as a product documenting the rule-governed nature of the young child's approach to literacy. At the age when we expected such a move to occur for Alison, we obviously, though not purposely, communicated this expectancy. Alison, at 5.6, obliged, although equally obviously she saw no reason, in settings where other constraints were operating, to test this particular set of hypotheses in this form.

While such sensitivity to context may initially surprise us, given the fact that semioticians have documented (Sebeok, 1977) that Hans, a horse, was reading the pupil dilations in his master's eyes in order to know when to stop tapping out the answers to addition problems—the Clever Hans Phenomenon—we should have no trouble believing a child even more sensitive to context. What seems surprising from one theoretical position about language looks eminently predictable from another.

From a research perspective, the importance of this experience lies in the fact that it clearly illustrates the difference between a psycholinguistic and a socio-psycholinguistic view of language use and learning. All language settings are not equal. To continue to collect developmental data with a blatant disregard for context can in the end only confuse us and do a disservice to children. Even Piaget's developmental statements, Margaret Donaldson teaches us (1978), merit close review. As educators, we know that statements emanating from such research all too often become the unexamined and assumptive frameworks of instruction. Language varies for each of us by situational context, and while we intuitively know this, it takes a sensitive observation of children and their writings for us to rediscover the applicability of this principle to written language learning and instruction.

How language use varies across instructional contexts is a contextual issue which enlarges our very notion of what is basic in literacy and literacy learning. Our Indianapolis sample of inner-city informants came from a single geographical area which included several preschools and elementary schools. Within particular age levels we had children, then, with distinct school writing histories. Because we collected our videotapes on site—though in special rooms set up solely for data collection purposes—and because, we suppose, we looked like teachers, often the constraints that operated in the classroom writing context became assumptive constraints operating in our research task.

In one particular school, children were taught to write in columns on lined school paper, a practice done, according to the teachers we interviewed, "to help them in forming their letters and in learning the difference between letters and words."

As shown in Figure 12.5, even in our letter writing task, first graders from this school maintained this writing form.

That this is clearly something learned in first grade in this school is evident when one examines the letters which kindergarten children in the same school produced. As shown in Figure 12.6, Sally's and Alpha's letters show no such constraint on form.

In School B, no such formatting criteria had been taught. Though the quality of the letters remains much the same (see Figure 12.7), indicat-

Figure 12.5. School A: First Grade Letter Writing Samples (Alanna, Natasha, LaShell).

FoRM Sally
I LIKMcRL
AnD L You

Dear Crryairr Nar
yrr Ysar AlPLoy
LIG Lrry SiSeM
SaYa

Figure 12.6. School A: Kindergarten Letter Writing Samples (Sally, Alpha).

Figure 12.7. School B: First Grade Writing Samples (Jake, Vincent, Chris).

ing, as we will show later, a commonality of other constraints operating across both settings, this formatting constraint is not one of them.

Of particular interest also is the fact that once a certain constraint was in effect, it seemed to affect other decisions which the children made. We note, for example, that the first graders' letters collected from School A are qualitatively different from the letters collected from School B. By contrast, the first graders' letters from School B seem much more well formed than do the first graders' letters from School A. In School A, the first graders seem to have taken Cicourel's interpretive procedure—the et cetera assumption—much too literally, not bothering to sign letterness via an opening, a closing, or for that matter, even a respectable amount of redundancy.

This phenomenon is particularly important, especially in light of the fact that kindergarten children in the same school do not seem to suffer from an "et cetera deficit." We note, for example, that the letters from kindergarteners in School A look more like the letters from first graders in School B than they look like the first-grade letters from their older and wiser peers in the same school.

What this phonemenon suggests is the notion of transaction. Constraints are not additive, leaving everything else the same, but transactive, altering the total composition of the event. Shanklin (1982) uses the metaphor of putting a drop of red dye in a beaker of water to discuss the notion of transaction. By establishing formatting constraints, first-grade children's knowledge of the personal letter form, as well as their handling of "exophoria"—text-context embeddedness—changes.

Probably the first graders in School A assume that if their teachers are so concerned about the shape and form of letters and words that they give explicit instructions, then each additional entry the children write, even when and if they have better linguistic information at their disposal, adds risks which are unnecessary, especially if the teacher's concerns are on quality of penmanship, not quality of writing. A second possibility also exists, that by accenting any particular constraint, attention and short-term memory are filled, making access and testing of other lin-

guistic hypotheses unlikely. Both of these effects seem deleterious to the evolution of literacy.

It should be noted that what is highlighted in these examples is the transactional effects of imposed constraints on language learning. Although from a language learning perspective we may or may not approve of imposing such constraints, regardless of our stance, the fact remains that a viable model of literacy must be able to explain both more productive and less productive instances of language learning.

Given the pervasive effects an imposed constraint dealing with something as simple as format can have on the writing process, we must predict that this effect will only be compounded as more writing contraints are added by the first-grade teachers in School A. Alison, who we can document (Harste & Burke, 1980) had been a written language user and producer from the age of 3, entered a very skills-centered first-grade reading and writing program. Despite the fact that she had been writing for years, by November, when requested to write at home, she announced amid tears, "But I can't write anymore!"

The compounded effects of form and spelling constraints at school had convinced her that all she had learned was somehow not useful, or, worse yet, wrong. While we very rapidly moved her beyond this moment of doubt by assuring her that she had been writing for years and that we could read anything she wrote, clearly, the effect of suddenly imposing constraints on the young child as writer in less supportive environments merits a full-scale investigation. We used to think that if children were off to a good start in literacy they could withstand any negative school experience. We don't think so any more.

That such effects need not be the outcome of instruction when constraints are allowed to develop naturally over time is best illustrated when letter writing across time is studied. Nanci Vargus (1982), one of the later members of our research team, corresponded with a group of first graders over the course of a semester. The in-depth study of how these children's letters changed over the course of the semester became the focus of her dissertation.

In comparing the letters we received from first graders (Figures 12.5 and 12.7) with the first letters which Nanci received, we see many similarities. As is illustrated in these examples, some letters seem long on form and short on context (LaShell & Vincent). Most deal with a single topic (Alanna, LaShell, Jake, Vincent, Chris), answer questions directly, assuming a continuity of context across what we see as events (see Alanna's "Cut and paste and go outside" in answer to the question, "What things do you like to do in school?"), and communicate little new information.

While the first letters which Nanci received look a lot like the letters we received, the changes over time which occurred as result of her

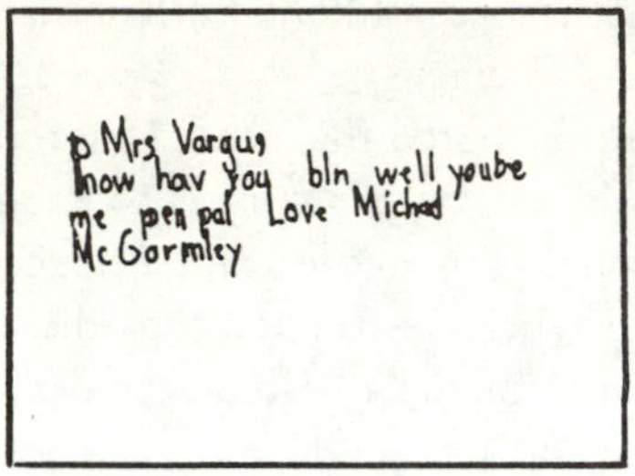

to Mrs. Vargus

*How have you been?
Will you be my pen pal?*

    Love Michael McGormley

*Dear Mrs. Vargus,
My puppy is getting big.
I will not be here when
school is out. I will be
in California. I will be
in a lot of places. I will
go on a roller coaster.*

    *Love
    Michael*

*Figure 12.8. Michael's First
and Ninth Letters (Vargus,
1982).*

continuing correspondence are impressive. Michael's first and ninth
letters are illustrative (see Figure 12.8). The letters become longer and
they show topic expansion and shift in responsibility. Children no longer
take refuge in ritualistic form and the answering of questions posed by
their correspondent, but take ownership and responsibility for generating and communicating new information.

The importance of these data is that they clearly demonstrate how
register evolves and changes over time. While first-grade children in our
study and Vargus's demonstrated that they had a particular register for
letter writing even in their first letters, what continued involvement
permitted was register expansion and exploration. Their letters seem to
move from high on form to high on content; yet, given the circumstances surrounding their first letters—to a stranger whom they barely
know—it should not surprise us that they have little to say, or little basis
other than the letter they have just received on which to make decisions
about what to say. What looks like a deficit is more a statement assessing
their perception of our research context than it is a comment on their
capabilities as young writers.

Theoretically, we might say that when language users are thrust into
an unfamiliar context they take refuge in those past registers which
provide the closest fit. To be successful in this new situation they rely on
text-context rules which they have abstracted out of past experience as
characteristic of language use in this setting. Within this frame, what
time does is to allow language users the opportunity to attend to and
orchestrate aspects of the specific field, mode, and tenor of the situation
in which they are involved more carefully. As constraints naturally

evolve and become perceptible, rather than restricting communication as imposed contraints do, they permit expansion of meaning potential.

Understanding this transactive relationship between context and meaning is important. What experience provides is potential, not only the opportunity to explore text potential, but in so doing, more fully to appreciate, to orchestrate, and to unleash human potential. That's what real literacy is all about.

Context has often been misunderstood as a variable which affects linguistic output. The cuts we have taken across our data in an attempt to explore context—with Zach by linguistic mode, with Hannah by literacy event, with Alison across home and school—show it to be not a variable but a transactive and transacting part of literacy process and sign. Text and context transact, together signing past and potential forms of psychological and sociological action. If Michael had written, "Will you be my pen pal?" in his ninth letter as he did in his first, the print only superficially would have remained the same; the text potential and hence meaning potential would have changed. To study text in isolation from context is at best to study only half the sign; at worst, to hopelessly confuse what is involved in scribbling and other literacy events.

Chapter 13
Text

It is shown that text is the basic unit of language.

THE YOUNG CHILD AS INFORMANT

From a cognitive processing perspective the basic unit of language is "text." "Text" presupposes a reader or a writer actively involved in making a unified chunk of meaning from experiences involving language.

Latrice, Marvin, Nathan, Terry, Patty, Towanna, Shannon, DuJulian, Robert, Jerry, and Heather, all age 3, were shown a photo of a Stop sign and asked what it said. Their responses respectively were "Stop," "Stop," "Stop," "Go this way," "Stop," "Stop," "Don't pass the sign," "Stop," "Danger," "Stop," "Stop," and "School."

What is interesting about this set of responses is that they all represent things one might find on street signs. They are, in other words, the right text for the right context.

To note that there is little or no graphemic involvement between some of these responses and the word Stop is to miss the textual event. Even responses such as "Danger," "Go this way," and "Don't pass this sign" are the right kind of print semantically and syntactically, and the right amount of print, organizationally, for this context.

Alison, age 6, but just prior to entering first grade, was asked by her father to prepare a shopping list as he finished the dinner dishes. Alison wrote each of the following items as they were dictated: MOLK (milk), VONOL (vanilla), ROSBOREJAM (raspberry jam), and BOD (bread). When she was asked to write "newspaper" she asked, "Can I draw that?" After Alison was assured that no one cared as long as they remembered the newspaper when they went shopping, she

---

PRINT SETTING
Stop
Stop
Stop
Go This Way
Stop
Stop
Don't Pass The Sign
Stop
Danger
Stop
Stop
School

MOK VONOL
ROS BOReJOM
BOD

ALISON
(ISO/(8

proceeded, drawing a newspaper replete with columns and layered sections of paper. On the bottom of her shopping list she signed her name and wrote the date 7/26/78.

Jason, age 9, was asked by his mother to start a shopping list by writing "blueberries" and "bacon" on it. He dutifully and literally hopped to the task. The list he prepared was a masterpiece of tidiness replete with the drawing of a sweet angelic child. In addition to his mother's entries, the shopping list had several additional items, however: 1 BAG OF DORITOS (LARGE); POP; SHOE STRINGS 29 INCHES; and KLETATS to indicate that he wanted a new pair of soccer shoes with "cleats." Anyone looking at this shopping list would know immediately that it was no ordinary list. Jason had created a surface text for a particular context. Through art, penmanship, and the placement of requests on his list, he had orchestrated available cues to create a text which he hoped signed not only his wishes, wants, and desires, but spoke of his fine character.

Wendy, Gregory, Tom, and Brett, all age 6, were asked to write Mr. Whiten, Brett's father, a Thank You letter for coming into their room and telling stories. Rather than allowing the children to write their own letters, the teacher wrote the following letter on the blackboard: "Dear Mr. Whiten: Thank you for coming to our room. Love _____ ." Each child was given a sheet of school paper and asked to illustrate the page, copy the letter, and sign it.

Wendy, Gregory, and Tom had no problem with the task. But Brett, who had quite a different relationship to the guest speaker, since Mr. Whiten was his father, found the "Dear Mr. Whiten" structure awkward. In the blank left for his name—the only slot left open to him by the teacher, he wrote DAD rather than signing his name.

The texts we create vary by the context of situation in which we find ourselves and reflect the tenor of the social relationships we have with the parties involved. Although we seemingly forget this, Brett demonstrates that he already knew this and refuses simply to comply. To focus on, or teach form and structure in language outside of context is to miss the orchestrated textual event which language use represents and is in the end to give children a dysfunctional view of the process.

Marci, Rhoda, Todd, and Mark, all age 6, were asked to complete the sentence, "(Blank) makes me happy," as a writing activity following a discussion of "happiness" in their first-grade classroom. Marci handled the assignment well, writing BIRDS MAKE ME HAPPY. Rhoda had more problems. She initially wrote MY BIGHCK {bike} MAKES ME HAPPY. In rereading her effort, she decided it wasn't a text and so added RIDEING {riding} to the front of her structure. The final product read RIDEING MY BIGHCK MAKES ME HAPPY. Todd's strategy was more evident. THIS IS MA SKADEPRSIN

{skate person} WRSKADEN *{roller skating}* MAKX *{makes}* ME HAPPY. *Todd initially had written, "Roller skating makes me happy"; his addition of "This is a skate person," suggests the cruciality of text to making sense of this task. Mark initially wrote* WHIN *{when}* i *{I}* GET A LETER *{letter} as his original contribution. In rereading, Mark decides "When I get a letter makes me happy" isn't much of a text. To solve this problem he adds* THIS *so his final text reads, "When I get a letter this makes me happy."*

In his search for text, Mark discovers clausal ellipses. What these data suggest are that text is a basic unit of language and that taking responsibility for the creation of text is much easier than taking someone else's partial text and trying to make a text out of it. The partial text structure, "(Blank) makes me happy" proved harder to deal with than would have a blank sheet of paper on which these children could have written their own text. By trying to simplify language we make it more difficult because we add yet another constraint which must also be dealt with and orchestrated in the response. Since under normal conditions we ourselves do not need to work within someone else's partial text conditions, we often, while having the best intent, make writing instruction more difficult than writing. The teacher in this instance had all of the children illustrate their texts, wanting to use them to create a bulletin board on the theme "happiness." Her decision to give the children the sentence frame," "(Blank) makes me happy," was done, no doubt, to support the literacy process and insure a set of usable products for the bulletin board. But it's important to realize that if practices such as this one are to continue they must be justified on the basis of our adult needs for tidiness, not because they support literacy learning.

As a unified chunk of meaning, "text" has both logical (propositional) and paralogical (nonpropositional, affective) dimensions. Literacy learning not only always involves these two dimensions, but is characterized by a search for unity across them and across other texts which have been created.

Robert, age 6, elected to write a story to go with the wordless book, A Boy, A Dog, and a Friend *(Mayer, 1961). On the final page in his book he wrote "the end" in black pen. Rescanning his work, he crossed it out, grabbed a color crayon, and wrote "the end" in a bold golden-colored script. "There," he said, "I wanted a rich ending."*

Given an opportunity to placehold his text in writing, Robert, like any writer, has to be concerned with signing his meaning. By using a combination of color and print, Robert overcodes his writing so that it better signs what he means. Whether or not another language user will read all of these signs is, of course, another issue. Robert, like the Impressionist painters who signed tree *by putting blobs of paint together to capture light reflections when the conventional sign of the times was different, is essentially faced with the problem of convincing the world of the value of his sign. The gold lettering of "the end" to Robert signs a rich ending and is an instance of semiosis. If and when Robert convinces other members of his interpretive community to read the sign as he does, his personal convention will have become public. Since gold in this society already has a rich coding, Robert demonstrates how convention serves invention and propels both our literacy and his own.*

Alison, age 3, knew that her father often carried children's literature books home in his briefcase. Whenever he arrived home Alison would immediately open his briefcase and look for books which she might have him read. One day, instead of a children's literature book, she pulled out a basal reader. As always she brought the book over to be read. The story they selected was about a baby monkey who wanted to know what he looked like. Whenever he asked his mother, she would respond, "You are baby monkey. You look just like what a baby monkey should. You are very beautiful." The story builds on this pattern: as baby monkey sees other baby animals he always asks if this is what he looks like, and his mother always responds, "No, you are baby monkey. You look just like . . ." Because the book was a teacher's edition of a basal reader, at the bottom of each page was a set of comprehension questions. Since Alison's father was as interested in comprehension as anyone else, he decided to ask Alison the questions suggested by the authors of the basal series as he read the book. Alison was on his lap sucking her thumb. When he finished the first page he asked, "What did Baby Monkey want to know?" Alison pulled her thumb out of her mouth and responded rapidly so as not to break the pace of her thumb sucking, "What he looked like." "And what did Baby Monkey's mother tell him?" Again Alison pulled out her thumb, "You look just like a Baby Monkey should." "And what do you think will happen next in the story?" At this point Alison extracted her thumb once more, and with body tense and fists clenched shouted, "O-O-O-O-O-O-Oh-h-h . . . READ!!!"

For Alison the questioning her father was doing was an interruption in the process of reading. Alison wanted to get on with reading, building a text world and living within it. The questions being asked by her father were an interruption; they lay outside of what the reading was all about. It is also interesting to note that Alison responded with emotion. Her "O-O-O-O-O-O-Oh-h-h . . . READ!!!" is overcoded with affect. How the book was read was affecting and coloring her lived-through textual experience.

Alison, age 4, was shown a paper cup from Wendy's and asked "What do you think it says?" Running her finger under the word, Wendy's, Alison responded "Wendy's" and running her finger under the word hamburgers, which also appears on the cup in bold print, "cup." Alison paused a moment after producing her response, as if in reflection, and added "That's a long word with a short sound."

The rule which Alison had obviously formulated is one that says that the sound of the word has some correspondence to the length of the word in written form. Given everything she knew about print in relation to context, this word should be "cup," and she concludes, "That's a long word for a short sound." Her decision here, from our perspective, is incorrect. In the long run, however, it is not. Need we help her? Not in a traditional corrective sense. All we need to insure is that she has continuing encounters with the process, for each encounter will allow her to test out the validity of her new hypothesis that sometimes no one-to-one correspondence exists between the graphemic length of a word and the phonetic length of the word.

From a cognitive processing perspective, what Alison's response indicates is a constant search for text. When reflecting, Alison is shifting psychological stances and becomes a monitor of her own participatory activities. In this role of monitor she looks at her current performance in light of what else she knows about language. This process represents a search for unity across this experience and other experiences she has had. It is this process of intertextual tying or the search for intertextuality which is a major driving force in literacy.

Writing does not entail simply taking what we know linguistically and translating it into written language, nor does reading entail taking written language and simply translating it into linguistic thought, but rather, involves other than linguistic ways of knowing. Semantic negotiation is a central characteristic of the psycholinguistic process involved in text creation. Such psycholinguistic activity takes place within the context of our personal histories of literacy, which include the past texts which we have created to make unified sense of our world. The search for unity both within the evolving text and with past texts creates psychological tensions which propel the reading, writing, and learning processes. The protocols and discussions which follow examine these ideas conceptually in order to understand literacy and literacy learning.

INTERDISCIPLINARY VIEWS

As a result of multidisciplinary work specifically in reading, we might characterize the last ten years of text research as having begun with a view of "text as object," moving from there to a view of "text as event," and finally to one of "text as potential." Importantly, these shifts in perspective reflect changes in the profession's notions about what is involved in literacy.

When text is viewed as an object, literacy is seen as a process of information transfer. Readers and writers are viewed as more or less faulty vessels. Good readers are defined as persons who reconstruct all implicit and explicit meaning (Adams & Collins, 1978). Good writers are defined as persons who are able to transcribe meanings from their heads onto paper in conventional form.

From this perspective texts can be rated, and readers and writers baited. And they often are. Current studies in cohesion (Halliday & Hasan, 1976; King & Rental, 1981), syntagmatic and paradigmatic overlap (Fries, 1980), transitivity relationships (Fillmore, 1976; Kintsch & van Dijk, 1978), ideational structure (Meyers, 1975, 1977; Stein & Glenn, 1978; Anderson, 1978), and propositional explicitness (Frederickson, 1975, 1977, 1978) are representative.

When text is viewed as an event, literacy is seen as a psychological and sociological partnership. Meaning is not something inherent in the print, but created in and through interaction. Text moves from being something on paper to being a psychological and sociological event. Anderson, Reynolds, Schallert, and Goetz (1977) show that what a reader brings to print strongly affects what he gets out of print. Carey, Harste, and Smith (1981) show that the situational context within which that event takes place contributes to schematization and hence to meaning. How meaning evolves in texts (Kintsch & van Dijk, 1978) and in classroom events over the course of time becomes a major area of study (Mehan, 1979; McDermott, 1976, 1977a, 1977b; Green & Wallat, 1978; Feathers, 1980; Siegel, 1980).

Just as studies of text as object led to and supported viewing text as event, so studies of text as event have led to and supported viewing text as potential. Text as potential is meant to capture not only the notion that text is an in-head phenomenon but that it is ever changing. What is out there is a "text potential"; what we create in our heads is "text."

Much confusion in current theory would be eliminated by a semantic distinction between surface text or the "text potential" and the "text." Teachers tell students to "take out their texts" when they mean their textbooks; researchers often endow their text (what we prefer to call a "text potential") with the kind of life which only a reader can find and create. Perhaps it is utopian to hope to change such entrenched confusions in critical terminology, but at least the present discussion will observe the following distinctions: "Text potential" designates a set or series of signs interpretable as iconic forms of psychological and sociological action. We use this rather roundabout phrasing to make it clear that the text potential is not simply the inked marks on the page but rather the sign complex formed by print and other communication systems in relation to situational context; that is, a print setting as it is encountered by a reader, or mental setting. In a reading situation "the text potential" may be thought of as the complex of available signs in a given print setting which demonstrate capacity to serve as iconic forms of psychological and sociological action for language users.

"Text," for our purposes, presupposes a reader or a writer actively involved with a text potential and refers, in reading, to what a reader makes of his or her encounters with a particular text potential at a given point in time. Text for a writer is an in-head phenomenon, some portion of which may never be signed in the surface text which is created. Writers, in creating a surface text, need to decide not only what elements of their text will be communicated, but how this portion of their text will be allocated and orchestrated (typically for most writers across and between art, context, implied gestures, and language) in an effort to sign their intended meanings. These decisions involve negotiation, defined as pragmatic and semantic shifts and moves on the part of a language user in an effort to find, create, and sign text (Harste, Burke, Woodward, 1981). A parallel process exists in reading, where negotiation is defined as pragmatic and semantic shifts and moves on the part of a reader in an effort to find and create text (Harste, Burke, Woodward, 1981).

From the time of birth to the present moment the world as we have experienced it is one continuous undifferentiated event (Smith, 1982). Given the limits of short-term memory, "texts" are those things which the mind creates in an effort to chunk the world of experience into meaningful and manageable units.

While "text" is a mental entity for language users, in creation it represents a series of psychological and sociological strategies. "Text" in reality must be thought of as an event in time. Rosenblatt (1978) captures this idea eloquently by stating that it happens during a coming together, "a compenetration," of a reader and what we have called a text potential. The texts we create have certain characteristics. They represent pieces of the world which for us have unity and contextual appropriateness, and represent our attempts to orchestrate and honor available signs.

Though we create texts from text potential, we assume intertextuality, i.e., that past texts we have created will be helpful in understanding the current text we are creating (De Beaugrande, 1980). From a semiotic perspective, texts sign other texts and hence act as both past and potential signs in their own right. This search for and discovery of suspected and unsuspected harmonies between past texts and current texts constitutes learning. Making sense of current texts in light of past texts constitutes comprehension.

The meaning of a text potential—textual meaning—is not fixed, but rather changes as a result of new experience. What experience does is to provide demonstrations of how the linguistic, behavioral, contextual, and affective elements of an experience are orchestrated and signed. With increased experience comes increased knowledge of, familiarity with, and use of these signs. Because reading, for example, is its own experience (Crafton, 1981), in rereading we have an opportunity to search for new unity and new forms of orchestration. This is one of the reasons young children can enjoy a book over and over again, never tiring of it long after we have convinced ourselves it has no new text potentials for us. It is, of course, why we can enjoy a good book a second and third time. Further, reading provides writers with multiple demonstrations of the writer's craft, so many in fact that no matter what our ability, a well-written document can serve us, as writers, as a veritable data source.

The relationship between thought and language insures that the texts we create always have a linguistic dimension. All that we know, however, is not linguistic in nature.

Some of what we know lies in and across alternate communication systems. In *Thought and Language*, Vygotsky (1962) emphasized "the weakness of traditional psychology" in separating the study of "intellect and affect." When this is done the thought process is "segregated from the fullness of life, from the personal needs and interests, the inclinations and impulses, of the thinker." He postulated "the existence of a dynamic system of meaning, in which the affective and the intellect unite" (p. 8).

James (1939) states that for him thought includes "every form of consciousness indiscriminately"—sensations, percepts, images, concepts, states or qualities of states, feelings of relations, feelings of tendencies. When viewed as an in-head potential, text is multidimensional.

In *Mind and Society* Vygotsky (1978) argues that when thought and language come together at about age 2, thought becomes linguistic and language becomes rational. The model we propose would argue that thought is never totally linguistic. In fact this is what's wrong with much current work in discourse analysis and comprehension. For us the notion of text includes linguistic and nonlinguistic thought. I. A. Richards's (1929) insightful analyses of "the plain sense" of a poem nicely captures how meaning often resides beyond the linguistic system itself:

In fact, a feeling that is quite pertinent seems often to precede any clear grasping of the sense. And most readers will admit that, as a rule, *the full sense, analysed and clearly articulated, never comes to their consciousness: yet they may get the feeling perfectly.* (p. 216)

Nor would we agree with those psychologists who would suggest that nonlinguistic thought is "muddle-headed" or nonlogical thought (Spiro, 1982). Knowledge in music, art, dance, etc., is organized, though quite possibly on some other basis than rationalism. We refer to the organizational structures underlying these alternate forms of knowing as paralogical thought to put them on an equal plane with language.

Aesthetics is operationally defined as the orchestration of signs across available communication systems such that more of the text potential or potential lived through experiences (psychological and sociological actions) have been signed. Rosenblatt (1978) states it this way:

The actual lived-through reading process is, of course, not a word-by-word summation of meaning, but rather a process of tentative organizations of meaning, the creation of a framework into which the reader incorporates ensuing words and phrases. . . . In aesthetic reading, the qualitative aspects, the voice, the tone that has been established, often have an important effect, not only on the emotive impact of the words that follow but on their meaning. (pp. 24, 25)

One can buy into the notion of macrostructural textual organization (Kintsch & van Dijk, 1978) without buying into or thinking about macrostructure as being only linguistic in form. Iser (1978) states:

The text itself simply offers "schematized aspects" through which the subject matter of the work can be produced, while the actual production takes place through an act of concretization. . . . From this we may conclude that the literary work has two poles, which we might call the artistic and the aesthetic: the artistic pole is the author's text and the aesthetic is the re-alization accomplished by the reader. In view of this polarity, it is clear that the work itself cannot be identical with the text or with the concretiza-tion, but must be situated somewhere between the two. It must inevita-bly be virtual in character, as it cannot be reduced to the reality of the text or to the subjectivity of the reader, and it is from this virtuality that it derives its dynamism. As a reader passes through the various perspectives offered by the text and relates the different views and patterns to one another he sets the work in motion, and so sets himself in motion, too. (p. 21)

"Texts," as used here, have some rationalistic characteristics in common with the notion of schema, though the term "text" is meant to capture and include both logical and paralogical ways of knowing which result, in reading, from sociological and psychological forms of action on the part of the reader.

Because inked marks on a page in a particular situational context together form one of the sign complexes of a text potential, alterations in the situational context necessarily alter the text potential. Illustration of

Figure 13.1. Alison's Note (Age 5.5).

the transactive relationship between text and context in writing, using young children's examples, began in the previous section of this book. What this section attempts to do is clarify other transactive relationships involved in text comprehension and production as these relate to literacy and literacy learning.

Not only are children's responses textual in the sense that they display internal and external unity, but further, they are textual in the sense that they are an orchestrated set of signs. Alison's POS DUNOT DOSDV (Please Do Not Disturb), in Figure 13.1, is a case in point.

Embedded and hence signed in the text is context. Not only is *Please do not disturb* a written language form (as opposed to its oral language form, "Please don't disturb me"), but since we are experienced language users the message and its accompanying form tell us that it is the kind of specialized environmental print one finds on doors in hotels when guests wish to sleep in, in schools when tests are being given, or in other situations where the person in authority wishes to exert control and does so by softening the superordinate-subordinate relationships involved with a "please."

Alison posted this note on her bedroom door after her older brother and his friend had repeatedly indicated that she was in their way on a rainy Saturday afternoon. In this instance the message and its accompanying form acknowledge Alison's sense of her rights; the "please" acknowledges the fact that while she knows she's in the right, she also knows she'd better not push it too far.

In addition to this unity (within the text itself and between text and context), we should also note that Alison used a black, thick-tipped magic marker with which to write her note. In so doing she lets us in on her current attitude as well as communicating the fact that she means business.

This, then, is the notion of orchestrated sign and text as involving not only linguistic, but affective, contextual, and indexical demonstrations. Captured in Alison's message is attitude, tone, and language which together constitute a complexly orchestrated set of signs.

Alison's "text" is for her brother and his friend a "text potential." Depending, of course, on their facility with written language, they may not read all of the available signs; or then again they may read more signs than what Alison had hoped to communicate, thus interpreting her message as, "She's getting uppity," or "The prissy little thing had better be taken down a notch."

All texts include affective as well as contextual complexes which operate as signs. A language story which illustrates both this notion and the notion of intertextual tying is that collected by David Whiten, a later member of our research team, and his wife (1981), in their attempts to understand evolving literacy.

Chris, age 4, liked to have stories read to him. His favorite was "The Three Little Pigs" which he insisted be read first at each session. One morning Phyllis, as usual, sat down to read stories. She began, of course, with "The Three Little Pigs."

Chris's next selection was Hans Christian Anderson's "Steadfast Tin Soldier." In this story the steadfast tin soldier meets one disaster after another. Finally on the last page he is shown in a rapidly deteriorating paper boat slowly sinking into the water. Phyllis paused as she finished the book. Chris reflected a moment and then with some disgust in his voice commented, "He should of built that boat out of bricks!!"

It is important to note that the past text—"The Three Little Pigs"—became the frame from and through which Chris attempted to make sense of this new text. As such this language story nicely illustrates the notion of intertextual tying and the assumption that the past texts we have created will be useful in understanding the current text we are creating. This binding of texts—where the current text signs past texts and where as a result a new synthesized text is created—is what learning is all about. From his experience with "The Three Little Pigs," Chris has abstracted a set of rules. His abstraction and his application of these rules—good wins over evil; diligence pays off; brick houses are stronger than wood and straw houses; smart people build with bricks—become the basis for evaluating and summarizing this experience.

Not only does this language story illustrate the notion of intertextual tying, but it also illustrates affective dimensions of text learning and use. Chris's "He should of built that boat out of bricks!!" is said with disgust and disappointment. While on one level we might productively study the linguistic propositions which make up his response, this is only a part of his text; the other component is affectively signed via intonation, tone, and accent. As in writing, the affective and linguistic dimensions of his reading response together constitute an orchestrated and complex signing of what this experience meant to him.

At age 3 Alison encountered the book *Prince Bertram, The Bad* (Lobel, 1963) in which Bertram lives in a "royal" nursery, breaks "royal" toys, pulls up "royal" flowers when he visits the "royal" garden and so forth. Days later, when she encountered the book on her own, her story line included, as we might suspect, "royal" everythings. Months later, on the grounds of the headquarters of Association of American Historians which is housed in an old historical mansion, she asked, "Is this 'the royal garden'?"

The importance of this instance of literacy lies in the fact that it clearly demonstrates the notion of text, as well as that of learning as the search for unsuspected textual harmonies across time. Alison assumed that the past texts she had created would be useful in her current attempts to make sense of the world. The texts she had created from a written language encounter served not only as frameworks for subsequent encounters with written language, but with the world. The lines which we as adults draw between written language texts and whole world texts are arbitrary, and both in fact interplay in the text worlds we create from language. Iser (1978) refers to these interplays as "tensions," and sees them as the basic force in literacy.

Whether certain parent-child interactions encourage this sort of intertextual tying, as Shirley Brice Heath's research indicates (1980), merits further study. From a socio-psycholinguistic perspective we are sure such a relationship exists. Importantly, from the perspective of text macrostructure, Alison's question, "Is this 'the royal garden'?" was triggered as much by the "aura" of the setting as it was by the referential objects: a castlelike house and its surrounding gardens.

The texts which children create during uninterrupted story writing bubble with affect and gesture and dance, only a "poor relations portion" of which actually gets recorded. Not only do children often literally hop, but their pens do too. Tasha (age 4) and her rabbit went hop, hop, hop with joy and spirit. The ink marks recording this event on the paper were poor relations—a series of dashes. In rereading, rather than being caught up in the story as she was when she was writing, she said, "And these are the bunny's tracks," thus signaling to us the change in her psychological relationship to the text. She made this statement, then paused, and shrugged her shoulders, thus signing her own disappointment at the gap between her original "text" and this "text potential." While the realization of discontinuity did not drive her to revision, partly because we had collected the pens, it is, we believe, this search for unity and the realization of discontinuity as we switch psychological stances that governs text creation and constitutes a self-corrected push toward literacy.

Donald's story is a semiotic event (see Figure 13.2). He began by drawing a man and a bat. As he later pointed back and forth between these forms he read, "A bat biting the man." His story also contained a dinosaur which chased a mouse which in turn made appropriate noises as it died. The wavy line in his product was initially the trail the mouse took, which only later became the back of his dinosaur as his story evolved. The extra little "n" markings on the dinosaur's back were "other mice coming out," all of which followed the same bloody trail and met the same bloody fate as did their predecessors. The text that he read was a poor second cousin to the text that he dramatized and told: "The bat is biting the man. And the dinosaur swallowed the rats."

The transcription of this event records important distinctions between "text" and "text potential." Further, it demonstrates the concept of negotiation as both a textual saga and strategy.

One of the decisions Donald faces, like all of us as writers, is what

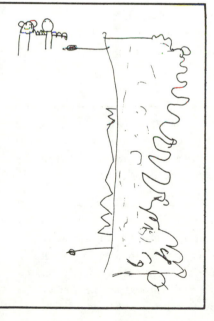

Figure 13.2. Uninterrupted Story Telling (Donald, Age 5).

portion of text to allocate to context, to art, to print, to gesture, or even to assumption. These semantic negotiations, as Donald shows us, are not without drama. The results of these decisions are often a disappointment not only to our readers, but to ourselves.

Yet, Donald's script shows us the potential in negotiation as much as it does "the saga" (Halliday, 1973). In moving to art Donald produces a set of signs which serve textual memorability and retrievability functions characteristic of more conventional scripts. These are not direct representations of referential objects, but abbreviated, abstracted, and arbitrary forms representing mental symbolism.

From his whole world experiences with mice Donald has abstracted out an image of how they move. This is not the meaning of the event to Donald but a code placeholding its meaning. This abstraction, he discovers in this setting, can be recorded via particular markings on paper. That they remind us more of art than writing is a distinction which leads us away from appreciating the written languagelike character, and the processes involved, as universal ones in literacy.

Donald is not imitating the movement of a mouse, but rather offering proof that from his past encounters he has abstracted out of the experience a code by which he can recreate it. If imitation were all that were involved there would be no evidence of inference, analogy, or imagination. This code serves a semiotic function, just as Donald's recording of this code now signifies the dinosaur-eating-mouse event in his story. Carey (1982), in discussing the applicability of a semiotic perspective for the study of reading, says:

Written texts owe their existence to the codes that we invent to process the world and create it. They remind *the reader of the codes and show him how they work. . . . Reading, then, like all other communicative activities, is the pursuit of signs. The reader engages in the prospect of grouping, comprehending, and capturing evasive signifying structures. (p. 13)*

"Writing," to borrow Carey's language, "like all other communicative activities, is the pursuit of signs. The writer engages in the prospect of grouping, creating, and capturing evasive signifying structures."

These are not new observations, though their importance in literacy learning may be. Piaget (as reported by Ginsburg & Opper, 1979) reports that his daughter Lucienne, upon observing him ride a bicycle, performed the same motions herself, swaying to and fro at about the speed of the bicycle.

Lucienne's and Donald's behaviors are forms of mental symbolism. The child's swaying back and forth later when the bicycle is not present signifies the bicycle event, just as Donald's mouse track signifies the dramatic events of mouse escape and fate.

While these are at one level abstract symbols, in text production and creation they are indexical traces and iconic images of psychological and sociological territory. Both Donald and Lucienne teach us that visual perception is as much an activity as is the placeholding of an event with paper and pen.

Theoretically we can say that the semiotic function involves signifiers— mental events, words, or things—which stand for something else. Signifiers signify or represent something to the individual. In the past semioticians have labeled signifiers as either symbol, index, or icon. What Donald and Lucienne demonstrate is that any signifier is all three: an index or trace of the event, an iconic image projecting the psychological and sociological territory, a symbol, or abbreviated abstraction of let this be that.

Signifiers may be *personal* or *conventional*. They may only signify things to us personally or they may signify things more generally to other members of our immediate culture or more distant cultures. This distinction is the difference between semiosis (personal) and a semiotic event (shared). For Donald the mouse trail signifies the event, for another child it may be a picture of a dinosaur actually eating the mouse (which despite some forms of detail is still an abstraction of the event itself), for a third child it may be the markings DIAUSOR (Matt, age 6). What is significant here is not so much the form it takes as the process which is involved. All represent the semiotic function or instances of real literacy. They differ only by virtue of their being variations on a common theme.

The semiotic function of literacy is not an all or none thing. Each of us has various elements in our world which we control at personal levels and others which we control at conventional levels. Donald can sign his name conventionally, though his signing of story lies somewhere between personal and social convention. (We note, for example, that though his story is placeheld in pictures, it has a story structure form.) Learning to mean in writing, Donald teaches us, involves transmediation from one form of knowing to another. This process is generative. As researchers we have found the strategies which children use in writing—negotiation, pretending—to be keep-going strategies for us too. We did not consciously know this before.

The complexity of semiotic terminology should not obscure the fact that the ability to form mental and physical representations is an achievement of great magnitude. Things no longer need to be present to be acted on. The ability to represent liberates the child from the immediate present (Vygotsky, 1978). He can imagine things that are both spatially and temporally separate from himself. He can create worlds where dinosaurs eat mice and placehold them by making marks on paper which capture the essence of his text. The use of such a system permits the child to transcend the contraints of space, distance, and time. Donald's scribbles, in short, offer him self-discovery of all that written language offers us.

In attempting to mean, children often freely move between writing and art; and just as often in this process border skirmishes result (Harste, Burke, Woodward, 1981). Erica, in writing a story about an animal, began with the letter *b* which she then turned into a fish and later into a "birdfish." Megan, in representing a castle, placeheld her notion with a jagged line which not only captures the characteristic jagged features of a castle wall, but takes on a written languagelike form. Mike on one occasion wrote his name quite conventionally, but on another occasion preserved his ideas via a combination of pictures and print. In reading what he wrote, Mike recalled the ideas placeheld by these border skirmish scribbles, but said as he came to each letter, "I don't remember what that says." Mike's scripting decisions looked a bit like those underlying hieroglyphs and the early writings of native Americans. It is significant that Mike's personal signs meant more to him than did his use of what we would call the conventional ones, as they indicate the order of things in literacy.

Alison (see Figure 13.3) wrote her story "in cursive," or so she said. She also said that she could write more if she added a picture, which she did before adding the other line of her story.

The interesting thing to note in each of the instances reported here is that the children not only seem to be inventing written language for themselves, but seem to be in the process of resolving for themselves all of the problems which the inventors of written language across various cultures have had to resolve. As a result of border skirmishes between writing and art, each of these children learned how they could write so that they could retrieve their texts over time.

Figure 13.3. Uninterrupted Story Writing (Alison, Age 5).

Alison, for example, could reconstruct her story almost word for word even weeks later. Her story read: "Once upon a time there was a girl named Alison. She was walking down the road and saw a little boy named Jack, I mean Jason. The little boy named Jason said 'Hello' to Alison. Alison said 'Hello' to Jason and they became friends so they played until it was suppertime. The end."

From such border skirmishes between art and writing, it may be but one metaphorically short step before other skirmishes arise, such as that between written language and sound. Megan, for example, initially drew a picture of a present to placehold her text. In reading, she said, "This says package." Then she reflected, "No, it doesn't!" crossed it out, and wrote PKPL.

What these examples demonstrate is that in scribbles is the origin of the written sign, which is not an heirloom passed on from generation to generation, but a process replete with the advantages which we, too, have discovered in written language over oral language. The fact that Donald's, Erica's, Mike's, Alison's, and Megan's markings are mere scribbles in relation to their original texts seems to us to be not unlike the relationship between this "text" as we envisioned it, and the "text potential" which readers will encounter in their reading of it.

Chapter 14
Demonstrations

The authors summarize both their perceptions on how language is learned and those transactions which they see as key to a new model of literacy.

THE YOUNG CHILD AS INFORMANT

By "demonstration" we mean a display of how something is done. As applied to written language and written language learning, any literacy event provides a variety of demonstrations which are available to language learners through the actions of the participants and the artifacts of the process. The learning of these demonstrations involves the active mediation of the language user.

Alison, age 6, was writing her timetable for watching her favorite television programs. She was copying from the TV Guide in the newspaper as she wrote: 6:30—Ch. 6—Mork & Mindy—7:00—Ch. 6—Wonder Woman. To make the spaces she used black squares. When her father looked at her timetable he said, "Alison, adults use blank spaces, not black squares to space." Alison replied, "Daddy, I'm not an adult."

Alison's response demonstrates that, through her encounters with the written language of newspapers, she has attended to how it is that members of her interpretive community separate their writing into units. Having inferred these rules she develops her own rule system, but has a different surface structure. Alison's behavior reflects the active role which the language learner plays in language learning. In light of what she currently knows, Alison develops a personal convention which, while different from ours, serves her at this time. She is not simply modeling or imitating what it is she has observed; rather, having observed a particular phenomenon she has inferred its function, and in light of her current interests, developed her own system.

Sarah, age 5, and Alison, age 6, both developed a new way to directly sign the fact that s's sometimes carry a z sound by making their s's under certain conditions

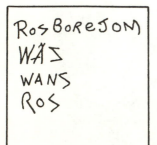

180

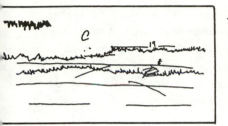

in the s *shape, but using the 45-degree straight line angle that we typically use in making the* z. *What is interesting is that both children made* s's *in other circumstances quite conventionally. All occurrences of this new letter in their texts were in those words in which the* s *carried a* z *sound, such as* raspberry, rose, *and* was. *While it is clear that this decision was intuitive, since the new letter also occurred for the* z *sound in* once, *it is interesting to note that these demonstrations and options are readily available in our written language system and represent an easy change which the inventors of our system might well have considered.*

Jerry, age 3, watched as his father diligently wrote out checks one evening after dinner. Since he was determined to help, his father gave him a pencil and paper with the outline of a check on it. In the upper left-hand corner Jerry made a series of very dark, dense marks where he had obviously noted the name and address were printed on checks. Using a finer stroke, he filled out the TO WHOM line, the dollar amount, and the signature block with a much finer wavy linear line and handed his check back to his father saying, "All done."

From his involvement in this literacy event Jerry learned a lot. His observations of the demonstrations involved in this literacy event not only informed him that writing was important and something he wanted to do, but also where to write and how to organize that writing. With these understandings he created a successful text, given this context.

There is no inherent sequence to the order in which the demonstrations involved in literacy are learned; rather, which demonstrations are learned are a function of which demonstrations are highlighted by a literacy event as they transact with the interests, purposes, and personal history of the language user.

Jennifer, age 8, had given us a copy of her book The Talking Egg Goes Camping. *We wrote her an official Thank You letter and suggested via a postscript that we would be happy to have copies of the other books in her series,* The Talking Egg Eats a Peanut Butter Sandwich, The Talking Egg Tries a Cigarette, *and* The Talking Egg Takes Up Jogging.

Jennifer had completed this whole series of books as part of her work with Vera Milz, a teacher attempting to support and encourage young children's reading and writing through functional classroom activities.

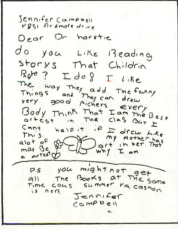

In response to our "business" letter, Jennifer wrote us a "business" letter back. Her letter began with a business address, JENNIFER CAMPBELL; (backward) 4 851 Ardmore Drive, followed by a salutation. Her letter read: DO YOU LIKE READING STORYS THAT CHILDREN RIGHT? I DO! I LIKE THE WAY THEY ADD THE FUNNY THINGS AND THEY CAN

DRAW VERY GOOD PICHERS. EVERYBODY THINK THAT I AM THE BEST ARTEST IN THE CLAS. BUT I CAN'T HELP IT IF I DRAW LIKE THIS (picture of a butterfly). MY MOTHER HAS A LOT OF ART IN HER. THAT MAY BE WHY I AM A ARTEST (picture of flower). To close her letter Jennifer added a postscript as we had done in our letter: P.S. YOU MIGHT NOT GET ALL THE BOOKS AT THE SAME TIME COUS SUMMER VACASHON IS HERE. JENNIFER CAMPBELL.

Jennifer obviously is a very self-confident young writer who knows a good deal about letter writing. What she is able to learn about business letter writing from this single encounter is truly impressive. From her experience as a reader and a receiver of a business letter, Jennifer noted several demonstrations and inferred their function: include a business address; add postscripts. With these data in tow, she actively goes about incorporating these ideas into what is already a well developed letter writing schema.

Alison, age 6, who we know was a written language user at 3 years of age, was asked by her first-grade teacher to make a Thanksgiving Book by copying a text from the blackboard onto school paper. Presumably this assignment used writing to support reading by using copying to get children to attend to print, discriminate between various letters, and in the process, learn their various forms. Since Alison and the other children we studied rarely demonstrated any of these inabilities, however, the worthiness of this activity seems questionable. The text Alison was asked to copy was about the pilgrims and read, "When they got to America they found corn and saw unfriendly Indians." Without commenting on the quality of this message's social studies content, it is interesting to note the difficulties Alison had with this assignment. Because of the lined school paper Alison tried to be extra careful. Her when *would have warmed the heart of a Palmer handwriting expert. When she got to the second word,* they, *she carefully made the* t *to fit the height of the half-line rather than the height of the full line; the* h *the height of the entire line; and the* e *and* y, *tail and all, to fit the half-line. Since both her* t *and* y *were written within the half-line space, her printing looked funny and unlike anything she had previously written without the benefit of lined paper.*

Concentrating on letter form she got worse rather than better, making decisions unlike any others she had ever made. The net result was a carefully done maze of crowded letters and words.

Interestingly, on the same day we invited Alison to write a Thanksgiving story at home. She thought awhile and then drew a pilgrim snowman and wrote the following text on unlined paper in two columns running the length of the picture: "The pilgrims had a long winter and built snowmen and one was a pilgrim snowman . . . The end . . . " spelling her message: THE POGROMS

*HOD A LONG WOTH AND BOLT SNOW MON AND WON WAS A
POGRA-M MAN SNOW MON THEE END.*

*Contrasted, the quality of these two writing experiences is striking. In the first
instance, what is being demonstrated is the importance of good penmanship. What
you write isn't important; how you write it is. Under these conditions Alison
attends to these demonstrations and produces a piece of writing which is nearly
illegible. By contrast, in the second setting what is demonstrated is faith in the
language learner. The assumption is that Alison has things to write about. She
rises to the challenge and assumes the pilgrims would like doing what she likes
doing, namely, building snowmen. Since there is nothing to sign the importance of
penmanship, she focuses on her story and the testing of her latest language
discoveries and hypotheses: when in doubt about a vowel use O; use a hyphen to
split words. From the perspective of literacy learning, the qualitative differences
between these experiences in terms of the demonstrations available and attended to
are startling. By using the child as informant, salient demonstrations in a
literacy setting can be identified. If the child is attending to demonstrations
which, given our present level of understanding of literacy, we theoretically believe
to be dysfunctional, then conducive environments can be established which highlight more functional demonstrations. For purpose of instruction, understanding
this relationship between literacy learning and available literacy demonstrations
is extremely important, and seems particularly meritorious of the profession's
immediate attention.*

Since attending to and making sense of available demonstrations is in
the self-interest of the language learner, language users of all ages are
extremely sensitive to any demonstrations which they perceive as potentially functioning as signifying structures in a literacy event. The search
for and orchestration of these signifying structures is governed psychologically by a search for text and the creation of unified meaning. In the
search, identification, and interpretation of signifying structures for the
purpose of creating text and unified meaning, language users make
active use of alternative communication systems and alternative expressions of language. Psycholinguistically and sociolinguistically what
these alternative communication systems and expressions of language
offer users are alternative stances whereby they can triangulate their
knowing. It is in this continual process of attending to and sorting out
available demonstrations in a literacy event as these relate to learning
written language, learning about written language, and learning through
written language, that the individual and societal potentials of literacy
in the service and expansion of the human potential occurs. The section
which follows examines these notions via protocol materials and a review
of pertinent literature in order to reconceptualize literacy and literacy
learning.

Smith (1982) argues that any language encounter provides a multitude of demonstrations:

The first essential component of learning, is the opportunity to see how something is done. I shall call such opportunities demonstrations, *which in effect show a potential learner "This is how something is done." The world continually provides demonstrations through people and through their products, by acts and by artifacts. (p. 108)*

In further building and explaining this concept, he suggests that a variety of process information is simultaneously demonstrated in any language event. In reading a book with a parent, for example, young children have demonstrated to them not only how enjoyable a book is, but that books are meaningful, and that book reading is important. Demonstrated also are what a story is, how authors put stories together, how pictures and print work together to form a surface text, and how you package the whole thing. Additionally children have demonstrated to them how pages in a book work, how to turn pages as you read, the order in which you read, and the relationship between page turning and movement through the story. Equally important are demonstrations about how one reads, how one corrects in reading, and how the speaking voice changes during reading. From still another perspective, children have demonstrated to them how language works, what it looks like, how it is chunked and formatted, as well as how it is distributed in this literacy setting. While not all of these demonstrations are attended to in any single instance of literacy, Smith argues that they are available.

It is important to understand that the information available is not content information per se, but process or strategic information. Smith's argument is important because it begins to explain why it is that we can repeatedly involve ourselves in reoccurring literacy events and still find them both valuable and enjoyable. Because literacy is an event rather than an act, a perpetual firstness (Peirce, 1931–58) is assured for both the young as well as the more seasoned learner. With repeated encounters we can attend to new demonstrations using choice as a self-motivating and context-capitalizing strategy.

When we say language use and learning involves orchestration, theoretically what we are saying is that the behavioral, affective, contextual, and linguistic demonstrations constituting an instance of literacy together and separately form a set of sign complexes which have meaning potentials. From this perspective a demonstration constitutes psychological and sociological actions associated with one set of these sign complexes. More successful and less successful instances of literacy revolve around the consistency and inconsistency of demonstrations, and the messages which they individually and collectively sign as they function in their role as a text or a text potential. The evolution of literacy involves awareness, familiarity, knowledge, and use of such demonstrations to sign and interpret meaning. With more and more encounters come more and more opportunities to become aware of, familiar with, and knowledgeable about the use of available and potential demonstrations. Literacy is never a glorified state one enters, but involves constant orchestration and reorchestration of the sign complexes of literacy as contexts change and evolve.

Because any instance of literacy contains multiple demonstrations, unity across demonstrations is an expectation which language users bring to the process. Unity, and the search for unity between and across sign complexes, becomes a driving force in text production and text comprehension; unity, and the search for unity across past and current texts, becomes the propelling force in literacy learning.

These observations are particularly powerful in explaining and in making sense of the data which we and others have collected during observation of the young child as writer. This section will further expand the notions of demonstration, orchestration, and unity as constructs for understanding literacy and the process involved in literacy learning.

Seating a child in front of paper and pen and announcing that "today we're going to write stories" proved to be a rather stark, but yet interesting setting for exploring key processes involved in literacy. Many younger children negotiated the task so that, rather than deal with story writing, they saw and took this as an opportunity to practice writing their letters and numbers. No other adult had ever approached them with such a request; surely, we must want what other adults wanted. Their search for unity across this setting and others led to negotiation of the task, but also to identification of a "text" which made orchestrated sense in light of current and past signs.

Those children that did engage were, of course, immediately confronted with two problems: what story should they produce and how should they begin? These problems were not independent of each other. Since the immediate environment offered little support in that we were busy writing our own stories, many children relied on past story settings in which they and we had been involved. Some accessed past prototypical stories; others accessed not only past stories, but an immediate past context which they saw as similar to the one in which they currently found themselves. Because of the nature of our research project this immediate past story context for many of our subjects involved their having read or having pretended to read—just three days previously—a book entitled *Ten Little Bears*. Under these conditions, not surprisingly, fully one-third of our subjects also wrote their stories on the topic of "bears." Jake, age 6, produced "The Three Little Pigs," an even more refined rendition of the story he elected to tell during our language experience story dictation task.

Because we were also writing a story, our very presence in the research setting provided the children with a variety of available demonstrations—where to begin, how to begin, and if they read over our shoulders, even what they might write about. The stories we had decided to write while the children were writing their stories were third-person narratives. We began in each instance by drawing a stick figure and then writing a brief story which included what we had learned about the child: "This is Tasha. . .Tasha likes to play in the sandbox with her friends, etc."

An examination of the stories which children produced under these conditions vividly illustrates not only that these demonstrations were available, but how influential such demonstrations are in literacy learning. Well over one-half of the children in our study included a picture in their story, many beginning with a picture as we had done. Natasha, age 6, even decided to cross out her first character and to make a puppy, which then became the basis of her story. That imitation or modeling is not the key phenomenon, but rather, a more general understanding of what strategies might be employed in this setting, is evidenced by the fact that she assured us, "I'm going to make something really different than you." Obviously, from past encounters, one of the things Natasha had learned was that imitation of content was inappropriate; reapplication of process, however, was acceptable.

Modeling for us involves the imitation of content or the aping of behaviors without an understanding of the underlying relationships or rules. Involved in the notion of demonstration is learning and the reapplication of abstracted strategic processing operations. Despite the fact, for example, that we drew, children still had to decide for themselves if they would draw. Given this demonstration as available, one-half of the children elected to ignore it as a strategic sign of how they might proceed. Choice is an integral part of a theory of literacy which perceives the language user as active.

Kibi, age 4 (see Figure 14.1), orchestrated a variety of strategic demonstrations which were available in this and past settings by electing the topic "bears" (a demonstration available in a past context) and by including in her story "illustrations" of her characters (a demonstration available in this context). Kibi nicely demonstrates not only the long arm of unity, but the significance of this search in terms of literacy.

An observation which Donald Graves (1980) has made relates to both this notion of demonstration and to Kibi's performance. Graves's observation is an important one: namely, that successful writers "live off the land," meaning they capitalize on the natural support systems available

*Figure 14.1. Uninterruped Story
Writing (Kibi, Age 4).*

Marc (Age 6)

LaShell (Age 6)

Figure 14.2. Uninterrupted Story Writing (LaShell & Marc.)

in their immediate context of situation.

In one of the schools, the room in which we did our videotaping contained several animal posters reflecting the tempo of the times. The posters had such pithy sayings as, "Love Will Keep Us Together," "Puppy Love," and "Skatebird." Since we felt these added to the decor of the setting rather than detracted from it, we decided to leave them up during our data collection.

Interestingly, several children saw these as available demonstrations and used them in their texts during uninterrupted writing sessions. Natasha's decision to write a story about a puppy no doubt was motivated by the fact that the posters available demonstrated to her the spelling of the word *puppy* and thus reduced the risk involved.

In addition, first-grade children coming from classrooms which had stressed spelling and letter formation seemed especially prone to solve their current writing problem using these posters as their major resources (see Figure 14.2). This is especially interesting because 5- and 6-year-old children demonstrated in other tasks that they knew more about writing and reading generally than did younger children who obviously had less experience, but who also felt less at risk. Their vulnerability was learned in classroom reading and writing programs which imposed constraints and demonstrated to them that what they already knew wasn't good enough.

This does not mean that "living off the land" is an inappropriate strategy, since it did help these children arrive at a text which they felt they could successfully handle given the constraints they perceived as operating. The strategy was in this sense very useful. It is important to understand, however, that the quality of a strategy is dependent upon the conditions of its use. Donald Graves and his research team have made an important contribution by demonstrating that under more natural conditions, instructional strategies—such as peer interviews prior to a writing experience—can be organized to facilitate literacy growth using as one's ideational source the natural support strategies which children themselves use.

Writing down the stories children dictate is advocated by proponents of the language experience approach because it provides support to children presumably before they can take ownership of both story composition and production. Upon analysis, story dictation proves to be an extremely complex language setting because children are expected to coordinate their evolving oral texts with the process of transcription when control of the setting is really in the hands of another language user—the person taking the dictation. Some children, of course, initially defy all odds and charge full-speed ahead.

Under these conditions one rapidly gets a feeling for what children already know about the process of story dictation, and for those less familiar with the setting, what demonstrations are available and how rapidly children learn from them. In this regard, we found, as did Sulzby (1981), several informants who initially did not seem to understand the requirement of story production. We also found, however, in studying our videotape protocols, that after even one repetition of a dictated story component—which we did to clarify what the child had dictated—children often began to pace their dictation of the story more realistically. While our research setting was not designed to be instructional, available demonstrations became signs which operated like instruction.

Further, although we were supposedly only there to take dictation, our presence led other children to ask hypothetical questions which in turn seemed to lead them to clarify for themselves what a story was and how one goes about creating one. Jason's story (age 5) is a classic instance of this phenomenon. He began by naming objects: "Dollar. Spoon. Case." He then posed a question which we must assume was in part at least stimulated by our presence, yet seemed to be said to no one in particular: "You know what you do with these?" What follows in his story dictation is more predictable, namely, connected discourse: "You take the spoon and you dip in chili and in cereal too, and you eat it." While Jason's story was a monologue, embedded in it are features of dialogue. Although, during dictation, we attempted only to ask questions for purposes of clarification, these, too, often served the same function that Jason's self-initiated and self-answered questions served him.

Equally interesting is the fact that several children who initially did not appear to understand what was involved in story dictation and transcription began to use metalinguistic terms such as *story* and *word*. But their use of these terms seemed to be more a result of our interactions with them during story dictation than a function of their understanding of these terms prior to story dictation.

In attempting to make sense of these data we found Halliday's insights extremely helpful. Halliday argues that any instance of language provides language users with an opportunity to learn language, learn about language, and learn through language (Halliday, 1980). Learning language involves learning how to mean in particular contexts. It involves language in use: the semantic and pragmatic functions of language. It was what our young language users were doing as they discovered for themselves, in process, what constituted a story and how to produce one in this setting.

Learning about language involves learning about language as a system. It involves an understanding of how language is used in particular contexts as well as language about language or metalinguistic knowledge. As we asked for repetitions of previously dictated content we caused these young authors psychologically to step back and reassess what was involved in the task, and how one talks about it. Through our sounding of their stories as we wrote, through interacting with them in attempting to communicate, we provided children with metalinguistic demonstrations which made sense and were rapidly learned.

Learning through language involves using language as a vehicle for cognition and for expansion of one's world. It encompasses what Halliday terms "the mathetic function" of language. Jason, in the process of story dictation, inventories what he knows and, in so doing, is led to the identification of what he might say. In this process he brings what he knows to a new level of awareness, and organization, understanding.

Any set of research protocols permits exploration of the relationship between available demonstrations and language learning. In reading environmental print, a simple "What?", said when we truly didn't hear the child's response, demonstrated disapproval to some of our subjects and more often than not resulted in their changing their responses. In our letter writing tasks the inclusion of an envelope on the table as our request was made acted as a complex sign which resulted in children more frequently engaging in the task we wanted—personal letter writing—than in the writing of letters of the alphabet—what "letter writing" meant to them given past experience at home and preschool. Initially we saw much of this as a problem in our research. In reassessing what is involved in literacy and literacy learning we now see it as data.

As we look across these and other data we must conclude that language is its own experience. Theoretically we might say that we, acting as representatives of our interpretive community in social interaction with our informants, helped them, and they in turn helped us, to identify what were significant demonstrations from among those which were available. Our own and their own speech and repeated actions, acted as ready signs for ongoing and expected forms of psychological and sociological action. As participants, both we and our informants expected that these settings, and what we would perceive in them, would make sense. Using signs available in the cue complexes formed by text in context, we and they accessed past and recent texts which shared key features and used these as an initial base upon which to create a text that was appropriate to this context. If and when conflicting information presented itself during the languaging event, that is, when either we or our informants sensed that these past texts were not serving us well, we began a search for new relationships among the demonstrations that were available, abstracting out of these key behavioral, linguistic, contextual, and affective cue complexes which signified for us the key demonstrations. These experiences expanded both their notions and ours of the potentials of language in this setting and caused us all to reorganize and reprioritize expectations about language in this setting. The process was cyclic. What they learned and what we learned from this language encounter became and becomes the anticipatory frame for subsequent encounters.

Chapter 15

A Summary: Synthesizing New Patterns in Literacy

Natural language situations always provide a multiplicity of data which are available as signs. A language user makes what they are personally capable of from each language setting. This concept generates new demonstrations and new literacy potentials.

This section summarizes each of the major patterns we have identified in our program of research in order to highlight key psycholinguistic and sociolinguistic processes involved in literacy and literacy learning. The function of this section is to synthesize these findings in order to redefine literacy and literacy learning. Because this summary represents a synthesis of what it is we believe we came to understand about the process of literacy and literacy learning from our program of research, a curriculum for both teachers and researchers is implicitly sketched.

Organization.   One of the first things we noted in our study of children's reading and writing responses was the variety and quality of organizational patterns they entailed. Children's written language responses were found to be organized pragmatically, semantically, syntactically, and graphophonemically. General organizational patterns were identifiable at each age level, while specific organizational patterns were found to be a function of culture, experience, and the latest discoveries and interests of the language user.

The organizational decisions which young children make do not appear to be made for different reasons, nor are they qualitatively different from the decisions other successful written language users continue to make at a conscious or intuitive level when involved in reading or writing. Psycholinguistically, what characterizes all written language users is that after they have perceived and inferred the function which a particular organizational pattern or signifying structure of written language serves, their attention is freed to sort out still other patterns. The organizational features or patterns to be attended to seem to be a function of what language features are highlighted in a particular instance of language use, given the language user's interests, prior experience, and purpose. There is no order in which organizational

190

features or patterns will be attended to, but rather, a simultaneous search for new signifying structures and surface text organizational structures by which to code and confirm linguistic discoveries as cognitive processing universals characterizing the literacy learning process.

Intentionality. One of the cognitive processing universals in literacy is the assumption, on the part of the language user, that written marks are signs which have the power of signification. This recognition of written marks as cultural objects, or signs which signify, occurs early and represents access to the fundamental structure of literacy. The very fact that children engage in the making of marks on paper attests to the fact that they have discerned this universal in literacy. This is true even before the child can report what the marks he or she has produced say. Sometimes young children, for example, make a mark on paper and ask, "What does this say?" (Angela, age 5), or "What did I write?" (Kibi, age 5). While these questions indicate that the child's markings do not sign a specific meaning to her, the very question itself means that the child is making the assumption that such markings should have the power to signify meaning. Given the fact that the writing of even the very youngest children reflects intentionality, such demonstrations are evidently readily available and are learned very quickly by children in this society as they encounter written language.

The assumption of intention and the access to literacy it represents govern any written language user's very first markings as well as his or her present ones. Readers and writers who produce what we initially perceive as nonsense appear to be an exception. Despite the fact that the intention another reader or writer may attribute to a sign may differ from the intention the child assumed was signed, from the child's perspective the sign is an attempt to make a meaningful response given what he or she perceives is called for in this context. Unconventionality does not deny intentionality.

The importance of the assumption of intentionality is that it is a propelling force in literacy, setting in motion cognitive search strategies whereby significance can be deduced. Further, it is this assumption which governs every literacy discovery, from the initiate's very first insight to our own latest accomplishment. Even when we have well-developed assimilative schema, the encountering of the unpredicted signs intentionality and sets into motion interpretive procedures and strategies. Prior literacy experiences may heighten sensitivity to objects which may serve as signs, but do not diminish the central role intentionality plays in all instances of literacy learning.

Generativeness. In use, language is an open system which permits the maintenance and generation of meaning. This observation describes any instance of language as well as the language process itself.

As a reader of our own writing we may decide that what we wrote was exactly what we wanted to say (even, when later, our editor tells us the thought is not written in sentence form), what we wrote was not what we meant, or even that we like what we wrote better than the thought that generated the process in the first place. As a reader we may be pleasantly surprised to find in rereading a book concepts and ideas we never knew were discussed, be dismayed when we cannot find something we wanted to quote because evidently the author never said it, decide upon hearing the author speak that he or she is a better writer than a speaker, or even that we can talk about the author's concepts better than the author can.

Such discoveries, whether the result of reading, writing, speaking or listening, force us to take a new cognitive stance about language. In this process we have new opportunities to learn how to use language to better serve our communicative ends, to think objectively about how language works, and to assess how what we said ties in with the other things we wrote and know. From a cognitive processing perspective, engagement and reengagement in the process increase the opportunities language users have for self-discovery of the generativeness and educative aspects of language in use. These functions within the process are inherent in the process itself and are universal. In use these functions are as available to the initiate written language user as they are to the more experienced.

The generativeness of language does not deny the value or importance of the meaning maintenance functions of language. Language psychologically and sociologically, however, is much more than convention as a medium in the process of literacy and literacy learning.

Risk-taking. Since language is an open sign system, risk-taking is necessarily a central feature of the process. Without risk there can be no exploration or discovery of the generative potentials of literacy. Overemphasis on the maintenance aspects of language discourages risk-taking.

Written language is an almost perfect medium for the mind to work with because cognitively, (1) all that we know about language cannot be attended to at once, and (2) our latest language discoveries are always more fun to think about than those which we already think we have sorted out. The process leaves a revisitable trail. In so doing, writing allows the mind an opportunity to do what it considers exciting—think about, attend to, and record the new—while simultaneously permitting, via the convenience of another literacy (reading, art, speaking, etc.) the opportunity to revisit, reflect, and orchestrate these latest discoveries with the known. Given the makeup of human cognition, this arrangement metaphorically allows us to have our cake and eat it. Cognitively it allows us to fine-tune not only language but thought. In writing it allows us to code and overcode demonstrations via the use or invention of signifying structures.

The trail we leave during the writing process reflects these penchants of the mind. Being psychologically, as opposed to conventionally, functional, the very process itself can scare both participants and observers. When this happens withdrawal from the process can occur. Since one cannot learn this process, to say nothing about fine-tuning it, except in use, such efforts to eliminate risk-taking are dysfunctional.

Since there is no good way nor is there any good reason to alter how the mind naturally works, understanding these penchants and the advantages they give to literacy is important. The psychological centrality of risk-taking is naturally supported sociologically by virtue of the fact that it is an event which occurs through time. What time allows is the opportunity for reengagement and refinement of the functional litter of literacy. The role risk plays in the literacy process needs to be supported, facilitated, and reflected in the advice and programs we provide and design for written language learners of all ages.

Social Action. Sometimes we seem to forget that language is, by its very nature, social. Not only do writers assume they have readers, and speakers assume they have listeners, but interaction with real or supposed social others involving all of the expressions of language is an integral part of any instance of the language and the language learning process. Because the psychological and sociological benefits of written language literacy are available to literates and even illiterates who are present in the event, print is a necessary, but not a sufficient, condition for understanding literacy and the processes involved in literacy learning.

While in the final analysis each language user and learner must function by him or herself, they are never psycholinguistically on their own. Psycholinguistic activities are sociologically available to language learners as they participate in a literacy event observing other language users engaging in the process. In a literate environment, identification of objects which are considered culturally significant signs (like written language), and what these signs signify in terms of psychological and sociological stances and actions are possible through observation of the participatory activities of others engaged in the events.

Understanding that one stops a car at a stop sign, eats at a McDonald's, or attends very carefully to story details to be successful in the classroom, is not something one learns by abstract thinking about print, but by inferring relationships between print and the actions of other participating representatives of the culture. While language labels (such as words) are arbitrary, the psycholinguistic and sociolinguistic actions they sign are concretely referenced through a variety of experiences and encounters with language in use. Language is a socio-psycholinguistic process, not just a psycholinguistic one.

These findings suggest that how one learns written language is not different from how one learns oral language. Further, they illustrate how valuable the opportunity to encounter literacy in a wide variety of written language events is for each of us. The socio-psycholinguistic process by which we made our last written language discovery is no different from how we learned our first. What makes a good written language learning environment for us makes a good written language learning environment for a child.

Context.   Often we mistakenly assume that print is the linguistic sign in literacy. In reality, the linguistic sign is formed by the union of text in context. This is why words mean different things in different settings. The S-T-O-P on a stop sign, signs "Stop." The same logo embedded in an advertisement with Ban Underarm Deodorant signs, "Ban stops wetness." Still another language user may interpret the sign as a confirmation of the regulatory function of all environmental print. Situational context is not something one can consider or not consider— it is not a variable; it is an inextricable part of the thing we call a linguistic sign.

Embedded in text is context. The contextual rules of language use (pragmatics) reflect themselves in the semantic, syntactic, and grapho-phonemic systems of language. Since context is embedded in language, it is also signed in the part of language we call print. In its function as a contextualized surface text, print psychologically and sociologically signs to the language user what interpretive actions to take and what activities to do. This is as true of the language of classrooms as it is of the language of research reports. Psycholinguistically and sociolinguistically, language is always "whole" in all instances of use. Since both language and classrooms are inherently social, classrooms have the potential to be qualitatively natural language learning environments in which quantitatively a greater number of opportunities for engagement in productive language learning circumstances can occur.

Text.   In the production of signifying structures in order to mean in writing, a surface text is created. This surface text is different from the real text which remains in the head of the originator. When someone else reads this surface text in search of signifying structures and interprets their significance, a new text is born. The constructive processes of creating texts in reading and writing are thus open. This openness is assured because our perception of signifying structures, and what they mean, is in part a function of the transactions which occur between context and the personal history of literacy we bring to the process.

Just as writing does not entail simply taking what we know linguistically and translating this into written language, so reading does not entail taking written language and simply translating this into linguistic thought. Because both of these processes involve other than linguistic ways of knowing, semantic negotiation and orchestration between and across communication systems are central characteristics of the psycholinguistic processes involved in text creation in reading and writing.

Such psycholinguistic activity takes place within the context of our personal histories of literacy, which include the past texts we have created to make sense of our world. The search for unity within the evolving text and with past texts creates psychological tensions which propel the reading and self-correction process, the writing and revision process, and the learning process more generally.

Demonstrations. It is through encountering the demonstrations of literacy in the actions and artifacts of the event that language learners come to perceive the organizational patterns or signifying structures involved in written language and what it is they are to make of them. Since attending to and making sense of available demonstrations is in the self-interest of the language learner, language users of all ages are extremely sensitive to any demonstration which they perceive to be a potentially predictable sign or signifying structure. Practically, this means that the language user is never bored with the process, no matter how many times he or she self-selects the opportunity to encounter or engage in a particular literacy event. Once the language user has perceived the significance of one organizational feature of language, the language user actively searches for unity for orchestrating and reorchestrating this discovery in terms of extant assimilative schema. If a tentative unity or an unresolvable disunity occurs, attention moves to other more interesting and compelling demonstrations in the setting. Because the mind is constantly learning and refuses to be bored by attending to what it already knows, when the language user decides there is nothing new to learn, or what there is to learn isn't worth the effort, his attention automatically shifts elsewhere.

This process of attending to and orchestrating available demonstrations is never-ending. Language is laced with organization and is an open system—meaning, in effect, that the language user can attribute organizational patterns or invent signifying patterns which from someone else's perspective are not there. Similarly, the communicative efficiency and effectiveness of a written language setting is enhanced when the complex of available demonstrations signs a unified meaning. Instructional settings designed to support written language literacy must be interested in which demonstrations are made available through not only the content of what they teach, but also through how they teach that content.

There is no sequence to the order in which the demonstrations involved are inherently learned. Which demonstrations are learned is a function of which demonstrations are highlighted. The context in which literacy learning occurs strongly affects the nature and direction of literacy learning. Since literacy growth can only occur in settings which contain or call for demonstrations for which we have only partial assimilative schema, good language learning settings are those in which language users are only tentatively satisfied, and where they assume that with continual engagement they would be able to code, overcode, or interpret other organizational features in the texts they read or produce.

The search for invention and the orchestration of these signifying structures is governed by the search for text and the creation of a unified meaning. Because of the human mind's penchant for cognitively setting aside the old while focusing on the new, signifying structures previously understood, but not functionally the focus of attention, reappear in surface texts when language users have continued opportunities to engage and reengage in the event.

In the search, identification, and interpretation of signifying structures in order to create a unified meaning, language users make active use of the alternative communication systems and the alternative expressions of language. Psycholinguistically and sociolinguistically what these alternate communication systems and expressions of language offer users are alternative stances whereby they can triangulate their learning of, about, and through written language. Within this continual process of learning written language, learning about written language, and learning through written language the individual and societal potentials of literacy in the service of and the expression of human potential occur.

Section
Three

Taking
Ownership

Chapter 16

Conceptual Implications

The authoring cycle is introduced as a demonstration curriculum reflecting natural language processing.

Science proceeds on the basis of belief, not fact. In designing research and in planning curriculum we must, in light of what we then know, take our best shot, while simultaneously designing settings where those beliefs are vulnerable to change and growth is possible. When old beliefs are found wanting, new beliefs, which better fit the data, need to be generated. This section revisits the working hypotheses upon which we built this program of research in order to clarify how our thinking has changed, and to identify what we see as the conceptual and methodological implications of these changes for the study of written language and written language learning.

THE SYSTEMS OF LANGUAGE

If linguistics and sociolinguists were right, no system of language could be studied in isolation from other systems of language. Figure 16.1 presents our conceptualization of language when we began this program of research. This model conceives of language as being made up of three systems of language: semantics (meaning), syntax (grammar), and graphophonemics (letter-sound). Language is conceived of as a sphere with meaning or semantics as the core. In written language this meaning is expressed in lexicogrammatical arrays; hence, sheathing this meaning core is the syntactic system and the graphophonemic system of language. We assumed that the focus of language in use was meaning (semantics) and that to operate, these outer systems had to be transparent. If they became opaque, that is, if the language user focused his or her attention on the outer systems, language did not work. The dotted lines in this model are meant to suggest that all systems are open and do not operate independently of each other. It is the openness of these systems which forms new subsystems of language like the morphemic system (ortho-

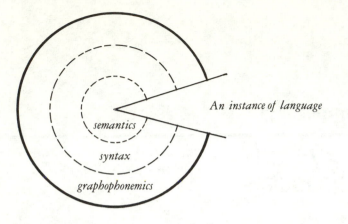

An instance of language

semantics

syntax

graphophonemics

Figure 16.1. Whole Language Model (Harste & Burke, 1977).

graphic patterns which sign meaning), story grammar (syntax of semantic system; i.e., the order of semantic chunks in narratives), and the like. The wedge in the model is meant to suggest that any instance of language contains all three systems when the focus of language is on meaning (see the selected writings of K. Goodman in Gollasch, 1982a, 1982b).

What this model meant for research purposes is that if we wanted to study what children knew about letter-sound relationships prior to coming to school, and we did, such a microanalysis had to be done from data collected in situations where all of the systems were available and operative. At the start of this study we suspected that children accessed the semantic system of language and that it was this access which led to control of the graphophonemic and syntactic systems. If such a belief were not tenable, that is, if control of the graphophonemic system were indeed a prerequisite to access of the reading or writing processes, the children's behavior would force us to abandon our initial beliefs.

In hindsight we have not had to abandon our model, although we have had to expand it because our initial hypothesis proved faulty. We no longer believe control of meaning precedes form in written language development; rather, in use, form and meaning transact: form clarifies and generates meaning, and meaning governs revision of surface text forms in both reading and writing. We introduced the concept of "text intent" to explain this phenomenon. Our data suggest that the decisions which children make are "orchestrated"; to make a semantic decision is to simultaneously make a syntactic and a graphophonemic one.

Given this insight we began to see the systems of language not as "real" in any sense of that word, but simply as linguistic devices researchers have used to discuss the complex phenomena called language. We have also come to understand and appreciate the conceptual advantage and danger of such a procedure. The advantage is that such taxonomies allow us to talk about complex processes. To date we, too, have no other alternative terminology and so only unfortunately continue this tradition. The danger is that once we and others put such reductionistic terminology and analytic devices on the floor, others, like cognitive psychologists, use them to think with and conceptualize cognitive processing models for language. Often, while they accept the reductionistic categories in the taxonomies, they do not accept the constraint that any system of language operates in isolation. While the models they develop often have data to support them, these data more often than not have been collected through research designs which violate this latter premise. As a consequence, this process leads to the positing of cognitive processing models for language which suggest that language users make a series of semantic, syntactic, and graphophonemic decisions in processing language. Soon the literature is replete with talk of "top-down" and "bottom-up" processing, or combinations of the two under different conditions, proficiency of reader, etc., and a "compensatory hypothesis" is born. The end result is that the taxonomic device, rather than moving the profession ahead, causes it to become sidetracked and confused with issues which were never real language issues in the first place.

We have, for example, no evidence from this program of research that children make a series of isomorphic decisions relative to each system of language in either learning or using language. Our data instead suggest that children made a single decision and that that decision is "textual." The principle that guides their search is: "What's the right text for this context?" We have found that even responses which appear to represent attention to the graphophonemic system (i.e., "Cro-Cro-Crost" [Leslie, age 7, when shown a Crest toothpaste carton and asked "What does this say?"]) are in reality textual. This first grader's experience in reading instruction focused on sounding out words, and because we looked like teachers and collected this data in a room in the school, Leslie's response of "Cro-Cro-Crost" also represented an attempt to interpret what she perceived to be the signifying structures available in this setting and to produce an orchestrated text to fit the context.

Further, and as a result of this program of research, we no longer believe in, nor would we again use the term "control" in relation to language. Imbedded in the use of this notion is a latent belief that language is a perfectable absolute. Our data show that language varies by the context of situation and that no two language events are exactly the same. Each and every instance of written language use calls for active, on-the-spot decision-making, based on one's interpretation of perceived signifying structures particular to this context, in an attempt to create a successful text.

We would call attention also to our use of the phrase "successful text."

We now prefer this term *successful* to others which we have tried. In our search we tried and abandoned the phrase "appropriate text," since that phrase reflects an outsider's, rather than an insider's, view of language. When one holds or adopts a theory-of-use perspective on language, and, a language user produces it, it has to be "appropriate." From the language user's perspective the text is appropriate; whether or not it is successful we and the language user can judge when given the subsequent course of the event itself.

For similar reasons we have also avoided as much as possible the use of the term *proficient*. The problem with this term is that the way it is currently used in most of the literature assumes that "proficient" is a monolithic state of being; either a reader or writer is proficient or he or she is not proficient. Used in this sense, proficiency becomes a blocking variable in many language studies. When used in this fashion, "proficiency" appears to be the state a language user enters and assumes literacy to be a monolithic skill.

Our data suggest language users are successful in some settings, but less successful in others. "Successful" is a term which, while not totally adequate, permits us for the time being to focus our attention, and that of those with whom we interact, on a particular instance of literacy without buying into what we have called the "light-switch theory of literacy" (either you have it or you don't).

This program of reseach has altered further our notions about systems of language by forcing us to discover pragmatics (the social rules of language use in a specific context) as a true fourth system of language. As a result of this program of research, we have come to see the linguistic sign not as phonemes (oral language) or graphemes (written language) + syntax + semantics + pragmatics, but rather as cue systems in transaction with each other and with the cue systems of other communication systems. Alter the context of situation, and the pragmatics (the rules of language use in this context of situation) changes, and with it, how the semantic, syntactic, and graphophonemic systems operate.

Figure 16.2 is an attempt to conceptualize our current model of language. This model suggests that pragmatics is the system that binds language users together in a language event. By viewing any instance of language as always involving two language users (even when one of them is a book or, more generally, written language), what rules operate in a particular language situation is open to negotiation between the participants in the event. This is why we may read a book for purposes which the author never intended, and also why studying the book will not in itself lead us to identify signifying structures and hence those processes involved in comprehension and comprehending.

The dotted lines in this model are meant to suggest that all systems are open. When pragmatic negotiation occurs any change in rules is reflected in how the semantic, syntactic, and graphophonemic systems operate.

An example of how this model applies involving settings used in this program of research might help clarify this point and the model itself. At first glance much environmental print, like the "Drive Thru" on the marquee at McDonald's, does not seem to have a true syntax. This, we now understand, is untrue. The rules of language use in environmental print settings (the pragmatics of the context of literacy) not only specify the syntactic patterns, but also specify and legitimize spelling patterns. In this instance, the spelling of the *through*, as T-H-R-U, in contrast to other spelling possibilities which also might be legitimized for use in this setting, operates as a potential sign. In our city, a competing restaurant went up across the street from McDonald's with a marquee which said "Drive Through" as opposed to "Drive Thru." Given what we know about language from this program of research we now would hypothesize that language users would search for signifying structures like this in this setting (Through vs. Thru), assume intentionality, and infer that this new restaurant was purposely attempting to say something different. By studying how language users interpret this new marquee in relation to the McDonald's marquee, we could come to understand its sign function and the interpretive procedures involved.

Research Implications. Because the basic premises underlying the model of language used in this program of research were expanded, but not found untenable, some of the conceptual implications for

Figure 16.2. Language as a Social Event.

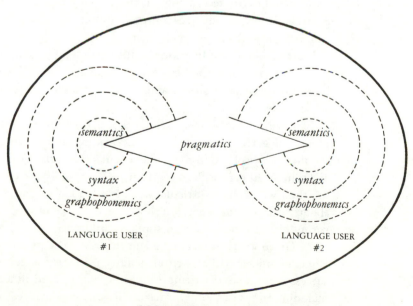

CONTEXT OF SITUATION

research of the position expressed in our revised model are the same as in the original. To clarify our current position, we sketch these and other implications for research involving the study of language and learning below. This list is meant to be suggestive, not exhaustive.

1. Since language only exists in use, functional real natural language settings, where all systems are allowed to transact, are more profitable ones for developing theory and curriculum than are controlled language settings that have built into them basic assumptions about language which are in need of testing.

2. Important research and curricular positions taken by the profession, which are based on research results that have attempted to isolate the systems of language for purposes of study, need to be replicated in functional language situations where all of the systems of language are permitted to operate simultaneously and in transaction with each other.

3. Because language use and learning is context dependent and a relationship always exists between constraints operating in a language setting and the linguistic resources called upon and used by language users in this setting, contrastive settings are helpful in highlighting these transactions and exploring key processes in language and language learning.

4. Given that reading and writing are social processes, researchers must recognize and accept pragmatic negotiations as real data, including in their analyses descriptions of their own involvement and influence during the course of the event. Further, because language is an event which takes time and which occurs between language users, researchers must attend to and record how the rules of language use change over the event, and how such changes continually alter and influence all aspects of language as well as the event itself.

Instructional Implications. Instructionally, the implications of perceiving language as a social event are far-reaching. The theoretically based instructional positions and activities which flow from this model are as follows:

1. Reading and writing are tools which language users use in the process of getting things done. The reading and writing curriculum should not be isolated from other curricular areas, but rather be a natural and functional part of the opportunities selected by the class for exploring their world. The curricular issue is not what we can teach children about written language, but how we can use reading and writing naturally and functionally to support children in their learning.

2. Given that written language learning occurs through written language use, and that written language literacy is central to school success, reading and writing should be highlighted in all classrooms, including the preschool. Our recommendation is that teachers litter the environment with print. We have found that when a reading center and

a writing center are located in or moved into the middle of the classroom, as opposed to a corner of it, children's involvement with books, paper, and pencil increases dramatically. Any and all opportunities to introduce print naturally should be taken.

3. Language users learn written language through meaningful encounters with print. Children, as active written language learners, should be given multiple opportunities to test their written language hypotheses in a low-risk environment. Open-ended language arts activities, in which the child is permitted to test and supported in the testing of his or her written language hypotheses, are recommended.

4. Written language varies by situational context. Teachers have a responsibility to introduce children to a wide variety of written language contexts as they provide children opportunities to expand, explore, and discover their world. Writing daily journals, newspapers, message boards, letters to pen pals, recipes, menus, reading environmental print, and other functional uses of written language, in addition to the use of stories and trade books in content areas, should be a natural part of all classroom environments. In preschool classrooms a play area with a note pad by the telephone, a "sign-in please" station where children take their own attendance, a grocery store, a restaurant, a post office, and other similar settings allow natural and functional uses of written language. Since language varies by the circumstances of its use, letter writing as well as story writing should be done under a number of different settings. Predictable books (Rhodes, 1981), jump-rope jingle books, and environmental-print walks (which can lead to the making of class- and child-composed product books [Milz, 1980]) are further suggestions. The role of the teacher is to help children understand the predictability of print in a wide variety of contexts.

5. Choice is an integral part of the language process. Participants in a language event have the right as responders, for example, to ask another question rather than to answer the question asked (pragmatic negotiation), or as writers, to decide to allocate parts of their texts to art, context, inference, etc. (semantic negotiation). These rights need to be respected in the classroom. Teachers' efforts to introduce new contexts of literacy and to expand the child's world should be handled as invitations. We have found that once a child engages in an activity and shares his or her work, even initially not-well-received invitations gain in popularity.

6. The focus of language in use is meaning. Instructional activities should not isolate the systems of language for formal study, but rather, should be natural and functional parts of the children's exploration of reading and writing as they use written language to explore their world. This does not mean that educators cannot identify materials which highlight particular organizational features in written language which they see as central to understanding literacy in a given context. But, it

does mean that any such feature identified must be naturally highlighted within real written language settings and the child's right respected to select or reject attending to that feature and test instead his or her own hypotheses.

Similarly, which features of written language are learned and in what order they are learned is a function of context, purpose, interest, and the background of experience of the language user. Analysis of a sample of children's writing and reading efforts over time permits identification of which organizational features have already been attended to as well as what the current interests and zones of proximal development in children are. In light of this information, particular instructional activities might be selected or developed to support children's exploration of literacy, since such activities represent real instances of written language use.

7. Written language learning and use involves orchestration of the cue complexes of literacy in a particular context. Free access to a wide selection of writing materials and writing instruments ought to be centrally available and a permanent part of the classroom so that children can choose items they see as appropriate given the context and purpose of their writing.

8. When reading and writing events take place in classrooms where participants have unequal social status, teachers must be particularly careful of not taking ownership of the process away from children. Our role as teachers is support of, rather than intervention in, the learning process. As teachers we can organize the social environment of the classroom to support the language user's perception, organization, and presentation of texts in reading and writing.

LANGUAGE IN A SYSTEM OF KNOWING

We believe in planning our research that in order to address language, we also had to address the relationship between language and thought more broadly. Alternative communication systems represent "alternative literacies" which transact to support and enrich any specific literacy (such as written language literacy). Conceptually, Figure 16.3 illustrates these notions by suggesting that the sum of what we as individuals or as a society know across alternate communication systems constitutes a "communication potential" of which language is but one system. Figure 16.3 suggests that what ties the humanities is a common semantic or meaning system, although it is not meant to suggest that all of what is known is equally accessible to a particular communication system. Rather, the sum of what is known across communication systems constitutes a meaning potential. By this view, society, and the school curricula which that society creates to further its ends, ought to be

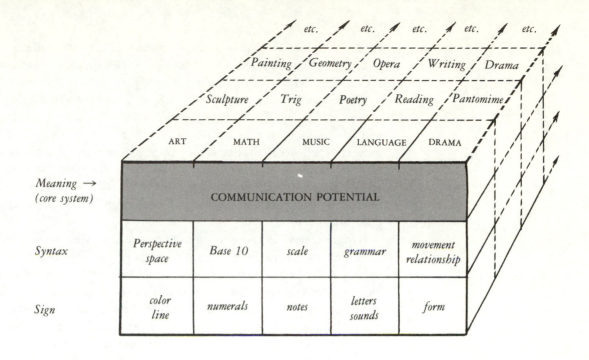

	ART	MATH	MUSIC	LANGUAGE	DRAMA
Meaning → (core system)	COMMUNICATION POTENTIAL				
Syntax	Perspective space	Base 10	scale	grammar	movement relationship
Sign	color line	numerals	notes	letters sounds	form

(Upper layers: Sculpture, Trig, Poetry, Reading, Pantomime; Painting, Geometry, Opera, Writing, Drama; etc.)

Figure 16.3. Communication Potential Model.

concerned with expanding communication potential rather than systematically shutting off certain forms of expression through overemphasizing some of the humanities and neglecting others (see Eisner, 1982).

We suspected, when we went into this study, that systems strong for the child (like art) could support weaker systems (like written language). We therefore wanted natural settings where alternative communication systems were an available part of the event. If such communication systems were not used by the language learner, or when available, were not facilitative but rather detracted from successful reading and writing, such data would force us to abandon our initial model and the beliefs which it entailed.

While the findings of this program of research support this position, our initial thinking about the relationships involved between language and alternative communication systems in the service of literacy learning proved extremely simplistic. We no longer believe that such neat distinctions between language and the alternative communication systems are possible. Not only do alternative communication systems support language, but language supports alternative communication systems. In our study, children as frequently moved from writing to art as from art to writing.

Further, we came to understand that in use, the "linguistic sign" is a cue complex which is multimodal in nature. Cue systems from alternative communication systems are embedded in and make up this linguistic cue complex. That this is readily evident we have shown in environmental print settings, the asides children make in reading, and in the surface texts which they produce in writing.

We believe that this is true for all surface texts whether or not they are the result of oral or written language encounters. We believe that this is why, for example, some poetry must be seen and other poetry heard in order to experience their effects. Each communication mode adds its own additional signifying structures which must be orchestrated, and only in unity with the signifying structures of other available communication modes does the potential meaning of a selection become a perceptual possibility.

Given the reading and writing responses of the children we studied, the multimodal nature of the linguistic sign is a key feature not only in literacy but in literacy learning. We now see meaning, in any instance of language, as conveyed simultaneously through linguistic (discursive) and paralinguistic (nondiscursive) aspects of the event. In written language this is done through formatting, type size and thickness, packeting, layouts, charts, graphs, and pictures, all of which in transaction with print are signifying structures with the potential in use to sign meaning. In oral language the use of gestures, intonation, and contextual referencing (pointing), contributes to the multimodal nature of oral expression. In short, our program of research forced us to abandon what in retrospect might be termed a "verbocentric" view of literacy and to adopt a semiotic one, in which the orchestration of all signifying structures from all available communication systems in the event have an integral part.

Research Implications.   Some of the methodological implications of this position for research are sketched below:

1. Since we do not fully understand what role signifying structures from alternative communication systems play in literacy learning, research and curricular studies should be conducted in functional natural language situations where transactions between and among these communication systems can be studied.

2. Methodologically, analytic devices for describing the patterns of linguistic and nonlinguistic signifying structures which emerge in the data from research and curricular studies need to be included in studies of literacy and literacy learning.

3. Cognitive processing models from which language and curricular studies are conceptualized must be capable of explaining how linguistic and nonlinguistic signifying structures are orchestrated by the language user and how they operate in literacy and literacy learning.

4. Since any language experience is multimodal, curriculum and research need to be designed so that *how* we teach or do research in relation to *what* we teach and do research about, are coordinated in terms

of the signifying structures demonstrated by each, and their impact on the literacy learning studied. Contrastive settings need to be identified where conflicting signifying structures are simultaneously demonstrated and these settings compared and contrasted with settings theoretically presumed to be more communicatively effective and efficient.

Instructional Implications.   In the final analysis the goal of the language arts program involves expansion of the child's communication potential. Activities which involve other than linguistic ways of knowing should be an integral and natural part of the language arts curriculum.

1. As an alternative to questioning, we have found that children can be asked to draw and share a sketch of what they think a story means. Acting out stories which they have read, pantomiming the actions of their favorite character, putting their stories to music, and other such activities heighten awareness and story appreciation. Similar activites can be used in content area reading.

2. Art can be used as a vehicle to help children organize their thinking prior to writing, or as a keep-going strategy when they experience writer's block. Pantomimes can help children get in touch with their feelings and facilitate quality writing. Music can be used to set a mood for reading or writing. Children can be encouraged to select music to go with their oral readings of the stories they write.

3. A wide variety of art and musical materials should be available in the classroom. Children should be encouraged to create their own props, put on their own plays, create story murals, conduct book sales, create bookmarks and flyers for their favorite books, etc., often in lieu of the traditional oral or written book report.

4. Signing one's meaning is a complex process. Children should be given ample opportunity to experiment with alternative ways of expressing their meanings in writing. At the writing center, crayons, colored magic markers, colored construction paper, glue, scissors, etc., should be available. Children should be encouraged to illustrate their books and other writing by exploring a wide variety of techniques by which they might better capture their meaning.

5. Reading and writing are aesthetic experiences in their own rights. Living through a story read aloud, sensing the rhythm of a poem, a well-written novel, a joke, a jump-rope jingle, are real written language experiences in their own rights. Written language experiences need not be formally dissected and analyzed for them to be good learning experiences. A particular favorite class poem, song, etc., can be illustrated by the child, kept in a folder, and revisited on a regular basis. Through repeated encounters children can attend to other demonstrations available in the event and their appreciation can be heightened.

Carolyn L. Burke has attempted to capture some of the essential notions of our thinking underlying the relationships of reading and writing in a system of language in a model she has entitled "The Linguistic Data Pool" (Harste, Burke, Woodward, 1981). The central notions which she attempts to portray (see Figure 16.4) are:

1. What language users learn from a language encounter feeds a common pool of linguistic data which can be drawn upon in a subsequent language encounter;
2. Oral language encounters provide data for written language encounters and vice versa;
3. Growth in a given expression of language must be seen as a multilingual event; in reading, for example, hearing a set of directions read, encountering written language with others, listening to a book, talking about a newspaper article, or attempting to write one's own story, all support growth and development in literacy.

Burke is not the only one to conceptualize language in this way (Moffett, 1968; Smith, 1980; King & Rental, undated). The importance of this conceptualization is that it proposes a parallel development for the language arts and seriously challenges existing notions relating to the supremacy of oral language in the development of written language (typically, listening is assumed to precede speaking, speaking to precede reading, reading to precede writing).

Oral language as primary is a notion that currently undergirds most formal language programs in this country. The model in Figure 16.4 is not meant to suggest that all of the expressions of language are the same, only that language shares much in common across expressions. This being the case, one strategy which initiate as well as seasoned language users can and do use is building on their available strengths in other expressions.

This model and the data we collected in this program of research did much to clarify our thinking about the relationship between reading, writing, reasoning, and the psycholinguistic processes involved in literacy and literacy learning. One of the first things we discovered, for example, was that a writing event involved much more than writing; also included in the event were speaking, listening, and reading. Similarly, we noted that from the child's perspective, creating a unified text in reading shared psycholinguistic similarities to composing a text in writing. Further, the rereading of one's own writing shared much in common, psycholinguistically, with a process called editing in writing.

From a cognitive processing perspective, the traditional distinctions between reading as a receptive activity and writing as an expressive activity did not hold up. Reading was as expressive as writing, and both

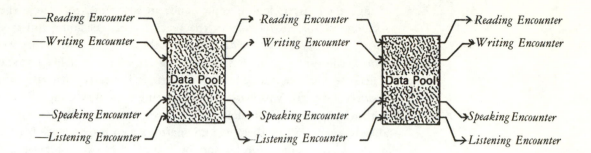

Figure 16.4. The Linguistic Data Pool.

entailed the creation of and search for a unified text.

Conceptually, Figure 16.5 depicts what we saw as occurring in light of our evolving model of language. What this model suggests is that underlying these expressions was a common language process, and that within a literacy event, pragmatic negotiation was possible between the expressions of language.

In this regard, we observed that shifts to alternative expressions of language (to pronounce a word orally during reading or spelling, to ask a

Figure 16.5. Reading and Writing in a System of Language.

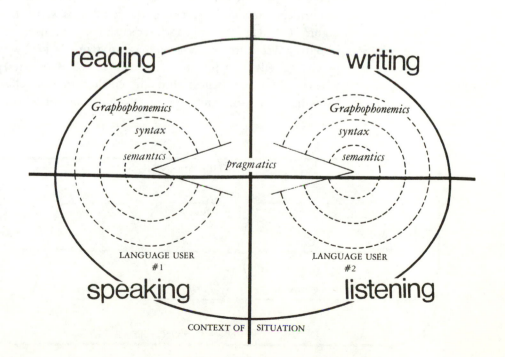

neighbor a question, to converse with a friend, to listen to a neighbor, to reread the evolving surface text) offered language users opportunities to change their psychological stance and, in so doing, to change their sociological role in relation to the text. As writers going full-speed ahead, language users were *participants* in the event; as readers they were *editors*, concerned with those signifying structures which editors are concerned with; as speakers their questions indicated that they were *monitors* of what they had written, contrasting what they wanted to write with what they knew or thought others would want to know or might already know. While there was no one-to-one correspondence between mode of expression and role, nor any guarantee of psychological shift, the opportunity for such negotiations of role was available at these points. More often than not the invitation to switch roles was accepted with the effect that there was a preceptible shift in stance toward the text.

We then noted that moves to alternative communication systems serve this same function psychologically for the language user, inviting and permitting semantic negotiation between the alternative communication systems. Conceptually, what these semantic and pragmatic negotiations offered the language user were invitations to take alternative perspectives of and on knowing.

Anthropologists use the term "triangulation" to describe a research procedure common to their discipline in which the participant-observer studies a phenomenon like marriage from the perspective of the bride and bridegroom and the parents of the couples, as well as from his own. Figure 16.6 likens the language user's use of alternative communication systems and the expressions of language to triangulation by positing that psychologically, they permit individuals (as well as societies) to triangulate or take other stances through which they can self-verify their knowing. Given the metaphor of triangulation, what such shifts and

*Figure 16.6. Triangulation:
A Psycholinguistic and
Sociolinguistic Processing Strategy
in Literacy Driven by the Search
for Text in Context and a Unified
Meaning.*

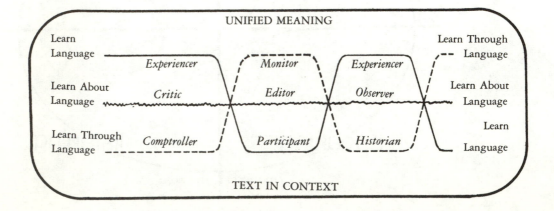

moves in literacy provide the individual are cognitive self-correcting strategies. As such, this model conceptually lays out what we now see as a fundamental process in literacy learning. It argues that a literacy event contains a number of signifying structures and simultaneous demonstrations which are potentially available for interpretation and signification by the language user. From the perspective of literacy and literacy learning these demonstrations provide the language user opportunities to learn how to use written language, to learn about written language and to learn through written language. Within a literacy event language users can and do shift to alternative communication systems and to alternative expressions of language. Each of these shifts allows the language user to take a new psychological stance and therefore also, a new sociological one in terms of his or her role and involvement with the text. Each new stance allows the language user an opportunity to marshall what it is he knows about language and to search for new arrangements of signifying structures and unity across such structures. In this process of using and, at the same time, learning written language, expansion and exploration of human and literacy potentials occur.

Research Implications.   Some of the conceptual implications for research suggested by this model are listed here:

1. Given the psycholinguistic and sociolinguistic processing similarities between reading and writing within and across a wide variety of literacy contexts, broadly conceived functional literacy programs are needed in which there are opportunities for both language learners and language researchers to further explore these transactive relationships.

2. If the distinctions between communication systems and the expression of language which we have drawn in the past are dysfunctional from a psycholinguistic and sociolinguistic processing perspective, then curriculum and research are better served using as their organizational structure functional literacy events where such transactions are possible.

3. Since we theoretically already know that not all classroom literacy programs are equally meritorious of study, initial selection of classroom research sites should be done using criteria based on our best information about the transactive relationship between context and the sociolinguistic and psycholinguistic processes involved in literacy. Collaborative arrangements should be built into the design of the study in order to further explore these relationships and to enhance the potential of classrooms as functional and natural literacy learning environments.

4. Given the complexity and universality of the psycholinguistic and sociolinguistic processes involved in literacy and literacy learning, settings involving young children and other initiate written language learners, where such processes might be studied in their unfrozen form, are encouraged to further needed theoretical work and its clarification.

Instructional Implications. Children can be supported in their reading and writing through activities which allow them to change their psychological stances, and thus give them an alternative perspective on the literacy process. Theoretically based instructional positions and activities which we have taken and which build on these insights are as follows:

1. Writing is an event, not an act. As such, writing is a process which occurs over time and which demands multiple and extended opportunities for engagement and reengagement. Classroom writing programs should be organized to reflect this process. Practically, this means large blocks of uninterrupted writing time and recognition of the role of writing as a functional and self-educative process. Convention is a natural part of the process, since selected drafts will be considered by children for revision, publication, and distribution to audiences beyond the classroom.

2. Teachers need to provide children multiple opportunities to experience the demonstrations available in the actions and artifacts of various types of written language literacies. To this end, teachers need to read and write with their children and to share their interpretations of selections. They also need to share their own writing when in draft form and seek help from the children. Further, as part of the language arts program, authors can be invited into the classroom. In a variety of other ways, teachers can help children develop functional notions of what is involved in writing. Because of their past histories of literacy, many children are overly concerned with conventions such as correct spelling and good grammar. An editor's table can do much to sign to the children that these concerns will be addressed at an appropriate point in the process, but that for now, they have to move ahead functionally by getting their thoughts on paper. Children must learn that no one can be an editor of their manuscript before they produce one.

3. Reading and writing are social events. Discussions with neighbors prior to, during, and after involvement are not disruptions to the process, but a natural part of the process itself. Successful writers use friends in order to discuss where they might go next and what arguments still need to be developed, and to verify for themselves that their writing has the effect they desire. Opportunities to build from the natural social support of the classroom should be a part of the language arts curriculum. During reading, children can be encouraged at selected points in the selection to say something to their neighbor about what they make of their reading up to that point. Cognitively, these discussions with their neighbors help children access assimilative schemas whereby they might further tie and integrate their understanding. An author's circle, in which authors could receive ideational and strategic support from other authors in the areas they wished, whenever they thought such support

would be helpful to them, might be a regular feature of the classroom.

4. From a cognitive processing perspective, reading and writing share much in common. Juxtaposing reading and writing in activities which highlight one or the other of these processes can do much to facilitate and support literacy learning. Before children write, books can be made available and children encouraged to read widely in a subject, take notes on 3" × 5" cards, organize these cards and use them as a global, but tentative plan for organizing their ideas for writing. Extended units where children read about a subject, write about that subject, read some more, write some more and so on, including experiences which involve the alternative expressions of language and the communication systems, should be explored. Dialogue journals (Staton, 1980), and written conversations (Burke, 1980) are informal but functional writing settings which juxtapose reading and writing and in so doing, offer language users the additional support they need.

5. Some of the potentials of literacy can only occur when language users have repeated opportunities to engage in the event over time. The opportunity for children to read a variety of books on a single topic or by a single author over a period of time allows them to identify those features which distinguish one author from another. Letter writing over time allows children to explore the potentials of this genre and to extend their own letter writing abilities. Asking children to read a selection a number of different times for a number of different purposes—once for the author, once for themselves, once to discover and think about what and why their neighbor underlined the things he or she did—can help children shift psychological stances and highlight appreciation for the reading process.

CONCLUSIONS

Figure 16.7 summarizes the conceptual insights we gleaned about literacy and literacy learning from a conceptual model we label "The Authoring Cycle." We see this authoring cycle as characterizing language learning generally, and reading and writing specifically. This model summarizes the key cognitive processes we came to see as involved in literacy by suggesting that:

1. Literacy is governed by the search for a unified meaning or "text." In beginning the cycle an abductive search of past experience or past "texts" serves as an anticipatory frame. The language learner's use of text to fine-tune text is a process we label, after De Beaugrande (1980), "intertextual tying." We see it as a fundamental process in literacy use and learning. Cognitively, intertextual tying and the evolution of a text specific to a particular context involve all the major forms of logic—abduction, induction, and deduction (see Deely, 1982). The cycle as represented in this model is further meant to suggest that any instance of

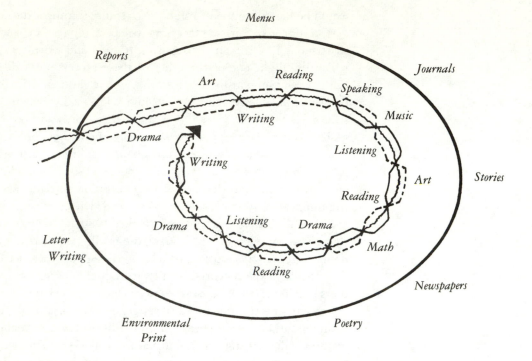

Menus
Reports
Journals
Art   Reading
Speaking
Music
Writing
Drama
Listening
Writing
Art
Stories
Reading
Drama
Listening
Drama
Letter
Writing
Math
Reading
Newspapers
Environmental
Print
Poetry

Figure 16.7 The Authoring Cycle

literacy is best seen as an event that occurs in time. As such, one's own history of literacy is an integral part of that process.

2. Literacy is multimodal. Involvement of alternative, available expressions of language (speaking, listening, reading, writing) and communication systems (language, art, math, music, drama, etc.) allow language users to psychologically and sociologically shift stances and get a new perspective on their knowing. We label these shifts and moves "negotiation" and the process involved "triangulation." These shifts and moves afford language users (following Halliday, 1980) the opportunity to simultaneously learn language, learn about language, and learn through language. Even further, the multimodal nature of language as well as the multimodal nature of the language event constitute a self-correcting potential inherent in the process itself.

3. The oval surrounding the authoring cycle is meant to suggest that literacy is context dependent. In its specific detail, the authoring cycle or any instance of the cycle is dependent on the context of situation in which it occurs. The labels on the outside of the oval represent alternative contexts of situation—journals, reports, newspapers, poetry, stories, environmental print, personal letters, etc.—and are meant to be suggestive of generalized but culturally specified contexts of literacy around which we might organize curriculum, and within which we

might study the particular circumstances of language use as well as the particular ways in which these cognitive processing universals are expressed.

It is important to understand that this model has conceptual implications not only for research but for curriculum. To illustrate the power of this model for rethinking research and curriculum, we close this section with a classroom language story and literacy lesson pulled from our most recent research files.

Mrs. Mattson invited the children in her kindergarten classroom to write stories. Kammi elected to write a story to go along with the pictures in a wordless book about a group of children finding and burying a dead bird.

Kammi began her story, "Once upon a time there was a dead bird," spelling it WANS APNATIM THAIR WAS A DED BRD. The next page read, " 'That bird is dead,' said Tommy" (THAT BRDA IS DED, SED TOMMY). " 'Oh, what a poor bird' " (OH WAT A POR BIRD). "The girl is crying" (THE GIRY IS CRING). "They're walking to the forest" (THAIR WOKING TO THE FORIST). "They're burying the bird" (THAIR BAIRING THE BIRD). "They are bringing flowers" (THEY R BRINGING FLOWRS). "They are sad" (THEY R SAD). "Tommy looked up at the sky" (TOMMY LOOKT UP AT THE SCI). "They are playing ball" (THEYR PLAIN BLL). Thus drafted, Kammi's story was added to the Writing-Reading Center.

The Writing-Reading Center was literally that: a combination table, bookshelf, post office, and writing supply area in the very center of Mrs. Mattson's classroom. It was here that the predictable books which Mrs. Mattson introduced to the children during one of her three daily Author Sharing Times were kept and made available. It was here that children like Kammi put the books they had drafted and written after they too, as authors, had first shared them during an Author Sharing Time. It was here that children found invitations to write—writing materials and a variety of pens for their every writing need. It was here children were given time simply to explore books, paper, and pens.

Almost a week to the day after Kammi had contributed her book to the Writing-Reading Center, one of Kammi's classmates, Stephanie, took a moment out of her busy day to read it. When she was done she commented, "Oh, Kammi, I like your book."

"Oh," reflected Kammi, "I don't think I much care for it anymore."

Overhearing the conversation, Mrs. Mattson remarked, "And, why is that?"

"Oh, I made a mistake. I shouldn't have just described the pictures. I should of have written about what they [meaning the characters in the pictures] were thinking."

"Well, there are more copies of the book at the Writing-Reading

Center. You might like to redo your story now that you've got a better idea. Most writers, I know, have to rewrite things several times to get them the way they want."

Kammi accepted the invitation. Her second version read: "Once upon a time there was a dead bird" (WANS A PON ATIME THAIR WAS A DEAD BRID). "Tommy said, 'Look at the poor bird' " (TOMMY SEID LOOK AT THT POR BRID). " 'I wonder how that bird got killed' " (I WUNDER HOW THAT BIRD GOT KILD). " 'Let's bury the bird,' said Tory" (LETS BARE THE BIRD, SAID TORY). "So Tory, Kammi, Tommy, and Dick all set out to bury the bird" (SO TORY KAMMI TOMMY AND DICK ALL SET OUT TO BARE THE BIRD). "So Tommy put the bird on the maple leaf so that they didn't have to carry him" (SO TOMMY PUT THE BIRD ON THE MAPLE LEFE SO THAT THAY DIDT HAF TO KAIRY HIM). "Kammi's bringing lots of flowers" (KAMMI'S BRINGING LOTS OF FLOWRS). "They scratched a sign on a rock" (THAY SCRATCHT A SINE NO A ROCK). "They all looked up at the sky to see how the bird got killed" (THEY ALL LOOKT UP AT THE SKY TO SEE HOW THE BIRD GOT KILD). "They were glad that they buried the bird" (THEY WERE GLAD THAT THEY BAIRED THE BIRD).

Before we compared Kammi's revision to her original story, it might be well to ask ourselves whether this would have been a good literacy experience if Kammi had decided not to revise, electing instead to leave her original story as it was?

Even before the revision, Kammi's involvement in the Authoring Cycle permitted her to test her growing understanding of storiness (Applebee, 1979; Stein & Glenn, 1978; Thorndyke, 1977), or wordness (Hiebert, 1978, 1981; Hill, 1980), of how one keeps ideas apart in writing (Clay, 1972, 1975, 1982), of how the sounds of language are mapped onto written letters (Ferreiro & Teberosky, 1982; Chomsky, 1979; Henderson & Beers, 1979, 1980; Read, 1975), of how one uses writing to mean (Bissex, 1980; Goodman & Goodman, 1979; and more (Teale, 1978; Heath 1979; 1980, 1981, 1982). Revision simply gave her an additional opportunity to orchestrate what she already knew by permitting her psychologically and sociologically to take new stances. As we watched her on videotape during the initial writing event, we saw that her reading and speaking—both to herself and neighbors—were an integral part of her writing process. These activities psycholinguistically and sociolinguistically provided much the same support that time and a functional setting provide authors outside classroom settings.

Rather than involving her as a written language user, or *participant*, as she was during the actual writing itself, the sociolinguistic and psycholinguistic "noisy pause" period between her first and second draft allowed Kammi to play other, pensive, writing roles, namely as *critic* and *monitor*.

By intuitively comparing and contrasting over time what she had written with what she already knew about language, stories, and what she wanted to say, she decided that her first effort seemed inadequate. She could do better. A theoretically based classroom environment—one purposely organized to support her involvement in the process sociolinguistically and psycholinguistically—permits Kammi to more fully explore and expand both her literacy potential, and the genre's.

What is impressive about Kammi's revision is that she not only follows through by speculating on what the characters were thinking about (First Draft: " 'That bird is dead,' said Tommy. 'Oh, what a poor bird.' "; Second Draft: "Tommy said, 'Look at that poor bird.' *I wonder* how that bird got killed.' "), but she:

1. explicates several key causal relationships (First Draft: "Tommy looked up at the sky"; Second Draft: "They all looked up at the sky *to see how* the bird got killed");

2. semantically elaborates all of the elements of her story structure (in the First Draft the reader has to infer the *Attempt* and *Reaction* categories (Stein & Glen, 1978); in the Second Draft these well-formed story categories are explicit);

3. reduces semantic redundancy by combining several sentences (First Draft: "Once upon a time there was a *dead bird.*" " 'That bird is dead,' said Tommy." " 'Oh, what a poor bird' "; Second Draft: "Once upon a time there was a dead bird." "Tommy said, 'Look at that poor bird' ");

4. lexicalizes her text by naming all of the characters (in her Second Draft she retains the character *Tommy*, but introduces *Kammi, Tory,* and *Dick*);

5. uses 92 words, of which 52 were different words; as opposed to 51 words in her First Draft, of which 32 were different words (an increase of 80 percent in total words or 65 percent when just new and different words are considered); and,

6. of the 20 common words across both the First and Second Drafts, Kammi spells 50 percent conventionally both times, moves 15 percent to conventional spelling from First to Second Draft (TIM-TIME; DED-DEAD; DRD-BRDA-BRID-BIRD), and moves another 15 percent toward convention; that is, when she used them a second time in the surface text, these words reflected an expanded consideration and orchestration of English spelling strategies (PN-PON; SED-SEID; BAIRING-BARE-BAIRED).

Even given the encouragement of Mrs. Mattson, the socially supportive environment of the classroom, and the semantic support which the pictures provided story composition, Kammi's behavior is truly impressive. Kammi is a 5-year-old going on 6!

How we conceive language and language learning is important. The authoring cycle represents our current best thinking about literacy and the cognitive processes involved in literacy use and learning. As such, it constitutes a curricular potential both for us and for children. It is from the basis of what we now currently know that we proceed.

Chapter 17

Methodological Implications

Teachers and students are invited to participate in literacy as a collaborative effort.

The great unfinished agenda item in language research is the identification and development of an appropriate methodology in light of what we know about language and language learning.

Whether you align yourself with those who view the current popularity of field-based studies as just one more passing fad, or with others who see field investigations as a panacea for all educational research, it is important to understand that this move by the profession has both theoretical and practical roots. In this section we trace recent shifts toward ethnography, to which this program of research has led us, in order to provide a curricular frame by which both teachers and researchers might more profitably proceed.

Some researchers have been drawn to ethnographic approaches because of a growing dissatisfaction with conventional experimental designs. Burton (1973) summarizes this position well:

"Research" has a highly positive connotation in American culture, suggesting the rational, scientific approach to truth and knowledge and is the premium of academe, though in the humanistic-oriented English teaching profession there has been an abiding uneasiness with quantitative methods and perhaps with the empirical approach generally. (p. 160)

From a theoretical perspective this dissatisfaction is more than just a dislike for numbers and a distrust of computers. Language is a particularly human phenomenon (Halliday, 1974). It is this concern for humanism and the role literacy plays in the search for and free expression of the human experience (Emig, 1982) that has led some language arts educators to seek out more theoretically consistent research paradigms.

221

Other language arts educators have been drawn to naturalistic paradigms because they are disappointed by the failure of much recent research to affect teaching and classroom practice. In attempting to play the important role of synthesizer (Goodman, 1979), these educators argue that research which is not understandable and relevant to classroom teachers and administrators fails to serve the educational functions for which it is designed. Kantor, Kirby, and Goetz (1981) argue this point most eloquently:

Educational inquiry should engage researchers and consumers in dialogue rather than isolate them from each other. The findings of descriptive, qualitative, naturalistic, and holistic approaches are often readily interpretable and couched in the language of English professionals. Such research strategies tend to work more with wholes than parts, with describable phenomena rather than inferential quantification, to use the language of the classroom teacher rather than the discourse of the laboratory researcher. (p. 294)

Theorists like Guba (1978), Mishler (1979), and Carey (1980) have argued that experimental inquiry emphasizes hypothesis-testing, control of variables, "stripping" of contexts, educational outcomes, reader-text interactions, generalizability, reductionism, and researcher detachment; while naturalistic inquiry is concerned with hypothesis generation, grounded theory, educational processes, reader-text transactions, contextual relationships such as the effect of the researcher and task on the language process, and participant observation. Without either confronting the issue of what constitutes truth (which we believe to be at the base of these methodological arguments), or buying into methodological eclecticism (a position we believe further demonstrates a failure to understand the fundamental issues), what we wish to do in this section is to acknowledge these discussions, but to add our own clarification by suggesting that the long overdue shift to ethnography represents an attitude and a paradigm which might guide language arts researchers and teachers.

THE ATTITUDE OF ETHNOGRAPHY

Research is not only a product and a process, but an *attitude*. The attitude of research, highlighted by the shift in the profession to ethnography, is "I can find out." This attitude is as important for teachers as it is for researchers. The attitude of ethnography suggests that good teachers act like good researchers and good researchers act like good teachers.

Often in our research and teaching we act as if we were the language informants, but such an attitude is misguided. The research attitude of "I can find out" is absolutely liberating, not only for teachers and researchers, but also for children. For us this new attitude allows a change from testing our language hypotheses to giving children the opportunity to test theirs. For children it allows a change from being language observers to language participants, from being tenants of our texts to owners of their own texts.

The most liberating experience we ever had both as teachers and as researchers, was in approaching language use and language learning with the find-out attitude embodied in the concept, "the child as informant."

The research attitude of "I can find out" often stands in contrast to the ways research is usually taught in institutions of higher education where the means and ends of research are presented as vehicles of proof, and where, because of this view, research is perceived as something one does in graduate education (knowledge production), but not teacher education (knowledge utilization). The attitude of ethnography argues that all gaps—between language theory and language practice, between the language researcher and the language teacher, between language research activities and language instructional activities, between language research settings and language instructional settings—are dysfunctional, and fail in the end to serve the profession.

This is not to suggest that there are not many research perspectives on truth, though it is to argue that some research language truths are more useful than others. It is the intention of this section not only to raise key issues in the ethnography of language arts research and teaching, but also to cast these in some conceptual frame by which the professional teacher-researcher and researcher-teacher might proceed even more productively.

THE PARADIGM OF ETHNOGRAPHY

In order to address and explore these and other research issues more formally, Figure 17.1 presents a theoretically based view of the language arts curriculum. This model represents current thinking about the relationship of teaching, research, and curriculum. Implicit in this model are suggestions that all language research and instruction are not equal; that certain forms of research and instruction are more useful than others; that eclecticism in research and teaching is not only illusionary, but also dangerous; that a relationship exists between what teachers and researchers know on the one hand, and the conditions under which they know it on the other; that to build practice upon practice constitutes anti-intellectualism; that our interest in the language arts as teachers and researchers is, in the final analysis, an interest in learning; that not all

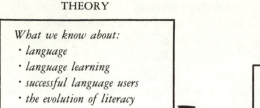

THEORY

What we know about:
· language
· language learning
· successful language users
· the evolution of literacy

THE CHILD AS INFORMANT

In light of what we know, how are these language users performing?

In light of what we know and how these language users are performing, what curricular support should I provide?

CURRICULAR SUPPORT

 = Classrooms as Natural Language Environments

Figure 17.1. A Theoretically Based View of the Language Arts Curriculum.

language settings which we could study are equally worthy of our attention; that classrooms can be made to be natural language environments; that supportive language environments are best not only for instructional decision-making, but also for assessing growth and development; that in the final analysis as a profession we are in this together to improve language arts instruction and to benefit children. This model, while looking quite innocuous, addresses the key issues involved in the ethnographic shift of the profession as they relate to transactions between language arts research and teaching.

The Role of Theory in Research and Instruction. Theoretically the paradigm depicts a transactional relationship between theory and practice. It is meant to argue that instruction must be rooted in theory, and by implication suggests that instruction not so rooted is not professionally productive and should be abandoned. The paradigm suggests four key theoretical areas upon which curriculum is built: what we know about language, what we know about language learning, what we know about successful language users, and what we know about the psycholinguistic and sociolinguistic processes involved in the evolution of literacy. By inference it suggests not only that are these areas and their counterparts (alternative communication systems, unsuccessful language users, etc.) fruitful areas for language study, but also that good language arts teachers and researchers are knowledgeable in these areas.

Implicit in the paradigm is a call for conscious awareness, for meta-researching and meta-teaching examinations of what one believes about language and language learning. What a teacher or researcher believes in these areas constitutes a set of relations upon which behavior is organized. While not stating it directly, the paradigm argues that all research and teaching in the language arts, whether examined or unexamined, is theoretically based (Harste & Burke, 1977), and that researchers and teachers owe it both to themselves and to the profession to lay out what they perceive to be key relationships in language learning.

Good language arts research and good language arts instruction not only lay out the theoretical positions they take across language, language learning, successful language users, and growth and development, but put such beliefs in a position of instructional and research vulnerability. The shift to ethnography argues that one of the major problems with much current research and instruction is a failure to examine assumptions—assumptions often deeply embedded in the what and how of teaching and research.

Some researchers and teachers even go so far as to suggest that while others are theoretically biased they are in a state of theoretical virginity, as if their decisions to look at what they looked at, or to select a worksheet over a blank sheet of paper, were made in innocence and purity. This paradigm does not ask researchers and teachers to be atheoretical—that's impossible—only honest. It condones neither mad-dog empiricism nor atheoretical ethnography.

Equally important, the paradigm suggests that only when theory and practice stand in equilateral relationship to each other is it possible for each to become a head taller than their current and single selves. When practice is built on practice we have a blatant disdain for research—an anti-intellectual stance—and wasted opportunities. When practice is built on theory, research results can feed back to identify and clarify theoretical constructs and practice. In transaction, then, both theory and practice can become more than either can become separately.

The power of this paradigm is its heuristic stance. It does not guarantee that teachers and researchers do not make mistakes, but only that we hope for fewer, and for those mistakes we do make, it calls for the practical and theoretical attention that they merit and demand. It is this generative function of language research and teaching, not the maintenance of our current assumptive language teaching and research, which makes the shift to ethnography by the profession so exciting.

The Child-as-Informant as a Self-Correcting Evaluative Strategy in Research and Instruction. A theoretically based view of the language arts suggests that an assessment which does not lend itself to improved theory or instruction should be abandoned. From a curricular perspective, the question to be addressed by evaluation is: "In light of what I know about language and language learning, how are these language users performing?"

All evaluation and all evaluation instruments are theoretically based. To the extent that they violate what we know about language and language learning, they must be abandoned and other more theoretically valid measures developed. When applied, this criterion often results in harsh judgments of current instruments and assessment practices.

Often in our attempt to assess the strengths which language users possess, we isolate them from peer support (for fear of cheating), give them materials to read which have no situational support by way of appropriate context (unlike natural reading situations, the reader under the conditions of testing never knows what the topic of his next selection will be), and ask them to deal with topics which they have little familiarity with or interest in (this is supposedly done to insure the actual reading of the materials and assure no reliance on background information). Equally often, what such data give us is a picture of what reading looks like under unnatural conditions. Under normal conditions we read things for which we have a background and in which we are interested, go to materials with a host of expectations about what we will find there, locate the materials in a situational context rich with signs to help us access appropriate anticipatory texts, and use colleagues and friends to discuss and clarify our understandings. We use this example to demonstrate that, given what we know about successful readers in real language situations, we can begin to improve research and instructional assessment. The shift to ethnography by the profession does not suggest that cleaning up assessment will be easy, only that it must be guided.

The view of evaluation proposed in Figure 17.1 suggests that we get our best language data when we put language users in situations which are rich with support, not isolated and deprived of the support available under normal conditions (Vygotsky, 1978). Theoretically this suggests that we must use whole, natural instances of language as settings within which to collect evaluative data. Since this same criterion holds for any instance of language instruction, this insight allows us to view classrooms as potentially natural language situations. All too often we go out of our way to make classrooms and research settings unnatural.

Interestingly, when we view classrooms in this light, what becomes accented is not only the unnaturalness of most current assessment and assessment conditions in language arts teaching and research, but the need, given the social nature of language, for the development of sociological models of learning. This insight, that current learning theory is rooted psychologically, whereas language and language learning are rooted sociologically, is a nice demonstration of the powerful transactions possible when theory and practice are juxtaposed, as is suggested by the recent shift by the profession to ethnography.

Supporting the Language Process in Research and Instruction.
In light of what we know and in light of what language users are doing, what support should be offered? Within "linguistically the least restrictive environment" (Watson, 1980), this support has two forms: (1) strategy instruction; and (2) the creation of a low-risk classroom aura.

If we are given, for example, an observation that when afforded opportunity to take text ownership, a child informant refused to write saying, "I can't spell," as teachers and researchers we immediately know several things. First, we have evidence that the child perceived the major constraint stopping him or her from engaging in the process to be spelling. This we theoretically suspect is a learned constraint. Because we know that successful language users cannot worry about spelling at "the point of utterance" and still be successful (Britton, Burgess, Martin, McLeod & Rosen, 1975), we also theoretically know that we must take action to help the child functionally reperceive this constraint, and that as long as this constraint governs initial writing efforts, the child is depriving himself or herself of the only vehicle—involvement in the process—whereby he or she can grow.

In this instance we might find that a simple, "I'm not interested in your spelling, I'm interested in your writing" would suffice to support the child in coming to see that functional writing is something all language users do. If our informant has learned his past instructional lesson too well we might have to be firmer and make recourse to such dysfunctional strategies more difficult: "No writer can worry about spelling and grammar and things like that while first trying to get his ideas down. We'll take care of those things later when and if we wish to make our writing public. Right now, let's just get our ideas down before they slip away. Let's get back to our writing; you made me lose my train of thought." In either of these instances curricular support grows out of theoretically based evaluations in the least restrictive linguistic setting. Such an environment gives us our best developmental data since it helps us sort out language behaviors which are an artifact of instruction from those which reflect communication potential. An ethnographic view of language tells us that there is a relationship between linguistic constraints and linguistic resources: Alter these constraints and you unleash new resources.

Other curricular support grows directly from theory (for various examples see Rhodes, 1978; Crafton, 1981; Hill, 1980). Many language users have been found to have extremely dysfunctional notions of writing (Britton, Burgess, Martin, McLeod & Rosen, 1975; Emig, 1971; Atwell, 1980; Kucer, 1982). The source of these dysfunctional notions can be readily recognized since no real writer could write under the conditions reported to surround much school writing (DeFord, 1979–1981; Graves, 1975; Applebee, 1981). To encourage more functional notions one instructional support unit might have as its focus acquainting children with successful writers through interviews with them in the classroom. Not only does this practice have roots in a theory of language in use, but it aids in the identification of strategies which may, when put into practice, cycle back to clarify the theoretical constructs from which they grew. Theory, because it affects practice, is much too important to be left in the hands of the theorist. An ethnographical view of language arts says that this is what has been wrong in the past.

Reading and reading instruction are not synonymous terms although they should be. Children, we have found, often have one set of perceptions for reading instruction and another for real reading. In conducting a written conversation (an instructional support strategy developed by Carolyn Burke after having observed real language users operate in real language settings), Susan Robinson, a doctoral student at our institution, asked one of her informants whether or not he had now learned to like reading. His telling response, "Which reading?" (Robinson, 1981).

Frank Smith (1981b) advises teachers who feel that they must have children engage in at least some of the pseudo reading tasks of much current skill instruction that the least they might do is to inform students that they are about to engage in a "funny kind of reading," and that they ought not confuse this with what they do when they really read. Smith argues that children can live with lots of adult peculiarities.

It shouldn't surprise us, given ethnographic insights into language, if children appear confused when we fail to provide them with support environments in which they might have demonstrated information on which to make better linguistic decisions (Smith, 1981a). The shift to ethnography by the profession suggests that the fastest way to clean up research and instruction is to throw out all practices not rooted in instances where real language users are operating in real language settings using real language.

In the opening of this chapter we asserted that it was important to understand that the move to ethnography by the language arts profession has both theoretical and practical roots. This chapter has attempted to develop the argument that this understanding is important because it represents a call for a new professionalism. At base this move to ethnography constitutes a challenge to past definitions of research, teaching, roles, truth, and who is in charge. A call for fundamental professional changes of this sort often creates dysfunctional gaps. This section has attempted to assert that if the move to ethnography is cast in the shape of an attitude and a curricular paradigm, it constitutes a low-risk, high-learning situation for teachers, researchers, and children. From this perspective, the essence of ethnography and of this report on our program of research is an open invitation to form a collaborative pedagogy.

Conclusion

A LANGUAGE STORY

As part of her Sunday School experience, Odette, age 8, was asked to be in the Christmas pageant being presented at her church. As she talked to her mother about her role in the play, it dawned on her mother that Odette had probably never heard the real Christmas story. Together they read the original story from the Bible. Odette found the experience fascinating. Afterwards, Odette decided to dictate and then write her own version.

She entitled it, "The Gospel According to St. Luke" by Odette.

Chapter 1
Once upon a time in the days of Herod the King, Mary was out washing the clothes when an angel of the Lord appeared and scared Mary half to death.
"You're going to have a baby and his name will be called Jesus."
"But, I'm a virgin."
"That's okay, God is the father. Besides, you know your cousin Elizabeth and Zachariah are having a baby. His name is going to be John."
Parenthetically, Odette seems to add: That's funny because they are old.

Chapter 2
Mary went over to Elizabeth's house to tell her about the baby.
She stayed three months, and then said, "Good-bye, I have to be going back to Nazareth to find a husband."
And it came to pass that she found Joseph who was a carpenter with a donkey.
It came to pass that it was good because they needed to go to Bethlehem.

229

Conclusion

Odette's story illustrates how written language is learned from the inside out in a socially supportive and conducive environment. Reading supports writing, just as speech—Odette and her mother's interchanges, art (the pictures that grace her surface text), and experience (her past and present encounters with print and her world)—support that process by permitting her to take alternate perspectives and stances on her knowing.

In the process of using written language, the child takes ownership of the written language learning process. Odette's text reflects not only her most recent literacy learnings, but her past history of literacy and the mental gyrations of orchestrating both: "You're going to have a baby . . . But, I'm a virgin. . . . I have to be going back to Nazareth to find a husband . . . And it came to pass that she found Joseph. . . . "

While we, as professional language educators and as adult members of the child's linguistic community, know a lot about language, children must discover it for themselves. In this social process of making it their own, children make their own language discoveries. An interesting thing happens to what the linguistic community knows about language in this process. Using the child as our informant, we learn more about language and about children's potential for language than what we initially knew.

Just as children must discover language from the inside out, so teachers and researchers must discover what others may have thought was already known. In this process of discovery—of making language our own—teachers and researchers also learn more about language and children's potential for language than we knew.

The contributions which we discuss in this volume sometimes confirm, but inevitably alter and extend what we all know. Language research, like language itself, is a potential. We argue that it is a potential the profession can use to explore and discover curricula, a better language cirriculum not only for children, but for itself.

Curriculum, in the final analysis, is the mental trip taken in the head of the language learner. Instructionally, what we hope to do as language educators is to put language learners in settings where they might come to experience and value the psycholinguistic and sociolinguistic activities we associate with successful written language use and learning.

In such a supportive and low-risk environment Odette makes abductions, tests hypotheses, and helps us appreciate the Christmas story and the process of literacy learning as we have never appreciated them before. Importantly, opportunity and engagement—at her level and on her terms—are the two ingredients which make this literacy event possible.

Just as the process of discovery gives the children's language its own quirks and personality, while earning them a linguistic birth certificate, so too, we endow past curricular efforts with our own personalities, our own quirks, our own birthmarks. This is not only a professional inheritance, but a professional right and responsibility.

What is true of literacy learning is true of literacy instruction. Just as Odette has taken the risk, so too, we have taken the risk . . . and so must all teachers.

When language teachers, like language learners, play it safe, no learning occurs, only curricular entrenchment and curricular estrangement. Under such conditions, not only literacy, but the teaching of literacy is at risk. But, as Odette and our other informants demonstrate, there is much to learn and many new potentials to explore.

Based on what we currently know, we can and must proceed. We offer no guarantee of correctness, but rather a formula for self-correction. Odette's personal theory of literacy and literacy learning directed her current explorations and growth. Our theories, too, must direct our exploration. Just as we do not have a right to ignore our history, so too, we do not have a right to ignore what we currently know. There is much we can do now. In the end, nothing is so practical as theory, and nothing so scientifically uncomfortable as not living out one's model.

Appendix

RESEARCH TASK DIRECTIONS

Task 1: Environmental Print

Task Sequence:

Condition 1	*Condition 2*	*Condition 3*
Packaged products	Two-dimensional graphics removed from products	Typed print

Researcher Script:

Condition 1
1. What do you think this says?
2. What things do you see that help you to know what this says?
3. Tell me some of the things you know about this.

Condition 2
1. What do you think this says?
2. What things do you see that help you to know what this says?

Condition 3
1. What do you think this says?

Task 2: Language Experience Story

Task Sequence:

1. Talk about favorite stories.
2. Display toys and discuss generally.
3. Pick one to three objects. '   Sequences to be videotaped.
4. Dictate to scribe.
5. Reread story.
6. Reread one day later.

Researcher Script:

1. I really like the story about Angus and the cat. When the cat first comes to live in Angus's house they fight. They fight over the food, and they fight over the places that they want to sit. The cat hits Angus and Angus chases the cat.

   But one day when the cat disappears, do you know what happens? Angus gets lonely. He misses the cat and he's very happy when the cat comes back.

   Another story that I really like tells all about cats and kittens. It tells how cats and kittens are alike. It tells that they both like milk, that they both hunt, and even that they both get mad.
2. What story do you like? What do you like especially about _____?
3. Today you are going to make up a story. I have lots of things in this box that you can use to tell a story. (Show child objects in box.)
4. Choose two or three things that you want to use in your story. Look at the things you've chosen and take a minute to think about the story you're going to tell.
5. Now you tell me your story and I'll write it down on the paper while you tell it. What do you want me to write first?
6. Here is your story. Read it for me.

ONE DAY LATER

7. Yesterday you chose some toys and wrote a story for me. What was your story about? (If you are having trouble remembering, why don't you think first about the toys you chose?)
8. Here is your story. (Put paper(s) on reading stand.) Now read or pretend to read your story for me.

Materials: *box of toys
         *writing paper and pencil
         *videotape

Task 3: Uninterrupted Writing and Drawing

Task Sequence:

Child is given blank paper and choice of pencils.
1. Write your name for me.
2. Now write or pretend to write anything else that you can write.
3. Can you write anything else? (Repeated until child stops process.)
4. Read me what you wrote. Show me what you wrote.
Child is given blank paper.
5. Draw a picture of yourself so that I can take it with me.

Directions for Observer:

1. Using Observation Sheet record with blue pencil each item produced by the child, placing it in an appropriate section of Observation Sheet.
2. Number each item designating sequence of production.
3. Note any significant behaviors or comments of child in relationship to item produced.

DURING CHILD'S REREADING

4. Record with red pencil each item read by child, placing notation above appropriate text (blue) item.
5. Number each item read designating sequence of production.
6. Note any significant behaviors or comments of child in relationship to item produced.

Materials:

*unlined paper, pencils, crayons (child will have a primary and regular pencil available from which to choose)
*audiotape/videotape
*observer/recorder sheet

Task 4: Reading a Book

Task Sequence:

1. Look through book, *Ten Little Bears*.
2. Read or pretend to read the book.

Researcher Script:

1. Here is a book that has a story in it. I want you to look through the book and find out about the story. When you have decided about the story I want you to read or pretend to read the story to me. While you're looking at your book I'll look at a book. (Researcher reads in silence while child reads.)
2. Now turn to the beginning of your story. (Wait until child has book prepared.) Read or pretend to read your story to me.

Materials:

*copy of *Ten Little Bears*
*book for researcher

Task 5, Phase 1: Receiving and Reading a Letter

Task Sequence:

1. Child receives letter in envelope.
2. Read or pretend to read letter.

Researcher Script:

1. Here is a letter that _____ has sent to you.
2. Open your letter and read it to yourself. (Silence while child reads.)
3. Now, read or pretend to read your letter to me.

Materials:

*letter addressed to child

Task 5, Phase 2: Writing and Reading a Letter

Task Sequence:
1. Compose letter.
2. Read letter.
3. Address envelope.
4. Read envelope.

Researcher Script:

1. Today we are each going to write a letter. I am going to write a letter to _____ . Who are you going to write a letter to?
2. All the things you need to write a letter are on the table. (Child and researcher write their letters.)
3. Read your letter to me.
4. Now, fix you letter so that it's ready to mail.
5. Now, read it (the envelope) for me.
6. I need to keep a copy of the letter that you wrote. So I'll mail your letter for you.

Task 5, Phase 3: Writing and Reading a Story

Task Sequence:

1. Write a story.
2. Read story.

Researcher's Script:

1. Here's a piece of paper for you, and one for me. We're going to

write stories. I'll write a story on my paper and you write, or pretend to write, a story on your paper. Then, when we're done, we will read our stories to one another.

2. Silent writing—researcher and child.
3. Now, read your story to me.
4. Researcher reads story to child.

Materials: *blank typing paper
            *pencil

SAMPLE CHARACTERISTICS
UPPER-MIDDLE/HIGHER SOCIOECONOMIC STATUS[1]

NAME	AGE	SEX[2]	BIRTHDATE[3]	RACE[4]	OCCUPATIONS
Nathan	3.1	M	9-19-74	W	Professor
Michelle	3.2	F	8-12-74	W	Professor[5]
Tyler	3.3	M	7-16-74	W	Dentist
Michelle	3.4	F	6-07-74	W	Insurance Salesman
Boyd	3.5	M	5-21-74	W	Professor
Alison	4.1	F	5-15-73	W	Professor
Megan	4.2	F	3-21-73	W	Dentist
Daniel	4.2	M	8-08-73	W	Engineer
Dawn	4.3	F	7-19-73	W	Professor
Jeremy	4.5	M	12-25-73	W	Professor
Dawn	5.1	F	8-22-72	W	Graduate Student
Charles	5.3	M	6-01-72	W	Graduate Student
Teddy	5.4	M	7-01-72	W	Professor
Mara	5.5	F	4-15-72	W	Teacher[5]
Jonathan	5.6	M	3-27-72	W	Graduate Student
Heather	6.0	F	9-22-71	W	Limestone Worker/ Supervisor
Emily	6.1	F	8-21-71	W	Accountant
Leslie	6.2	F	7-20-71	W	Teacher
Justin	6.4	M	5-25-71	W	Graduate Student[5]
Denver	6.5	M	4-02-71	W	Apartment Manager/Disabled

[1]The following criteria were used in the selection of upper-middle/higher socioeconomic children:

    a) Years of formal education by father (or mother in single-parent families).

    b) Parental occupation (needed to fall within or at the upper-middle levels of prestige occupations as listed by Duncan, 1971).

    c) Residential area (Selected by suburbs where professionals lived).

[2]F=Female; M=Male

[3]Only children who ranged in age from 3.0−3.6; 4.0−4.6; 5.0−5.6; 6.0−6.6 were included in sample

[4]W=White

[5]Single-parent families

SAMPLE CHARACTERISTICS
LOWER SOCIOECONOMIC STATUS[1]

NAME	AGE	SEX	BIRTHDATE	RACE	EDUCATION LEVEL MOTHER	EDUCATION LEVEL FATHER	OCCUPATION MOTHER	OCCUPATION FATHER
Latrice	3	F[2]	4-17-76[3]	B[4]	10	—[5]	Housewife	——
Marvin	3	M	7-29-76	B	11	12	Labor	Line Worker
Nathan	3	M	7-27-76	W	12	8	Housewife	Common Labor
Terry	3	M	4-29-76	B	11	—	Line Worker	——
Patty	3	F	6-20-76	W	10	—	Housewife	——
Towanna	3	F	5-19-76	B	10	—	Floor Clerk	——
Kibi	4	F	6-21-75	B	10	12	Clerk Typist	Warehouse Worker
Angie	4	F	7-20-75	W	9	12	Housewife	Unemployed
Benjamin	4	M	6-24-75	B	9	9	Kitchen Supervisor	Layoff-Chrysler
Charles	4	M	4-7-75	W	12	10	Insurance Clerk	Newspaper Handler
Michael	4	M	4-7-75	W	12	10	Insurance Clerk	Newspaper Handler
Stephanie	4	F	7-28-75	W	9	—	Housewife	——
Greg	5	M	8-28-74	B	6	—	Housewife	——
Angela	5	F	6-20-74	W	10	—	Housewife	——
Dan	5	M	9-27-74	W	12	8	Housewife	Plasterer
Dawn	5	F	9-27-74	W	12	8	Housewife	Plasterer
Crystal	5	F	4-18-74	B	12	—	Sales	——
Frank	5	M	6-22-74	B	12	—	Nurse's Aide	——
Christopher	6	M	5-18-73	W	12	12	Housewife	Inspector-Ford
Gerald	6	M	3-21-73	B	10	11	Line Worker	Navy
DeShonna	6	F	9-10-73	B	10	—	Housewife	——
Latisha	6	F	8-6-73	B	12	11	Housewife	Bus Driver
Gina	6	F	7-25-73	W	6	12	Housewife	Checker-Ford Motor
Vincent	6	M	8-28-73	W	12	12	Teacher's Aide	Custodian

[1] The following criteria were used in the selection of SES:
  (A) Years of formal education completed by parents (low SES = high school or less).
  (B) Parental occupation (needed to fall within low prestige occupations as listed by Duncan, 1971).
  (C) Income. All children selected came from families which qualified for federal assistance based on total income and family size at their respective school; all children 3, 4, and 5, with the exception of 3 (Kibi, Michael, and Charles) came from families whose total income qualified them for 80% federal subsidy of their child's preschool program.
  (D) Residence. All children in low SES sample came from School 114 attendance area, a lower class neighborhood in Southeastern Indianapolis. Children bused into School 114 were excluded from the sample. Most children lived in federal housing projects which bordered School 114.
[2] F = Female; M = Male
[3] Only children who ranged in age 3.0—3.6, 4.0—4.6, 5.0—5.6, 6.0—6.6 at the time of data collection were included in the sample population. This criterion meant that only children born between March and August were included in the population sampled.
[4] B = Black, W = White
[5] Single-parent families

SAMPLE CHARACTERISTICS
MIDDLE SOCIOECONOMIC STATUS[1]

NAME	AGE	SEX	BIRTHDATE	RACE	EDUCATION LEVEL MOTHER	FATHER	OCCUPATION MOTHER	FATHER
Shannon	3	F[2]	4-3-76[3]	W[4]	12	14	Computer Operator	Small Business-Owner
D.J.	3	M	5-24-76	B	16	15	Postal Clerk	Factory Worker
Robert	3	M	4-17-76	W	12	12	Secretary	Env. Control Spec.
Jerry	3	M	5-7-76	W	13	14	LPN	Journeyman
Taisha	3	F	5-27-76	B	14	12	Fork Lift Operator	Painter
Heather	3	F	6-3-76	B	12	12	Assembler	Machinist
Misty	4	F	7-6-75	W	12	12	Driver	Security Manager
Ben	4	M	9-29-75	W	17	17	Teacher	Teacher
Mike	4	M	7-22-75	W	12	12	Assembler	Machinist
Tassha	4	F	3-23-75	B	14	16	Secretary Supervisor	Musician
Brandyce	4	F	9-2-75	B	12	16	Secretary	Small Business-Owner
Charvin	4	M	9-30-75	B	16	16	Teacher	Accountant
Sally	5	F	7-9-74	W	17	16	Teacher	Finance Manager
Jill	5	F	5-29-74	W	12	12	Secretary/Bookkeeper	Supervisor
Alpha	5	F	4-14-74	B	17	16	Psychological Consult.	Government Accountant
Jeff	5	M	5-23-74	B	12	12	Order Analyst	Screw Machinist
Donald	5	M	9-4-74	B	14	17	Communications Spec.	Teacher
Jason	5	M	7-11-74	W	12	13	Secretary	Taxi Driver
Jake	6	M	9-1-73	W	16	19	Housewife	IBM
LaShell	6	F	8-8-73	B	15	14	Teacher	Parts Inspector
Eugene	6	M	8-20-73	B	14	15	Cashier	Greyhound Bus Driver
Natasha	6	F	5-17-73	B	15	15	Secretary	Dock Supervisor
Marc	6	M	7-18-73	W	15	16	Police Officer	Social Ins. Rep.
Alanna	6	F	7-26-73	W	15	12	Legal Secretary	Machinist

[1] The following criteria were used in the selection of middle SES:
  (A) Years of formal education completed by parents (middle SES = high school or more, but not above masters).
  (B) Parent occupation (needed to fall within or very near middle prestige occupations as listed by Duncan, 1971).
  (C) Income. Families of children selected did not qualify for federal assistance; several families where occupation and years of formal eduction just met our criteria for middle SES occupation and education sent their child to a private school for day care or preschool and thus were included in the middle SES sample—this was true of Heather (#50), Mike (#53), Jeff (#60), and Jason (#62).
  (D) Residence. All children in middle SES sample came from outside the immediate area surrounding School 114; most 3-, 4-, and 5-year-olds were involved in private day care or preschool experiences which required a tuition for enrollment; several 6-year-olds were bused to School 114 from outside areas; most children came from School 82's attendance area, a distinctly middle class residential area.

[2] F = Female; M = Male

[3] Only children who ranged in age from 3.0—3.6, 4.0—4.6, 5.0—5.6; 6.0—6.6 were included in the sample population. This criterion meant that only children born between March and August were involved in the population sampled.

[4] B = Black; W = White

Bibliography

Adams, M. J., & Collins, A. 1978. *A schema-theoretic view of reading* (Technical Report No. 32). Urbana, IL: University of Illinois, Center for the Study of Reading. (Also in R. J. Spiro, B. C. Bruce, & W. F. Brewer, eds. *Theoretical issues in reading comprehension*. Hillsdale, NJ: Erlbaum.)

Altwerger, B. 1980. Research generated from a psycholinguistic model of reading: Metaphor processing. Speech presented at the Annual Convention of the National Reading Conference, San Diego.

Altwerger, B., & Strauss, S. 1983. Readers' understanding of figurative language: Implications of linguistic theory for psycholinguistic research. In R. Tierney & P. Anders, eds. *Understanding readers' understanding*. Hillsdale, NJ: Erlbaum.

Anderson, R. C., Reynolds, R. E., Schallert, D. L., & Goetz, E. T. 1976. *Framework for comprehending discourse* (Technical Report No. 12). Urbana, IL: University of Illinois, Laboratory for Cognitive Studies in Education. (Also in *American Educational Research Journal*, 1977, 14: 367–381.)

Anderson, T. H. 1978. *Study skills and learning strategies* (Technical Report No. 104). Urbana, IL: University of Illinois, Center for the Study of Reading.

Applebee, A. 1978. *The child's concept of story: Ages two to seventeen*. Chicago: University of Chicago Press.

———. 1979. Sense of story. Paper presented at Annual Meeting of the International Reading Association, Atlanta.

———. 1981. Writing and learning in school settings. In M. Nystrand, ed. *What writers know: Studies in the psychology of writing*. New York: Academic Press.

Applebee, A., Lehr, F., & Austin, A. 1980. *A study of writing in the secondary school* (Final Research Report to Department of Education). Washington, DC: National Institute of Education.

Atwell, M. 1980. The evolution of text: The interrelationship of reading and writing in the comparing process. Unpublished doctoral dissertation, Indiana University.

Austin, J. L. 1962. *How to do things with words*. Oxford: Clarendon Press.

Baghban, M. J. M. 1979. Language development and initial encounters with written language: A case study of preschool reading and writing. Unpublished doctoral dissertation, Indiana University.

Baker, R. G. 1980. Orthographic awareness. In U. Frith, ed. *Cognitive processes in spelling*. London: Academic Press.

Baron, R. W. 1980. Visual and phonological strategies in reading and spelling. In U. Frith, ed. *Cognitive processes in spelling*. London: Academic Press.

Bartlett, E. J. October 1981. Learning to write: Some cognitive and linguistic components. In R. W. Shuy, ed. *Linguistics and literacy (Series: 2)*. Washington, DC: Center for Applied Linguistics.

Bates E. 1976. *Language and context: The acquisition of pragmatics*. New York: Academic Press.

———. 1981. Just as syntax evolves from semantics, so semantics evolves from pragmatics. Presentation given to Faculty and Graduate Students in Reading, Indiana University, Language Education Departments.

Berthoff, A. E. 1975. The problem of problem solving. In W. R. Winterowd, ed. *Contemporary rhetoric*. New York: Harcourt Brace Jovanovich.

Bigge, M. L. 1982. *Learning theories for teachers*. 4th ed. New York: Harper & Row.

Bissex, G. 1979. Written language development: A case study. Paper presented at the Annual Meeting of the Elementary Language Arts Division of the National Council of Teachers of English, Hartford.

———. 1980. *Gnys at wrk: A child learns to write and read*. Cambridge: Harvard University Press.

———. 1980. Patterns of development in writing: A case study. *Theory into Practice*, 19:197−201.

Bloome, D., & Green, J. 1982. The social contexts of reading: A multidisciplinary perspective. In B. A. Hutson, ed. *Advances in reading/language research*. Greenwich, CT: JAI Press.

Bobrow, D. C., & Collins, A. M., eds. 1975. *Representation and understanding: Studies in cognitive science*. New York: Academic Press.

Bouffler, C. 1983. A case study exploration of functional strategies in spelling. Doctoral dissertation proposal, Indiana University.

Brandt, D. 1983. Writing and the significance of context. Unpublished dissertation, Indiana University.

Britton, J. N. 1970. The student's writing. In E. Evertts, ed. *Explorations in children's writing*. Urbana, IL: National Council of Teachers of English.

———. 1977. Language and the nature of learning: An individual perspective. *The teaching of English* (Seventy-sixth Yearbook of the National Society for the Study of Education). Chicago: University of Chicago Press.

———. 1978. The composing process and the functions of writing. In C. Cooper & L. Odell, eds. *Research on composing: Points of departure*.

Urbana, IL: National Council of Teachers of English.

Britton, J., Burgess, T., Martin, N., McLeod, A., & Rosen, H. 1975. *The development of writing abilities (11−18)*. London: Macmillan.

Brown, R. 1973. *A first language: The early stages*. Cambridge: Harvard University Press.

Bruner, J. 1982. The formats of language acquisition. *Semiotics*, 3(1):1−6.

Burke, C. L. 1980. A comprehension-centered reading curriculum: Videotape. In D. J. Strickler (Director & Producer), *Reading comprehension: An instructional television series*. Bloomington, IN: Indiana University, Language Education Departments.

———. 1980. The reading interview (1977). In B. Farr & D. Strickler, eds. *Reading comprehension handbook*. Bloomington, IN: Indiana University, Language Education Departments.

Burton, D. 1973. Research in the teaching of English: The troubled dream. *Research in the Teaching of English*, *I*, 160−169.

Calkins, L. M. 1983. *Lessons from a child*. Exeter, NH: Heinemann.

Carey, R. F. 1980. Empirical vs. naturalistic research? *Reading Research Quarterly*, 5:412−415.

———. 1982. The effect of text structure on comprehension. Paper presented at the Annual Meeting of the American Educational Research Association, New York.

———. 1982. Meaning in context: The semiotics of literacy. Paper presented at the Annual Meeting of the International Reading Association, Chicago.

———. 1982. Toward holistic theory: Some methodological considerations for language researchers. Paper presented at the Annual Meeting of the International Reading Association, Chicago.

Carey, R. F., & Harste, J. C. 1982. Reading and writing in semiotic perspective. Speech given at the Annual Meeting of the International Reading Association, Chicago.

Carey, R. F., Harste, J. C., & Smith, S. L. 1981. Contextual constraints and discourse processes: A replication study. *Reading Research Quarterly*, 1981, 6:201−212.

Cazden, C. B. 1965. Environmental assistance to the child's acquisition of grammar. Unpublished doctoral dissertation, Harvard University.

———. 1966. Subcultural difference in child language development: An interdisciplinary review. *Merrill-Palmer Quarterly*. 12:185—214.

———. 1972. *Child language and education*. New York: Holt, Rinehart & Winston.

———. 1978. Toward educational linguistics. Paper presented at the Annual Meeting of the National Council of Teachers of English, Kansas City.

Cazden, C. B., John, V., & Hymes, D. H., eds. 1972. *Function of language in the classroom*. New York: Teachers College Press.

Chomsky, C. 1971. Write first, read later. *Childhood Education*. 47:296—299.

———. 1979. Approaching reading through invented spelling. In L. B. Resnick & P. A. Weaver, eds. *Theory and practice of early reading*. Vol. 2. Hillsdale, NJ: Erlbaum.

Chomsky, N. 1965. *Aspects of the theory of syntax*. Cambridge: MIT Press.

Christensen, F. 1965. A generative rhetoric of the paragraph. *College Composition and Communication*, 16(4):155—161.

Cicourel, A. V. 1974. *Cognitive sociology*. San Francisco: Free Press.

Clay, M. 1972. Reading. *The patterning of complex behavior*. Auckland: Heinemann.

———. 1975. *What did I write?* London: Heinemann.

———. 1982. *Observing young readers: Selected papers*. Exeter, NH: Heinemann.

Corsaro, W. 1980. Script recognition, articulation and expansion in children's role play. *Discourse Processes*, 8:21—43.

Crafton, L. 1981. The reading process as a transactional experience. Unpublished doctoral dissertation, Indiana University.

Culler, J. 1980. Literary competence. In J. P. Tompkins, *Reader response criticism*. Baltimore, MD: Johns Hopkins University Press.

De Beaugrande, R. 1979. *Modeling text processes for research on reading*. University of Florida Monograph. Gainesville, FL: Department of English.

———. 1980. *Text, discourse, and process*. Norwood, NJ: Ablex.

———. 1981. Design criteria for process models of reading. *Reading Research Quarterly*, 16:261—315.

Deely, J. 1982. *Introducing Semiotic: Its history and doctrine*. Bloomington, IN: Indiana University Press.

DeFord, D. E. 1978. A validation study of an instrument to determine a teacher's theoretical orientation to reading instruction. Unpublished doctoral dissertation, Indiana University.

———. 1979. Written language acquisition: After instruction. Paper presented at the Annual Meeting of the International Reading Association, Atlanta.

———. 1980. Young children and their writing. *Theory into Practice*, 19:157—162.

DeFord, D. 1979—1981. Young children's developing concepts about reading and writing. NCTE, Research Grant. Carbondale, IL: Southern Illinois University, Department of Curriculum, Instruction and Media.

Dijk, T. A. van. 1976. *Pragmatics of language and literature*. Amsterdam: North Holland Publishing Company.

———. 1977. Semantic macro-structures and knowledge frames in discourse comprehension. In M. A. Just & P. A. Carpenter, eds. *Cognitive processes in comprehension*. Hillsdale, NJ: Erlbaum.

———. 1979. From text grammar to interdisciplinary discourse studies. Paper given at La Jolla Conference on Cognitive Science, University of California at San Diego, La Jolla, August 13—16. Mimeographed.

———. 1979. *Macro-structures*. Hillsdale, NJ: Erlbaum.

Dijk, T. A. van, & Kintsch, W. 1978. Cognitive psychology and discourse: Recalling and summarizing stories. In W. U. Dressler, ed. *Current trends in text-linguistics*. Berlin & New York: Walter de Gruyter.

Dijk, T. A. van, & Petofi, J. S., eds. 1977. *Grammars and descriptions*. Berlin & New York: Walter de Gruyter.

Doake, D. 1979. Book experience and emergent

reading behavior. Paper presented at the Annual Meeting of the International Reading Association, Atlanta.

Donaldson, M. 1978. *Children's minds*. Glasgow: William Collins & Son.

Downing, J. 1970. Children's concepts of language in learning to read. *Educational Researcher*, 12:106–112.

———. 1979. Cognitive clarity and linguistic awareness. Paper presented at the International Seminar on Linguistic Awareness and Learning to Read, University of Victoria, Canada.

Durkin, D. 1977. Comprehension instruction: Where are you? *Reading Education Report #1*. Urbana-Champaign, IL: Center for the Study of Reading, University of Illinois, October.

Eco, U. 1976. *A theory of semiotics*. Bloomington, IN: Indiana University Press.

———. 1979. *The role of the reader: Explorations in the semiotics of text*. Bloomington, IN: Indiana University Press.

Eisner, E. W. 1982. *Cognition and curriculum*. New York: Longman.

Emig, J. 1971. *The composing process of twelfth graders* (Research Report No. 13). Urbana, IL: National Council of Teachers of English.

———. 1976. Writing as a mode of learning. *College Composition and Communication*, 10:122–128.

———. 1982. Literacy and freedom. Speech presented at the Conference on College Composition Annual Meeting, San Francisco, April.

Feathers, K. M. 1980. Comprehension as extended text. Speech presented at the Annual Meeting of the National Reading Conference, San Diego.

———. 1982. Non-obtrusive, continuing evaluation procedures for natural language use. Inquiry Methodology, Minor Qualifying Paper, Indiana University.

———. 1983. Semantic features of text: Their interaction and influence on reading behavior. Unpublished doctoral dissertation, Indiana University.

Ferreiro, E., & Gómez-Palcio, eds. 1982. *Nuevas perspectivas sobre los procesos de lectura y escritura*.

Mexico City, Mexico: Siglo Veintiuno Editores.

Ferreiro, E., & Teberosky, A. 1982. *Literacy before schooling*. Trans. K. Goodman Castro. Exeter, NH: Heinemann.

Fillmore, C. 1976. Frame semantics and the nature of language. In S. R. Harnad et al., eds. *Origins and evolution of language and speech*. Vol. 80. New York: Annals of the New York Academy of Sciences.

Firth, J. R. 1957. The techniques and semantics. *Transactions of the Philosophical Society*, 1:21–34. (Also in *Papers in linguistics* 1934–1951. London: Oxford University Press.)

Fish, S. 1980. *Is there a text in this class?* Cambridge: Harvard University Press.

Fleck, L. 1979. Genesis and development of a scientific fact (1935). Chicago, IL: University of Chicago Press.

Flower, L. S. 1981. A cognitive model of the writing processes of adults. In A. Humes, B. Cronnell, J. Lawlor, & L. Gentry, eds. *Moving between practice and research in writing*. Los Alamitos, CA: SWRL Educational Research & Development, pp. 37–39.

Flower, L., & Hayes, J. 1980. A cognitive process theory of writing. Paper presented at the Annual Meeting of College Composition and Communication Association, Washington.

Frederiksen, C. H. 1975a. Acquisition of semantic information from discourse: Effects of repeated exposures. *Journal of Verbal Learning and Verbal Behavior*, 14:158–169.

———. 1975b. Representing logical and semantic structure of knowledge acquired from discourse. *Cognitive Psychology*, 7:371–458.

———. 1977. Semantic processing units in understanding text. In R. Freedle, ed. *Discourse production and comprehension*. Norwood, NJ: Ablex, pp. 57–88.

———. 1977. Structure and process in discourse production and comprehension. In M. A. Just & P. A. Carpenter, eds. *Cognitive processes in comprehension*. Hillsdale, NJ: Erlbaum, pp. 313–322.

Frederiksen, C. H., Frederiksen, J. D., Humphrey, F. M., & Ottsensen, J. 1978. Discourse inference: Adapting to the inferential demands of school texts. Paper presented at the Annual Meeting of the American Educational Research Association, Toronto.

Freedle, R. O., ed. 1977. *Discourse production and comprehension*. New York: Ablex.

———. 1980. Children's recall of narrative and expository prose: The acquisition of an expository schema. Paper presented at Annual Meeting of the American Educational Research Association, Boston.

Freedle, R. O., & Carroll, J. B., eds. 1972. *Language comprehension and the acquisition of knowledge*. Belmont, CA: V. H. Winston & Sons.

Fries, P. 1980. The role of thematic information in edited prose. Paper given at Center for Expansion of Language and Thought Rejuvenation Conference, University of Missouri, Columbia.

Gesell, A. 1925. *The mental growth of the preschool child*. New York: Macmillan.

———. 1940. *The first five years of life*. New York: Harper & Row.

Gibson, E. J. 1976. Trends in perceptual development: Implications for the reading process. In H. Singer & R. B. Ruddell, eds. *Theoretical models and processes of reading*. Newark, DE: International Reading Association.

Ginsburg, H., & Opper, S. 1979. *Piaget's theory of intellectual development*. 2d ed. Englewood Cliffs: Prentice-Hall.

Gollasch, F. V., ed. 1982a. *Language and literacy: The selected writings of Kenneth S. Goodman. Volume 1: Process, theory, research*. London: Routledge & Kegan Paul.

———. 1982b. *Language and literacy: The selected writings of Kenneth S. Goodman. Volume 2: Reading, language and the classroom teacher*. London: Routledge & Kegan Paul.

Goodman, K. S. 1967. Reading: A psycholinguistic guessing game. *Journal of the Reading Specialist*, 4:126–135.

———. 1980. El proceso lector en niños normales. In L. Bravo Valdivieso, ed. *El niño con dificultades para aprender*. Santiago de Chile: Unicef & Pontificia Universidad Catolica.

———. 1980. Bridging the gaps in reading. In J. C. Harste and R. F. Carey, eds. *New perspectives in comprehension*. Bloomington, IN: Monographs in Language and Reading Studies, School of Education.

Goodman, K. S., & Emig, J. 1979. The reading and writing process: Comparisons and contrasts. Audiotape. Tucson, AZ: University of Arizona.

Goodman, K. S., & Goodman, Y. M. 1979. Learning to read is natural. In L. B. Resnick & P. A. Weaver, eds. *Theory and practice of early reading*. Vol. 2. Hillsdale, NJ: Erlbaum.

Goodman, Y. M. 1982. The compositions of Papago children: Research, classroom applications, and implications. Speech made at the Annual Meeting of the National Council of Teachers of English, Washington.

Goodman, Y. M., & Burke, C. L. 1972. *Reading miscue inventory*. New York: Macmillan.

Goodman, Y. M., Burke, C. L., & Sherman, B. 1980. *Strategies in reading: Focus on comprehension*. New York: Holt, Rinehart & Winston.

Graves, D. H. 1973. Children's writing: Research directions and hypotheses based upon an examination of the writing process of seven-year-old children. Unpublished doctoral dissertation, State University of New York-Buffalo.

———. 1975. An examination of the writing process of seven-year-old children. *Research in the Teaching of English*, 9:227–241.

———. 1978. Handwriting is for writing. *Language Arts*, 55:352–363.

———. 1980. Research update: A new look at writing research. *Language Arts*, 57:913–919.

———. 1981. Research update: Writing research for the eighties: What is needed. *Language Arts*, 58: 197–206.

———. 1983. *Writing: Teachers and children at work*. Exeter, NH: Heinemann.

Green, J., & Wallat, C. 1978. Sociolinguistic ethnography: A methodology for identification of social interaction contexts. Paper presented at the Annual Meeting of the International Reading Association, Houston.

Grice, P. 1975. Logic and conversation. In P. Cole & J. Morgan, eds. *Syntax and semantics III: Speech acts*. New York: Academic Press, pp. 41–58.

———. 1978. Further notes on logic and conversation. In P. Cole, ed. *Syntax and semantics IX:*

Pragmatics. New York: Academic Press, pp. 113–127.

Guba, E. 1978. *Toward a methodology of naturalistic inquiry in educational evaluation*. CSE Monograph Series in Evaluation, Los Angeles, CA: Center for the Study of Evaluation, U.C.L.A., Graduate School of Education.

Halliday, M. A. K. 1973. *Explorations in the functions of language*. London: Edward Arnold.

———. 1974. *Language and social man*. London: Longman.

———. 1975. *Learning how to mean: Explorations in the development of language*. London: Edward Arnold.

———. 1978. Meaning and the construction of reality in early childhood. In H. L. Pick, Jr. & E. Saltzman, eds. *Models of perceiving and processing information*. Hillsdale, NJ: Erlbaum.

———. 1980. The sociolinguistic constraints of literacy. Speech given at the Annual Meeting of NCRE, Boston.

Halliday, M. A. K., & Hasan, R. 1976. *Cohesion in English*. London: Longman.

———. 1980. *Text and context: Aspects of language in social-semiotic perspective*. Sophia Linguistica VI. Tokyo: Sophia University Press.

Harris, T. L., & Hodges, R. E. 1981. *A dictionary of reading and related terms*. Newark, DE: International Reading Association.

Harste, J. C., & Burke, C. L. 1977. A new hypothesis for reading teacher education research: Both the teaching and learning of reading are theoretically based. In P. D. Pearson, ed. *Reading: Research, theory and practice* (Twenty-sixth Yearbook of the National Reading Conference). Minneapolis, MN: Mason Publishing Co.

———. 1980. Examining instructional assumption: The child as informant. *Theory into Practice*, 19: 170–178.

———. 1982. Predictibilidad: Un universal en lectoescritura. In E. Ferreiro & M. Gomez-Palacio, eds. *Nuevas perspectivas sobre los procesos de lectura y escritura*. Mexico City, Mexico: Siglo Veintiuno Editores, pp. 50–67.

Harste, J. C., Burke, C. L., & Woodward, V. A. *Children, their language and world: The prag-*

matics of written language use and learning. NIE Final Report #NIE-G-80-0121. Bloomington, IN: Language Education Departments.

———. 1981. Children's language and world: Initial encounters with print. In J. Langer & M. Smith-Burke, eds. *Bridging the gap: Reader meets author*. Newark, DE: International Reading Association.

———. 1983. *The young child as writer-reader and informant*. Final Report #NIE-G-80-0121. Bloomington, IN: Language Education Departments.

Harste, J. C., & Carey, R. F. 1979. Comprehension as setting. In J. C. Harste & R. F. Carey, eds. *New perspectives in comprehension*. Indiana University Monographs in Language and Reading Studies. Bloomington, IN: School of Education Publications.

Harste, J. C. & Feathers, K. 1979. A propositional analysis of Freddie Miller, scientist. *Occasional papers in language and reading*. Bloomington, IN: Indiana University, Language Education Departments.

Hasan, R. 1979. On the notion of text. In J. S. Petofi, ed. *Text vs. sentence*. Australia: Helmut Buske Verlag.

———. 1980. The identity of a text. Speech given at the CELT Rejuvenation Conference, University of Missouri, Columbia, Missouri.

Havighurst, R. 1952. *Developmental tasks and education*. New York: Longmans.

Heath, S. B. 1979. Language beyond the classroom. Paper prepared for the Delaware Symposium on Language Studies, University of Delaware.

———. 1980. The functions and uses of literacy. *Journal of Communication*, 29:123–133.

———. 1980. *What do bedtime stories mean? Narrative skills at home and school*. Paper prepared for the Terman Conference, Stanford University.

———. 1981. *Ways with words: Ethnography of communication, communities and classrooms*. Palo Alto, CA: Stanford University, School of Education.

———. 1981. Toward an ethnohistory of writing in American education. In M. Whiteman, ed. *Variation in writing: Functional and linguistic cultural differences*. Vol. 1. Hillsdale, NJ: Erlbaum.

———. 1982. Protean shapes in literacy events: Ever shifting oral and literature traditions. In D.

Tannen, ed. *Spoken and written language*. Norwood, NJ: Ablex.

———. 1983. *Ways with words: Language, life, and work in communities and classrooms*. New York: Cambridge University Press.

Henderson, E., & Beers, J. W. 1979. A study of developing orthographic concepts among first graders. Paper presented at the Annual Meeting of the International Reading Association, Atlanta.

———, eds. 1980. *Developmental and cognitive aspects of learning to spell*. Newark, DE: International Reading Association.

Herzfeld, M. 1982. Signs in the field: Prospects and issues for semiotic ethnography. Keynote address given at the Annual Meeting of the American Anthropological Association, Los Angeles, 1982. Mimeographed; to be reprinted in special 1983 issue of *Semiotica*.

Hiebert, E. H. 1978. Preschool children's understanding of written language. *Child Development*, 49:1231–1234.

———. 1981. Developmental patterns and interrelationships of preschool children's print awareness. *Reading Research Quarterly*, 16:236–259.

Hilgard, E., & Bower, G. 1975. *Theories of learning*. 4th ed. Englewood Cliffs, NJ: Prentice-Hall.

Hill, M. W. 1978. Look I can write: Children's print awareness from a socio-psycholinguistic perspective. Unpublished graduate research, Reading Department, Indiana University.

———. 1980a. Parenting and language education: A theoretical view of parental role in children learning to read and write. Unpublished doctoral dissertation, Indiana University.

———. 1980b. Preschoolers' print awareness: An in-depth study of 3 and 4-year old children. In M. L. Kamile & A. J. Moe, eds. *Perspectives in reading research and instruction*, Twenty-ninth Yearbook of the National Reading Conference.

———. 1982. Written language learning as social event. Westminster College, research in progress.

Holdaway, D. 1979. *The foundations of literacy*. Exeter, NH: Heinemann Books.

Hudleson, S. 1977. Children's use of contextual cues in reading Spanish. *Reading Teacher*, 30:735–740.

Hunt, K. W. 1970. *Syntactic maturity in school children and adults*. Monograph of Society in Child Development. Chicago: University of Chicago Press.

Hunt, R. A. 1983. Teaching Clever Hans to write: Whole language in freshman composition. Paper given at the Penn State Conference on Rhetoric and Composition.

Hymes, D. H. 1967. Models of interaction of language and social setting. *Journal of Social Issues*, 23:34–98. (Also in J. J. Gumperz & D. H. Hymes, eds. 1972. *Directions in Sociolinguistics*. New York: Holt, Rinehart & Winston.)

Iser, W. 1978. *The act of reading: A theory of aesthetic response*. Baltimore, MD: Johns Hopkins University Press.

James, W. 1939. *Talking to teachers on psychology*. New York: Holt.

Kantor, K. J., Kirby, D. R., & Goetz, J. P. 1981. Research in context: Ethnographic studies in English education. *Research in the Teaching of English*, 4:293–309.

King, D. F. 1982. Curriculum: What we can learn from a language user. Paper presented at the First Annual CEL Conference, Winnipeg, March.

King, M. L. 1982. Language foundations for writing: A research perspective. Presentation given at the Language in Education Conference at The Ohio State University.

King, M. L., & Rental, V. M. 1981. *How children learn to write: A longitudinal study*. Final Report #s NIE-G-79-0137 and NIE-G-79-0039. Research Foundation, The Ohio State University, Columbus, Ohio.

King, M. L., & Rentel, V. Toward a theory of early writing development. The Ohio State University, Columbus. Mimeographed.

Kintsch, W., & Dijk, T. A. van. 1978. Toward a model of text comprehension and production. *Psychological Review*, 85:363–394.

Kohl, H. 1983. Examining closely what we do. *Learning*, 12(1):28–30.

248

Kucer, S. B. 1982. A message based model of discourse production. Unpublished doctoral dissertation, Indiana University.

———. 1982. Text coherence from a transactional perspective. Paper presented at the Annual Meeting of the National Reading Conference, Clearwater Beach, FL.

Kuhn, T. 1970. *The structure of scientific revolutions*. 2d ed. Chicago: University of Chicago Press.

Labov, W. 1982. Beyond functionalism in language. Speech given at the Linguistics Society of Indiana University.

Lewin, K. 1935. *A dynamic field-theory of personality*. New York: McGraw-Hill.

———. 1942. *Field theory and language*. Forty-first Yearbook of the National Society for the Study of Education. Chicago: University of Chicago Press.

Lindfors, J. W. 1980. *Children's language and learning*. Englewood Cliffs, NJ: Prentice-Hall.

Lobel, A. 1963. *Prince Betram, the bad*. New York: Harper & Row.

Malinowski, B. 1923. The problem of meaning in primitive languages. Supplement to C. K. Ogden & I. A. Richards, *The meaning of meaning*. London: Kegan Paul.

Marcel, T. 1980. Phonological awareness and phonological representation. In U. Frith, ed. *Cognitive processes in spelling*. London: Academic Press.

Marsh, G. M., Friedman, V., Welch, D., & Desberg, P. 1980. The development of strategies in spelling. In U. Frith, ed. *Cognitive processes in spelling*. London: Academic Press.

Mattingly, I. G. 1972. Reading, the linguistic process, and linguistic awareness. In J. F. Kavanagh & I. G. Mattingly, eds. *Language by ear and by eye: The relationship between speech and reading*. Cambridge: MIT Press.

———. 1979. Reading, linguistic awareness, and language acquisition. Paper presented at the International Seminar on Linguistic Awareness and Learning to Read, University of Victoria, Canada.

McDermott, R. P. 1976. Kids make sense: An ethnographic account of the interaction management of success and failure in one first-grade classroom. Unpublished doctoral dissertation, Stanford University.

———. 1977a. The ethnography of speaking and reading. In R. Sharp, ed. *Linguistic theory*. Newark, DE: International Reading Association.

———. 1977b. Social relations in contexts for learning in school. *Harvard Educational Review*, 47:198–213.

Mehan, H. 1979. *Learning lessons: Social organization in the classroom*. Cambridge: Harvard University Press.

Meyers, B. J. 1975. *The organization of prose and its effect on recall*. Amsterdam: North-Holland.

Meyers, B. J. F. 1977. What is remembered from prose: A function of passage structure. In R. O. Freedle, ed. *Discourse production and comprehension*. Norwood, NJ: Ablex, pp. 307–333.

Milz, V. 1980. The comprehension-centered classroom: Setting it up and making it work. In D. J. Strickler & B. P. Farr, eds. *Reading comprehension: Resource guide*. Bloomington, IN: Indiana University, Language Education Departments.

———. 1980. The comprehension-centered classroom: Making it work: Videotape. In D. J. Strickler (Director & Producer), *Reading comprehension: An instructional television series*. Bloomington, IN: Indiana University, Language Education Departments.

———. 1980. First graders can write: Focus on communication. *Theory into Practice*, 19:179–185.

Milz, V. E. 1980. *Young children can write: The beginnings*. Pontiac, MI: Oakland Schools, English Department.

Minsky, M. 1975. A framework for representing knowledge. In P. H. Winston, ed. *The psychology of computer vision*. New York: McGraw-Hill.

Mishler, E. G. 1979. Meaning in context: Is there any other kind? *Harvard Educational Review*, 49:1–19.

Moffett, J. 1968. *Teaching the universe of discourse*. Boston: Houghton Mifflin.

Montessori, M. 1964. *The Montessori method* (1912). Cambridge, MA: Robert Bentley.

National Assessment of Educational Progress. 1980. *Reading comprehension of American youth: Do they understand what they read?* Denver, CO: Educational Commission of the States.

National Institute of Education. Undated. Teaching and learning. Washington, DC: United States Department of Health, Education, and Welfare Pamphlet.

Neisser, U. 1976. *Cognition and reality.* San Francisco: Freeman.

Olson, D. 1977. From utterance to text: The bias of language in speech and writing. *Harvard Educational Review,* 47:257−281.

Paley, V. G. 1981. *Wally's stories.* Cambridge: Harvard University Press.

Peirce, C. S. 1931−1958. *Collected papers.* Cambridge: Harvard University Press.

Perl, S. 1979. The composing process of unskilled college writers. *Research in the Teaching of English,* 13:317−336.

Piaget, J. 1970a. *Genetic epistemology.* New York: Norton.

———. 1970b. *Structuralism.* Trans. C. Maschler. New York: Basic Books.

———. 1973. *The language and thought of the child.* New York: World.

Piaget, J., & Inhelder, B. 1969. *The psychology of the child.* New York: Basic Books.

Pollack, J. 1979. Psycholinguistic research: Fifteen years later. Presentation given at the Annual Meeting of International Reading Association, Houston.

Pratt, M. 1977. *Toward a speech act theory of literary discourse.* Bloomington, IN: Indiana University Press.

Propp, V. 1928. *The morphology of the folk tale.* Bloomington, IN: Indiana University Press.

Read, C. 1975. *Children's categorization of speech sounds.* Technical Report No. 197. Urbana, IL: National Council of Teachers Committee on Research.

Rhodes, L. K. 1978. The interaction of beginning readers' strategies and texts reflecting alternate models of predictability. Unpublished doctoral dissertation, Indiana University.

———. 1979. Visible language acquisition: A case study. Symposium on Beginning Reading and Writing: Before and After Instruction. Annual Meeting of the International Reading Association, Atlanta. Mimeographed paper and videotape data.

———. 1981. I can read! Predictable books as resources for reading and writing instruction. *Reading Teacher,* 34:511−519.

Richards, I. A. 1925. *Practical criticism.* New York: Basic Books.

———. 1936. *The philosophy of rhetoric.* New York: Oxford University Press.

Robinson, S. 1981. Which reading? A language story. Unpublished manuscript prepared in completion of doctoral requirements, Indiana University.

Rosenblatt, L. M. 1938. *Literature as exploration.* New York: Appleton-Century Crofts.

———. 1969. Toward a transactional theory of reading. *Journal of Reading Behavior,* 10:31−43.

———. 1978. *The reader, the text, the poem.* Carbondale, IL: Southern Illinois Press.

———. 1980. What facts does this poem teach you? *Language Arts,* 53:386−394.

———. 1981. Focus on literature. Paper presented at the Fourth Annual CELT Rejuvenation Conference, May, Rochester, MI.

Rumelhart, D. E. 1977. Understanding and summarizing brief stories. In D. LaBerge & S. J. Samuels, eds. *Basic processes in reading: Perception and comprehension.* Hillsdale, NJ: Erlbaum.

Rumelhart, D. E., & Ortony, A. 1977. The representation of knowledge in memory. In R. C. Anderson, R. J. Spiro, & W. E. Montague, eds. *Schooling and the acquisition of knowledge.* Hillsdale, NJ: Erlbaum.

Schank, R. C. 1980. Reading and understanding: A perspective from artificial intelligence. Paper presented at Annual Meeting of the National Reading Conference, San Diego.

Schank, R. C., & Abelson, R. P. 1977. *Scripts, plans, goals and understanding: An inquiry into human knowledge structures.* Hillsdale, NJ: Erlbaum.

Searle, J. R. 1969. *Speech acts.* London: Cambridge University Press.

———. 1975. A taxonomy of illocutionary acts. In K. Gunderson, ed. *Minnesota studies in the philosophy of language*. Minneapolis, MN: University of Minnesota Press.

———. 1979. The philosophy of language. Speech delivered to the Modern Linguistic Study Group Seminar, Indiana University.

Sebeok, T. A., ed. 1968. *Approaches to semiotics: Cultural anthropology, education, linguistics, psychiatry, psychology*. The Hague: Mouton.

———. 1975. *The tell-tale sign: A survey of semiotics*. Lisse: Peter de Ridder.

———. 1976. *Contributions to the doctrine of signs*. Lisse: Peter de Ridder.

———. 1977. *A perfusion of signs*. Bloomington, IN: Indiana University Press.

Shanklin, N. K. 1982. *Relating reading and writing: Developing a transitional model of the writing process*. Bloomington, IN: Monographs in Teaching and Learning, School of Education.

Shuy, R. W. 1979. On the relevance of recent developments in sociolinguistics to the study of language learning and early education. In O. Garica & M. King, eds. *Language, children, and society*. Oxford: Pergamon Press.

Siegel, M. 1980. Discourse processing from the perspective of speech act theory. Speech presented at the Annual Meeting of the National Reading Conference, San Diego.

———. 1983. Reading as signification. Unpublished doctoral dissertation, Indiana University.

Skagestad, P. 1981. *The road to inquiry: Charles Peirce's pragmatic realism*. New York: Columbia University Press.

Skinner, B. F. 1950. Are theories of learning necessary? *Psychological Review*, 57:193–216.

———. 1978. Why I am not a cognitive psychologist. In B. F. Skinner, ed. *Reflections on behaviorism in society*. Englewood Cliffs, NJ: Prentice-Hall, pp. 97–112.

Smith, E. B., Goodman, K. S., & Meredith, R. 1978. *Language and thinking in school*. 2d ed. New York: Holt, Rinehart & Winston.

Smith, F. 1978. *Understanding reading*. New York: Holt, Rinehart & Winston.

———. 1980. The language arts and the learner's mind. In D. J. Strickler & B. P. Farr, eds. *Reading*

comprehension: Resource guide. Bloomington, IN: Indiana University, Language Education Departments.

———. 1981a. Demonstrations, engagement and sensitivity: A revised approach to language learning. *Language Arts*, 52:103–112.

———. 1981b. *The learning mind*. Speech given at the Edwardville Reading Conference, Edwardville, MO.

———. 1982. *Writing and the writer*. New York: Holt, Rinehart & Winston.

———. 1983. *Essays into literacy*. Exeter, NH: Heinemann.

Spiro, R. J. 1977. Remembering information from text: The "state of schema" approach. In R. C. Anderson, R. J. Spiro, & W. E. Montague, eds. *Schooling and the acquisition of knowledge*. Hillsdale, NJ: Erlbaum.

———. 1982. Simple-minded and muddle-headed thinking: Schema and beyond. Speech given at Language Education Departments Seminar, Indiana University, October.

Staton, J. 1980. Writing and counseling: Using a dialogue journal. *Language Arts*, 57:514–518.

———. 1981. Analysis of writing in dialogue journals as a communicative event. In A. Humes, B. Cronnell, J. Lawlor, & L. Gentry, eds. *Moving between practice and research in writing*. Los Alamitos, CA: SWRL Educational Research & Development, pp. 86–90.

Stein, N. L. 1978. *How children understand stories: A developmental analysis* (Tech. Rep. No. 69). Urbana, IL: University of Illinois, Center for the Study of Reading.

Stein, N., & Glenn, C. G. 1978. *An analysis of story comprehension in elementary school children*. Washington, DC: Washington University, Department of Psychology.

Steiner, E. 1968. Development of theory in the curriculum field. *Samplings*, 1:1–30.

———. 1978. *Logical and conceptual analytic techniques for educational researchers*, Washington, DC: University Press of America.

Sulzby, E. 1981. *Kindergarteners begin to read their own compositions: Beginning readers' developing knowledges about written language project*. Final Report to the Research Foundation of the National

Council of Teachers of English. Evanston, IL: Northwestern University.

Taylor, D. 1983. *Family literacy: Young children learning to read and write*. Exeter, NH: Heinemann.

Teale, W. H. 1978. What studies of early readers tell us. *Language Arts*, 55:922–932.

———. 1982. Toward a theory of how children learn to read and write naturally. *Language Arts*, 59(6): 555–570.

Tenny, Y. J. 1980. Visual factors in spelling. In U. Frith, ed. *Cognitive processes in spelling*. London: Academic Press.

Thorndyke, P. W. 1977. Cognitive structures in comprehension and memory of narrative discourse. In R. O. Freedle, ed. *Discourse processing: Multidisciplinary perspectives*. Hillsdale, NJ: Ablex.

Tierney, R., & Mosenthal, P. 1982. Cohesion as a reader-based as opposed to text-based phenomenon. Paper presented at the Annual Meeting of the CCCC, San Francisco.

Thomas, D. W. 1977. *Semiotics I: Signs, language and reality*. 2d ed. Lexington, MA: Ginn Custon.

Turner, A., & Greene, E. 1977. *The construction and use of a propositional text base*. Technical Report No. 63. Institute for Study Intellectual Behavior, University of Colorado, Boulder, CO, April.

Vargus, N. R. 1982. Letter writing over time: Socio-cognitive constraints in transition. Unpublished doctoral dissertation, School of Education, Indiana University.

Vygotsky, L. S. 1962. *Thought and language* (1934). Cambridge: MIT Press.

———. 1978. *Mind in society* (1938). M. Cole, V.

John-Steiner, S. Scribner, & E. Sonberman, eds. Cambridge: Harvard University Press.

Watson, D. J. 1980. Learning about the reader: Videotape. In D. J. Strickler (Director & Producer), *Reading comprehension: An instructional videotape series*. Bloomington, IN: Indiana University, Language Education Departments.

———. 1980. Whole language for whole children. Speech given at the Third Annual Reading Conference, Columbia, MO.

———. 1980. Strategies for a comprehension-centered reading program: Videotape. In D. J. Strickler (Director & Producer), *Reading comprehension: An instructional television series*. Bloomington, IN: Indiana University, Language Education Departments.

———. 1981. *A description of teacher-student language interaction, student language productions and attitudes in two first grade classrooms*. Columbia, MO: University of Missouri-Columbia, Department of Elementary Education (in process).

Woodward, V. A. 1977. *Comparison of early readers and non-readers in strategies of organization in intellectual tasks*. Sabbatical Leave Research Report, Indiana University, Bloomington, IN.

Young, R. E., Becker, A. L., & Pike, K. L. 1970. *Rhetoric: Discovery and change*. New York: Harcourt Brace Jovanovich.

Zutell, J. 1978. Some psycholinguistic perspectives on children's spelling. *Language Arts*, 55: 844–850.

———. 1979. *Linguistic and psycholinguistic perspectives on brain mechanisms and language*. Columbus, OH: Ohio State University, Early and Middle Childhood Education.

Index

AUTHOR INDEX

Adams & Collins, 89, 112, 122, 168, 242
Altwerger, 123, 242
Altwerger & Strauss, 123, 242
Anderson, 169, 242
Anderson, Reynolds, Schallert & Goetz, 89, 169, 242
Applebee, 32, 115, 218, 227, 242
Applebee, Lehr, & Austin, 242
Atwell, 35, 37, 69, 80, 105, 134, 135, 227, 242
Austin, 242

Baghban, 79, 242
Baker, 242
Baron, 96, 242
Bartlett, 242
Bates, 112, 243
Berthoff, 243
Bigge, 68, 243
Bissex, 96, 218, 243
Bloome & Green, 243
Bobrow & Norman, 89, 243
Bouffler, 80, 99, 243
Brandt, 64, 69, 243
Britton, 243
Britton, Burgess, Martin, McLeod & Rosen, 134, 227, 243
Brown, 56, 112, 243
Bruner, 60, 243
Burke, 117, 215, 243
Burton, 221, 243

Calkins, 69, 243
Carey, 51, 123, 145, 176, 222, 243
Carey & Harste, 149, 243
Carey, Harste & Smith, 169, 243
Cazden, 60, 243
Cazden, John & Hymes, 244
Chomsky, C., 96, 218, 244
Chomsky, N., 55, 56, 244
Christensen, 103, 244

Chubb, 34
Cicourel, 155, 156, 160, 244
Clay, 69, 218, 244
Corsaro, 156, 244
Crafton, 80, 123, 127, 170, 227, 244
Culler, 122, 244

De Beaugrande, 101, 122, 170, 215, 244
Deely, 215, 244
DeFord, 227, 244
Dijk, 103, 115, 244
Doake, 244
Donaldson, 65, 159, 245
Downing, 245
Durkin, 32, 245

Eco, 53, 116, 122, 245
Eisner, 245
Emig, 63, 134, 221, 227, 245

Feathers, 80, 169, 245
Ferreiro & Gomez-Palcio, 245
Ferreiro & Teberosky, 55, 61, 66, 67, 218, 245
Fillmore, 112, 169, 245
Firth, 146, 245
Fish, 122, 245
Fleck, xiii, 245
Flower, 116, 245
Flower & Hayes, 116, 135, 245
Fredericksen, 103, 112, 169, 245
Fredericksen, Fredericksen, Humphrey & Ottensen, 245
Freedle, 122, 246
Freedle & Carroll, 246
Fries, 103, 169, 246

Gesell, 68, 246
Gibson, 147, 246
Ginsburg & Opper, 90, 176, 246
Gollasch, 200, 246

Goodman & Burke, 127, 246
Goodman & Emig, 134, 246
Goodman & Goodman, 13, 61, 112, 121, 218, 246
Goodman, Burke & Sherman, 246
Goodman, K., 60, 80–81, 112, 122, 200, 222, 246
Goodman, Y., 69, 246
Graves, 32, 69, 186–87, 227, 246
Greene & Wallat, 169, 246
Grice, 112, 155–56, 246
Guba, 51, 222, 247

Halliday, 22, 91, 100, 112, 113, 134, 146, 149, 155, 176, 188, 216, 221, 247
Halliday & Hasan, 64, 103, 112, 156, 169, 247
Harris & Hodges, 117, 141, 247
Harste & Burke, 7, 77, 161, 225, 247
Harste & Carey, 134, 247
Harste & Feathers, 124, 247
Harste, Burke & Woodward, 14, 34, 56, 81, 103, 137, 170, 178, 210, 247
Hasan, 103, 247
Havighurst, 64, 247
Heath, 175, 218, 247–48
Henderson & Beers, 96, 218, 248
Herzfeld, 53, 248
Hiebert, 218, 248
Hilgard & Bower, 68, 248
Hill, 31, 40, 45, 62, 79, 80, 147, 149, 158, 227, 248
Holdaway, 69, 248
Horn, xii
Hudleson, 248
Hunt, K., 248
Hunt, R., 67, 248
Hymes, 112, 134, 155, 248

Iser, 122, 175, 248

James, 171, 248
Joyce, 30

Kantor, Kirby & Goetz, 222, 248
King, M., 69, 248
King, M. & Rental, V., 61, 102, 169, 210, 248
Kintsch, 123
Kintsch & Dijk, 103, 104, 112, 169, 172, 248
Kohl, 73, 248
Kucer, 69, 80, 107, 123, 135, 227, 249
Kuhn, xi, 249

Labov, 57, 249
Lavoisier, xi
Lewin, 134, 249

Lindfors, 55, 249
Lobel, 174, 249

Malinowski, 146, 249
Marcel, 96, 249
Marsh, Friedman, Welch & Desberg, 96, 249
Mattingly, 63, 249
Mattson, 217
McDermott, 169, 249
Mehan, 169, 249
Meyers, 169, 249
Milz, 205, 249
Minsky, 89, 249
Mishler, 51, 222, 249
Moffett, 210, 249
Montessori, 64, 249

NAEP, 32, 250
Neisser, 89, 91, 250
NIE, 54, 250

Olson, 63, 250

Paley, 250
Palmer, xii
Peirce, 50, 148, 184, 250
Perl, 134, 250
Piaget, 64–66, 90–93, 159, 176, 250
Piaget & Inhelder, 250
Pollock, 112, 250
Pratt, 102, 250
Propp, 115, 250

Read, 96, 218, 250
Rhodes, 79, 205, 227, 250
Richard, 146, 148, 171, 250
Robinson, 228, 250
Rosenblatt, x, 122, 170, 172, 250
Rumelhart, 112, 250
Rumelhart & Ortony, 89, 250

Schank, 112, 250
Schank & Abelson, 89, 250
Schulz, 9
Searle, 112, 250–51
Sebeok, 159, 251
Shanklin, 69, 91, 123, 134, 135, 158, 160, 251
Shuy, 112, 251
Siegel, 69, 80, 169, 251
Skagestad, 50, 251
Skinner, 55, 251

Smith, E. B., Goodman, K. S. & Meredith, R., 135, 251

Smith, F., xvii, 60, 61, 89, 90, 112, 123, 170, 184, 210, 228, 251

Spiro, 89, 171, 251

Staton, 215, 251

Stein, 251

Stein & Glenn, 115, 169, 218, 251

Steiner, 251

Sulzby, 69, 251

Taylor, 252

Teale, 60, 218, 252

Tenny, 97, 252

Thomas, 148, 252

Thorndyke, 115, 218, 252

Tierney & Mosenthal, 103, 252

Turner & Greene, 123, 252

Van Neurath, 50

Vargus, 80, 137, 161, 252

Vygotsky, 65, 91, 113, 115, 121, 128, 136, 171, 177, 252

Warriner, xii

Watson, 227, 252

Whiten, D., 173

Whiten, P., 174

Woodward, 77, 252

Young, Becker & Pike, 252

Zutell, 96, 252

SUBJECT INDEX

accommodation, 90–91

age, 95

alternate communication systems, xi, 16, 18, 19, 20, 29, 33, 35, 171, 172, 183, 206–9, 216

art, 93

assimilation, 90

assumptions, 90, 110–11
   developmental stages, 54, 64–68
   emergent reading, 54, 69
   oral language supremacy, 61–63
   print as decontextualized, 63–64
   randomness, 90, 110–11
   readiness, 54, 68–69

authoring cycle, x, xii, 215–20

behavioral view, 54–55, 58

beliefs, ix

case grammar, 95

child as informant
   assumptions about language, 7, 59
   and curriculum, xii
   and hypothesis testing, 8
   relationship to study, 74

cognition, 90

cognitive confusion, 95

cognitive dissonance, 74

cognitive psychology, xi

cognitive structures, 90

cognitive view. 54–56, 58, 60

coherence, 80, 105–7

cohesion, 75, 80, 93

collaboration, xiii, 221

communication potential, 207

comprehension, 90, 211

context, ix, 81, 151–63, 211

convention, xii, 29, 30
   as fringe benefit, xii
   and language learning, 15, 26, 27

cue complexes, orchestration of, 8, 10–13, 20, 24, 26, 28, 96, 208

curriculum, xii, 224
   common confusions, xii
   criteria for, xii
   as human potential, xii
   as mental trip, xii, 73
   and teacher planning, xii

decontextualization, 63–64, 96

demonstrations, 180–89

development, xi, xii

developmental stages, x, 54, 64–69

disciplines, bridging the gaps, xi, 80, 81

discovery vs. intervention, xi

emergent reading, 54, 69

environment, and learning, 54, 56, 58

equilibration, 91

ethnography, 221–31

experience, and literacy learning, x, 15, 22, 23, 78

fine-tuning language, xi

form and function, 9, 22, 31

functional writing, xi

generativeness, 81, 118–29, 177

graphophonemic correspondence, 95, 96, 199–202

growth and experience, 15, 22, 23, 91

hypothesis testing, 8, 9, 11

imitation, 57–59

inferencing, and schema theory, 90

instruction, xiii
   assumptions about, 3–5
   and learning, 12–14, 32

intentionality, 81, 84, 108–17

interaction, role in literacy learning, 80

interdisciplinary perspectives, 89–107, 112–21, 129, 134–42, 145–50, 154–63, 168–79, 184–89

interpretive community, 84

intertextual tying, 173–74

invented spelling, x, 96

invention vs. discovery, xi

language
   as multimodal, xii, 216
   as open systems, 195, 199–200
   as a social event, 9, 28, 31, 46
   as system of knowing, 206–15
   systems of, 199

language encounters, 45, 48

language learning, 188, 212
   behavioral view, 58
   cognitive universals in, 12, 87, 189
   cognitive view, 58
   and convention, xii, 15, 16, 27
   environment for, 14, 22, 27
   and the home, 42, 43, 44
   hypothesis testing, 8

and metalinguistics, 188
orchestration in, 8, 10–13, 20, 24, 26, 28
as social event, 91
as socio-psycholinguistic phenomena, 82, 92
support for, xi
transactional view, 58
learning
   assumptions about, 4, 5
   correlates of, 41–48, 95
   and schema theory, 89–91
linguistic data pool, 117, 210–11
linguistics, 77
literacy
   as collaboration, 221
   as context dependent, 75, 202–6, 216
   and convention, xii
   correlates of, 77, 95
   as event, 183, 184
   increasing demands, xiii
   indicators of, 78
   key patterns, 73–196
   as potential, xii, 12, 78
   search for text, 215
literacy learning, 78, 219–20
literary criticism, xi

meaning generation, 80
metalinguistics, 188
models, 54–70
morphemic, 96

name writing, 83, 94
natural language learning, 34, 46, 47
naturalistic inquiry, 221–31
negotiation, xi, 170, 177, 202, 205, 216, 224

oral language, 61–63
orchestration, 8, 10–13, 99, 101, 200
organization, 81, 82–107
   early patterns, 93–95
   later patterns, 95
ownership, 32, 199–228, 230

patterns in literacy 73–81
   context, 81, 151–63, 194
   demonstrations, 81, 180–89, 195
   generativeness, 81, 118–29, 191–92
   intentionality, 81, 108–17, 191, 203
   organization, 81, 82–107, 190
   risk taking, xi, 14, 22, 81, 130–42, 192–93
   social action, 81, 143–50, 193

a synthesis, 190–98
   text, 81, 164–79, 194
perception, 90
phonemic, 96
Piagetian theory, and authors' position, 91–93
pragmatics, 11, 12, 28, 33, 95, 202–6
predictability, 90
process and product, 15, 34
program of research
   case studies within, 78
   characteristics of, 74–77, 80, 239–41
   conceptual implications, 199–220
   curricular studies within, 80
   description, ix, xiii, 73–78, 233–38
   identifying key patterns, 76
   in interdisciplinary perspective, xi
   methodological implications, 221–28
   taxonomies, 76
   in theoretical perspective, x
propositional analysis, 104–7
psycholinguistics, 77

race, 41, 77
readiness, 54, 68–69
reading
   emergent, 54, 69
   graphophonemic system, 99
   syntactic system, 101
   in system of language, 211
reading comprehension, 90
register changes, 80
research
   beliefs as important, 73
   and consistency, 75
   and functional language settings, 79
   and generalizations, 75
   insights into, 74
   as theoretically based, 73
   and variation, 75
risk taking, xi, 14, 22, 27, 81, 130–42, 192–93

scaffolding, 60–61
schema theory, 89, 90, 95
   and Piagetian theory, 91
scribbles, x, 33, 93, 117, 178–79
semantic field, 95
semantics, 86, 95, 102, 199–202
semantics of syntax, 95
semiosis, 177
semiotics, x, xi, 33, 77, 80, 177
sex, 41, 77

signifiers, personal/conventional, 177–78
signifying structures, 84, 86, 172, 183
social action, 81, 143–50, 175, 203
socioeconomic status, 41, 77
sociolinguistics, 77
spelling strategies, 80, 87, 95, 96
strategies, x, 86
successful text, 201–2
surface text organization, 95, 96, 100, 102
syntax, 95, 100, 199–202
syntax of semantics, 95

teacher, 4, 5, 73
teaching, xiii, 73, 74
text, xi, 81, 164–79, 183, 201–2
  and coherence, 80, 105–7
  and context, 96, 173, 189, 201, 212
  as decontextualized, 96
  as an event, 169
  as an object, 168

  as potential, 169–70, 172–73, 179
  as sign, 173, 196
  surface feature organization, 95
  and thought, 172
text organization, graphophonemic perspective, 96
text unity, 86
theory and practice, xi, 89
thought collective, xiii
time-on-task, 32, 48
transactional view, 54, 56–58
transitivity relationships, 95
transmediation, 80, 177
triangulation, 212–13, 216

variation, role in research, 75

whole language, 199–200
writing, 93, 211
writing instruments, 34, 44

INFORMANT INDEX

Aaliya, thank you, 87
Abigail, oral language ("fetch"/"get"), 137
Alanna
    Letter writing, 159, 161
    Name writing, 76
    Story telling, 86
Alison
    Book reading, 174–75
    Cursive story script, 11
    "Do not disturb" sign, 173
    Finger puppet, 12
    Functional spelling, 132–33, 180–81
    Hyphen, 98
    Language experience story, 7
    Letter to grandmother, 13
    Longitudinal case studies, 79
    Oral language examples
    —"Close the door," 143
    —"Tree," 57
    —"Unconcentrative," 3
    Overwriting—school-initiated writing, 6
    Parent–teacher notice, 4
    Reading environmental print, 8–9, 24, 29, 110, 145,
        167–68
    Scribble, 179
    Shopping list, 164–65
    Signature, 28
    Signatures, 12
    Story reading, 167
    Story to wordless book, 10
    Story writing, 178
    Thanksgiving book, 182–83
    TV schedule, 180
    Underwriting—school-initiated writing, 4
    Uninterrupted story writing, 158, 163
    Uninterrupted writing, 14
Alpha
    Letter writing, 160
    Name writing, 76
    Story reading, 121
Angela
    Name writing, 76
    Uninterrupted writing, 191
Angie, name writing, 76
Annika, writing as social action, 147
Ariel, thank-you note, 87

Barbara, uninterrupted writing, 83–84
Becka, oral language example ("fetch"/"get"), 137

Ben
    Name writing, 76
    Reading environmental print, 118
Benjamin
    Name writing, 76
    Story reading, 130
Beth, uninterrupted story writing, 113–15
Bill, reading environmental print, 131
Boyd
    Reading environmental print, 24, 29
    Uninterrupted drawing, 109
    Uninterrupted writing, 130–31
Bradley, functional spelling ("dinosaur"), 132
Brandyce
    Name writing, 76
    Story reading, 121
Brett, thank you, 165

Carol, sign in, 132
Catherine, uninterrupted writing, 83–84
Charles
    Name writing, 76
    Reading environmental print, 24, 29, 110–11
Charvin
    Name writing, 76
    Reading environmental print, 86
    Story writing, 119–20
    Uninterrupted writing, 29–30
Chris
    Letter writing, 160, 161
    Name writing, 76
    Oral language example ("S–N–A–K–E"), 109–10
    Story beginning, 103
    Story reading, 174
Crystal, name writing, 76

Dan, name writing, 76
Daniel, reading environmental print, 24, 29
David
    Newspaper reading, 59–60
    Thank you, 87
    Uninterrupted writing, 131
Dawn
    Name writing, 76
    Reading environmental print, 24, 29
    Storytelling and reading, 123–29
    Uninterrupted writing, 82, 92
Dawn B., reading environmental print, 29
Denver, reading environmental print, 29

Deshonna
  Name writing, 76
  Uninterrupted writing, 153
Donald
  Name writing, 76
  Uninterrupted storytelling, 175–79
DuJulian
  Name writing, 76
  Reading environmental print, 164
  Uninterrupted writing, 47
  —and drawing, 92–93

Emily, reading environmental print, 29
Erica
  Envelope, 87
  Longitudinal case studies, 79
  Story writing, 178, 179
Eugene
  Name writing, 76
  Storytelling, 120

Frank
  Name writing, 76
  Reading environmental print, 108

Gerald, name writing, 76
Gina, name writing, 76
Gita, longitudinal case studies, 79
Greg
  Letter reading, 108–9
  Name writing, 76
Gregory, thank you, 165

Hannah, shopping list and story, 157–58, 163
Heather
  Language experience story, 46
  Name writing, 76
  Reading environmental print, 24, 29, 144, 164
  Storytelling, 120–21

Ian, reading environmental print, 152

Jake
  Letter writing, 160, 161
  Name writing, 76
  Story writing, 186
Jason
  Functional spelling, 27, 87–88
  Name writing, 76
  Oral language examples, 57
  Shopping list, 165
  Storytelling, 120

Story writing, 19, 133, 188–89
—and reading, 19
Jeff, functional spelling, 96
Jeffrey, name writing, 76
Jennifer
  Business letter, 181–82
  Thank you, 87
Jeremy, reading environmental print, 29
Jerry
  Check, 181
  Name writing, 76
  Reading environmental print, 164
  Uninterrupted drawing, 94
  Uninterrupted writing, 83
Jill
  Name writing, 76
  Story beginning, 103
  Story reading, 111
Jodi, name writing, 111
Joe, reading environmental print, 151–52
Jonathan, reading environmental print, 24, 29
Joshua, story reading, 152
Justin, reading environmental print, 24, 29

Kammi
  Spelling, 88
  Story writing, 217–19
Kara
  Basal story reading, 110
  Longitudinal case studies, 79
Kibi
  Name writing, 76
  Story writing, 186
  Uninterrupted writing, 108, 191

LaShell
  Language experience story, 46
  Letter writing, 159, 161
  Name writing, 76
  Oral language example ("I ated"), 56
  Story writing, 187
Latisha
  Name writing, 76
  Story beginning, 103
Latrice
  Name writing, 76
  Reading environmental print, 86, 164
  Story reading, 121
  Story writing, 115
  Uninterrupted writing, 83
  —, drawing, and name samples, 33–40

260

Leslie
  Reading environmental print, 29, 144–45, 201
  Uninterrupted writing, 131
Lisa, name writing, 87
Lucienne, mental symbolism, 176

Mara
  Reading environmental print, 24, 29
  Say something, 144
Marc
  Name writing, 76
  Reading environmental print, 24
  Story writing, 187
Marci, sentence writing, 165
Mark, sentence writing, 165–66
Marvin
  Name writing, 76
  Reading environmental print, 88–89, 164
  Uninterrupted writing and drawing samples, 15
Matt
  Story writing, 87
  Uninterrupted writing, 95–106
Megan
  Longitudinal case studies, 79
  Reading environmental print, 24, 29
  Scribble, 179
  Story and letter writing, 109
  Story writing, 178
Michael
  Letter writing, 162
  Name writing, 76
Michelle
  Letter writing, 21
  Reading environmental print, 23–25, 29
  Uninterrupted writing, 20, 87
Michelle S., reading environmental print, 29
Mike
  Name writing, 76
  Scribble, 179
  Story writing, 178
  Uninterrupted writing, 29–30
Misty, name writing, 76

Najeeba, uninterrupted writing—multiculture, 82–92
Natasha
  Letter writing, 159
  Name writing, 76
  Story reading, 19
  Story writing, 19, 186
  Uninterrupted writing, 47
Nathan
  Name writing, 76

Reading environmental print, 29, 118–19, 143, 164
  Uninterrupted writing, 83
Noah, worksheets, 152–53
Nora, say something, 144

Odette, story writing, 229–31
Ofer, uninterrupted writing—multicultural, 82–92

Patty
  Name writing, 76
  Reading environmental print, 164
  Uninterrupted drawing, 94
  Uninterrupted writing, 83

Ranee, thank you, 87
Rebecca, spelling, 88
Redzuen, thank you, 87
Rhoda, sentence writing, 165
Robert
  Language story, xv–vi
  Name writing, 76
  Reading environmental print, 164
  Story writing, 135, 139–41, 166–67
  Uninterrupted drawing, 94
Robin, notes, story, letter, 85

Sally
  Letter writing, 160
  Name writing, 76
  Oral language example ("She rided"), 56
  Storytelling, 86
Sara, uninterrupted writing, 95–105
Sarah, functional spelling, ("S"–"Z"), 180–81
Saul
  Say something, 144
  Thank you, 87
Shannon
  Name writing, 76
  Reading environmental print, 164
  Uninterrupted drawing, 94
  Uninterrupted writing, 82, 116
Stephanie
  Birthday list, map, letter, story, 84–85
  Name writing, 76

Taisha
  Name writing, 76
  Uninterrupted writing, 16
Tasha
  Name writing, 76
  Reading environmental print, 143–44
  Story writing, 175, 186

Terry
    Name writing, 76
    Reading environmental print, 164
    Story beginning, 104
    Uninterrupted writing and drawing samples, 16–17
Todd, sentence writing, 165–66
Tom, thank you, 165
Towanna
    Name writing, 76
    Reading environmental print, 164
    Story beginning, 103
Tyler, reading environmental print, 23–25, 29

Vincent
    Letter writing, 160, 161
    Name writing, 76
    Story beginning, 103
    Story writing, 19

Wendy, thank you, 165

Zach
    Story reading, 163
    Story writing, 156–57

CHILDREN'S SAMPLES INDEX

Basal story reading, Kara, 110
Birthday list, map, letter, story, Stephanie, 84–85
Book reading, Alison, 174–75
Business letter, Jennifer, 181–82

Check, Jerry, 181
Cursive story script, Alison, 11

"Do not disturb" sign, Alison, 173

Envelope, Erica, 87

Finger puppet, Alison, 12
Functional spelling
    Alison, 132–33, 180–81
    Jason, 27, 87–88
    Jeff, 96
Functional spelling ("dinosaur"), Bradley, 132
Functional spelling ("S"–"Z"), Sarah, 180–81

Hyphen, Alison, 98

Language experience story
    Alison, 7
    Heather, 46
    LaShell, 46
Language story, Robert, xv–xvi
Letter reading, Greg, 108–9
Letter to grandmother, Alison, 13
Letter writing
    Alanna, 159, 161
    Alpha, 160
    Chris, 160, 161
    Jake, 160, 161
    LaShell, 159, 161
    Michael, 162
    Michelle, 21
    Natasha, 159
    Sally, 160
    Vincent, 160, 161
Longitudinal case studies
    Alison, 79
    Erica, 79
    Gita, 79
    Kara, 79
    Megan, 79

Mental symbolism, Lucienne, 176

Name writing
    Alanna, 76
    Alpha, 76
    Angela, 76
    Angie, 76
    Ben, 76
    Benjamin, 76
    Brandyce, 76
    Charles, 76
    Charvin, 76
    Chris, 76
    Crystal, 76
    Dan, 76
    Dawn, 76
    Deshonna, 76
    Donald, 76
    DuJulian, 76
    Eugene, 76
    Frank, 76
    Gerald, 76
    Gina, 76
    Greg, 76
    Heather, 76
    Jake, 76
    Jason, 76
    Jeffrey, 76
    Jerry, 76
    Jill, 76
    Jodi, 111
    Kibi, 76
    LaShell, 76
    Latisha, 76
    Latrice, 76
    Lisa, 87
    Marc, 76
    Marvin, 76
    Michael, 76
    Mike, 76
    Misty, 76
    Natasha, 76
    Nathan, 76
    Patty, 76
    Robert, 76
    Sally, 76
    Shannon, 76
    Stephanie, 76
    Taisha, 76
    Tasha, 76
    Terry, 76

Towanna, 76
Vincent, 76
Newspaper reading, David, 59–60
Notes, story, letter, Robin, 85

Oral language example
   "Close the door," Alison, 143
   "Fetch/get"
   —Abigail, 137
   —Becka, 137
   "I ated," LaShell, 56
   "S–N–A–K–E," Chris, 109–10
   "She ried," Sally, 56
   "tree," Alison, 57
   "unconcentrative," Alison, 3
Oral language examples, Jason, 57
Overwriting—school-initiated writing, Alison, 6

Parent–teacher notice, Alison, 4

Reading environmental print
   Alison, 8–9, 24, 29, 110, 145, 167–68
   Ben, 118
   Bill, 131
   Boyd, 24, 29
   Charles, 24, 29 110–11
   Charvin, 86
   Daniel, 24, 29
   Dawn, 24, 29
   Dawn B., 29
   Denver, 29
   DuJulian, 164
   Emily, 29
   Frank, 108
   Heather, 24, 29, 144, 164
   Ian, 152
   Jeremy, 29
   Jerry, 164
   Joe, 151–52
   Jonathan, 24, 29
   Justin, 24, 29
   Latrice, 86, 164
   Leslie, 29, 144–45, 201
   Mara, 24, 29
   Marc, 24
   Marvin, 88–89, 164
   Megan, 24, 29
   Michelle, 23–25, 29
   Michelle S., 29
   Nathan, 29, 118–19, 143, 164
   Patty, 164
   Robert, 164

Shannon, 164
Tasha, 143–44
Terry, 164
Towanna, 164
Tyler, 23–25, 29

Say something
   Mara, 144
   Nora, 144
   Saul, 144
Scribble
   Alison, 179
   Megan, 179
   Mike, 179
Sentence writing
   Marci, 165
   Mark, 165–66
   Rhoda, 165
   Todd, 165–66
Shopping list
   Alison, 164–65
   Jason, 165
Shopping list and story, Hannah, 157–58, 163
Sign in, Carol, 132
Signature, Alison, 28
Signatures, Alison, 12
Spelling
   Kammi, 88
   Rebecca, 88
Story and letter writing, Megan, 109
Story beginning
   Chris, 103
   Jill, 103
   Latisha, 103
   Terry, 104
   Towanna, 103
   Vincent, 103
Story reading
   Alison, 167
   Alpha, 121
   Benjamin, 130
   Brandyce, 121
   Chris, 174
   Jill, 111
   Joshua, 152
   Latrice, 121
   Natasha, 19
   Zach, 163
Storytelling
   Alanna, 86
   Eugene, 120
   Heather, 120–21

Jason, 120
Sally, 86
Storytelling and reading, Dawn, 123–29
Story to wordless book, Alison, 10
Story writing
Alison, 178
Charvin, 119–20
Erica, 178, 179
Jake, 186
Jason, 19, 133, 188–89
Kammi, 217–19
Kibi, 186
LaShell, 187
Latrice, 115
Marc, 187
Matt, 87
Megan, 178
Mike, 178
Natasha, 19, 186
Odette, 229–31
Robert, 135, 139–41, 166–67
Tasha, 175, 186
Vincent, 19
Zach, 156–57
Story writing and reading, Jason, 19

Thank you
Aaliya, 87
Brett, 165
David, 87
Gregory, 165
Jennifer, 87
Ranee, 87
Redzuen, 87
Saul, 87
Tom, 165
Wendy, 165
Thank-you note, Ariel, 87
Thanksgiving book, Alison, 182–83
TV schedule, Alison, 180

Underwriting—school-initiated writing, Alison, 4
Uninterrupted drawing
Boyd, 109

Jerry, 94
Patty, 94
Robert, 94
Shannon, 94
Uninterrupted storytelling, Donald, 175–79
Uninterrupted story writing
Alison, 158, 163
Beth, 113–15
Uninterrupted writing
Alison, 14
Angela, 191
Barbara, 83–84
Boyd, 130–31
Catherine, 83–84
Charvin, 29–30
David, 131
Dawn, 82, 92
Deshonna, 153
DuJulian, 47
Jerry, 83
Kibi, 108, 191
Latrice, 83
Leslie, 131
Matt, 95–106
Michelle, 20, 87
Mike, 29–30
Natasha, 47
Nathan, 83
Patty, 83
Sara, 95–105
Shannon, 82, 116
Taisha, 16
Uninterrupted writing and drawing
DuJulian, 92–93
Marvin, 15
Terry, 16–17
Uninterrupted writing, drawing, and name sample,
Latrice, 33–40
Uninterrupted writing—multicultural
Ofer, 82–92
Najeeba, 82–92

Worksheets, Noah, 152–53
Writing as social action, Annika, 147